W9-BPO-648

THE NEW
DINOSAUR DICTIONARY

Restoration of *Bactrosaurus* prepared for this
book by William Stout.

THE NEW

CITADEL PRESS SECAUCUS, NEW JERSEY

Early restoration of the duck-billed
dinosaur *Hadrosaurus* by Charles
R. Knight. Courtesy of the American
Museum of Natural History.

DINOSAUR DICTIONARY

DONALD F. GLUT

KRAXBERGER SCHOOL LIBRARY

567.903
Glu

6430

Restoration of *Homalocephale* prepared for this
book by William Stout.

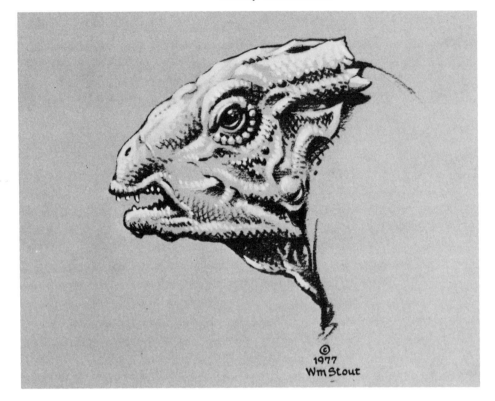

830227

First Edition

Copyright © 1982 by Donald F. Glut
All rights reserved
Published by Citadel Press
A division of Lyle Stuart Inc.
120 Enterprise Ave., Secaucus, N.J. 07094
In Canada: Musson Book Company
A division of General Publishing Co. Limited
Don Mills, Ontario
Manufactured in the United States of America by
Halliday Lithograph, West Hanover, Mass.
Designed by A. Christopher Simon

Library of Congress Cataloging in Publicaton Data

Glut, Donald F.
  The new dinosaur dictionary.

  Bibliography: p. 283
  Includes index.
    1. Dinosaurs—Dictionaries. I. Title.
QE862.D5G65   1982   567.9′1′0321   81-38530
ISBN 0-8065-0782-9   AACR2

Dedicated to
ROBERT A. LONG and RALPH E. MOLNAR,
for their encouragement,
enthusiasm and help in the
preparation of this book.

Also dedicated to
Edwin H. Colbert, the late Alfred Sherwood Romer and David Techter,
for their assistance with the original *Dinosaur Dictionary*.

Restoration of *Efraasia* prepared for this book
by William Stout.

ACKNOWLEDGMENTS

Sincere thanks are due the following, both living and deceased, who either directly or indirectly contributed to this volume and to the field of paleontology:

Othenio Abel, Roy Chapman Andrews, Joseph Augusta, Donald Baird, Robert T. Bakker, Lawrence G. Barnes, José F. Bonaparte, M. Borsuk-Bialynicka, Michael Brett-Surman, Barnum Brown, Dean William Buckland, George Callison, Carol J. Campbell, Sankar Chatterjee, Edwin H. Colbert, Walter P. Coombs, Jr., Edward Drinker Cope, Georges Cuvier, Jeffrey G. Eaton, Gordon Edmund, Peter Galton, Charles Whitney Gilmore, Orville Gilpin, Jacques van Heerden, H. Stanton Hill, Edward Hitchcock, John R. Horner, Friedrich von Huene, Werner Janensch, James A. Jensen, Zofia Kielan-Jaworowska, Lawrence Lambe, Robert A. Long, James H. Madsen, Jr., Gideon Mantell, Othniel Charles Marsh, Sylvia Massey, John S. McIntosh, Ralph E. Molnar, Michael Morales, Ferencz Nopcsa, Mary Jean Odano, George Olshevsky, Henry Fairfield Osborn, John H. Ostrom, Richard Owen, H.P. Powell, Alfred Sherwood Romer, Dale A. Russell, Charles S. Sternberg, W.E. Swinton, David Techter, Diana Thatcher, R.A. Thulborn, Mary Wade, Samuel P. Welles and Rainer Zangerl.

And to: Forrest J. Ackerman, John Allison, Jorge Arenal, Keith Bennett, Zdenek Burian, Larry M. Byrd, L. Sprague de Camp, Greg Chalfin, Sohn Cotte, Jim Danforth, Marcel Delgado, J. L. Dunning, Steve Glut, Jim Harmon, Ray Harryhausen, Waterhouse Hawkins, Ron Haydock, Richard Hescox, Cathy Hill, Rick Hoberg, Larry Ivie, Helen B. Jones, C. W. Kirby, Charles R. Knight, Allen G. Kracalik, Roy G. Krenkel, Joe Kubert, Jerri Long, Russ Manning, David M. Massaro, Norman Maurer, Helen J. McGinnis, E. V. Nelson, Willis O'Brien, Neave Parker, Winifred Reinders, Franc Reyes, D. Scott Rogo, Martin Sara, Tom Scherman, Edward Schneider, Scott Shaw!, Pete von Sholly, Arthur Smith, Ferenc Solyomi, Adam Spektor, William Stout, Lyle Stuart, Gordon Thomas, Bill Warren, Allan J. Wilson, Robert W. Wilson, William Wray and Rudolph Zallinger.

Special thanks to Julia Glut, my mother, for her tolerance and endurance. When I was a child she took me to such prehistoric animal havens as Dinosaur Park in Rapid City, South Dakota, with its life-sized dinosaur statues, and read many a novel while I gazed with a great sense of wonder at the paleontology exhibits in the museums of the United States.

My deepest apologies to anyone I may have neglected to mention.

In every possible instance I have attempted to credit illustrations and secure permissions for their reproduction when such permissions were required.

The following institutions and companies have been more than cooperative in supplying me with data and illustrative material: The Academy of Natural Sciences of Philadelphia; The Ackerman Archives, Hollywood, California; American Museum of Natural History, New York; British Museum (Natural History), London; Carnegie Museum, Pittsburgh; Charles Scribner's Sons; Dinosaur National Monument; Field Museum of Natural History, Chicago; Greater London Council; the *Illustrated London News;* Los Angeles County Museum of Natural History; Museum of Comparative Zoology (The Agassiz Museum), Harvard University, Cambridge, Massachusetts; Museum of Paleontology, University of California, Berkeley; National Museums of Canada, Ottawa, Ontario; Peabody Museum of Natural History, Yale University, New Haven, Connecticut; Polska Akademia Nauk, Zakad Paleobiologii, Warsaw, Poland; The Prehistoric Gardens, Port Orford, Oregon; Princeton University, Princeton, New Jersey; Queensland Museum, Queensland, Australia; Rand McNally and Company; Royal Ontario Museum, Toronto; School of Mines and Technology, Rapid City, South Dakota; Sinclair Oil Corporation; United States National Museum, Smithsonian Institution, Washington, D.C.; University Museum, Oxford University; University of California, Los Angeles; The University of New South Wales, Australia; The University of Wyoming, Department of Geology, Laramie, Wyoming; University of Southern California; and the Utah Museum of Natural History, University of Utah, Salt Lake City.

CONTENTS

Two duck-billed dinosaurs of the genus *Brachylophosaurus* flee from a hungry tyrannosaurid. Restoration by Robert T. Bakker. Courtesy of the National Museums of Canada.

Modern sculpture of *Tyrannosaurus* by Sylvia Massey Czerkas. Photograph by Robin Robin.

PREFACE TO
THE NEW EDITION

Paleontology is not, contrary to the notions of some critics, a dead science with as little future as the extinct denizens it studies. Rather it is in a perpetual state of flux. Old concepts are constantly being relegated to obsolescence as new and exciting discoveries are made and fresh, oftentimes revolutionary, opinions and theories are postulated.

The first edition of *The Dinosaur Dictionary* was published in 1972. Three years later the world became dinosaur-conscious as the paleontological society embarked on what became popularly known as a "Dinosaur Renaissance."* A veritable revolution in paleontological thinking was suddenly upon us as dinosaur specialists directed their attention with new outlooks to these fantastic animals. "Facts" that had proliferated in paleontology texts since before the turn of the last century were seriously challenged and oftentimes entirely rejected. The 1970s were truly the years of a vast Golden Age of Dinosaurs, during which more paleontologists than ever before focused their attention upon these former rulers of this planet. In the light shed by this "Renaissance," the

*The term became popularized after Robert T. Bakker's article "Dinosaur Renaissance" was published in the April 1975 issue of *Scientific American*.

9

first edition of *The Dinosaur Dictionary* has become embarrassingly dated.

This new edition of *The Dinosaur Dictionary* has been thoroughly revised. Upon comparing this volume with the old edition, the reader will readily note some of the more obvious changes. Many new entries have been added to the body of the text; and, as there are yet new dinosaurs that have not been formally named or described (though some may have been between this writing and the date of the book's publication), you will find an added section on "unnamed" genera. Certain genera covered at length in the first edition have been reduced to a mere mention, as they are now known to be simply junior synonyms of genera with name priority, or not dinosaurs at all. In some instances a genus once believed to embrace numerous species (six species of *Corythosaurus*—*C. casuarius*, *C. brevicristatus*, *C. intermedius*, *C. bicristatus*, *C. frontalis* and *C. excavatus*—being pictured in the first edition) is now regarded as having but one (*C. casuarius*).

Many of the illustrations in the first edition have been replaced by new material prepared especially for this edition by artists Richard Hescox, Cathy Hill, Rick Hoberg, George Olshevsky, Scott Shaw!, Pete von Sholly, William Wray, my former wife Linda L. Glut, and especially William Stout. I have added an illustrations index which essentially solves two problems that surfaced in the first edition—cropped paintings depicting more than one genus, which disrupted the layout intended by the artist, and the frequent mismatching of illustration with its respective text entry, a problem that any professional art director should easily understand. Dinosaurian classification has been considerably revamped in the past few years (i.e., dinosaur families), and I have included with each entry the genus' author and the date of original publication.

During the preparation of this second edition of *The Dinosaur Dictionary*, I received the special and much appreciated help of five persons who actively and enthusiastically contributed their opinions, criticisms and suggestions:

Donald Baird, Director of the Museum of Natural History at Princeton University, has sent me correspondence regarding dinosaurian ichnites.

Michael K. Brett-Surman, now of George Washington University, has permitted me access to his yet unpublished M.A. thesis on a revision of the Hadrosauridae.

George Olshevsky, in his computer printout compilation *The Dinosaurian Taxa* and subsequent publication *Mesozoic Meanderings*, has kept me up to date on valid genera and synonyms.

And most active and enthusiastic of all . . .

Robert A. Long of the Department of Paleontology, University of California, Berkeley, who supplied so many photographs and drawings of dinosaur specimens and provided me with an unforgettable "dinosaur weekend" at his home, during which time he answered every question I could cram into three fascinating days. And . . .

Ralph Molnar, now of the Queensland Museum, Australia, who has been corresponding with me regularly for well over six years, during which time he has answered perhaps more questions about dinosaurs than ever before in his life, and who has kept me supplied with regular and welcomed shipments of illustrations for use in this book.

To these latter two gentlemen, I offer an additional thanks for their examination of and annotations to this manuscript.

DONALD F. GLUT
North Hollywood, California, 1981

Restoration of the sauropod *Barosaurus* prepared for this book by William Stout.

Restoration of the carnivorous dinosaur *Daspletosaurus* by Patricia R. Haldorsen. Courtesy of the National Museums of Canada.

INTRODUCTION 1

Hollywood sports various societies and organizations. Some of these are scholarly, some mundane, and some, I am sure, are downright outré.

At least once a year my wife delivers me to the Oakland airport, and I, like an excited little boy, board a plane in anticipation of a remarkable Hollywood adventure. You see, I have the privilege of being an honorary member of one of those societies.

As my plane leaves Oakland, a blueprint of the next two or three days clicks through my head—banquets and parties with the famous and to-be famous, including movie-makers, painters, sculptors, animationists, authors, museum technicians, and scientists. One of the central figures in this gifted menagerie is Donald F. Glut.

The common denominator that brings these people together once a month from all over California is *dinosaurs*. Dinosaurs represent not only an interest to these people, but also an obsession. More often than not, their vocations involve the dinosaur, be the result a book, a scientific paper, a movie, a painting, or a sculpture.

As a paleontologist, I have deep admiration for this remarkable group of people. It is their intelligence and skills that will bring the prehistoric animal beyond the often limited and guarded domain of the scientist to the public.

The New Dinosaur Dictionary is just such an example. It is the result of nearly a decade's research by Mr. Glut, with the cooperation of paleontologists from around the world. Glut's first *Dinosaur Dictionary*, published in 1972, is perhaps the largest selling dinosaur book yet written. However, it has become somewhat dated because of the tremendous strides made by dinosaurian paleontologists in the last decade. This much enlarged and updated *Dinosaur Dictionary* is a long-awaited and greatly needed volume. It will be of benefit to scientists and laymen alike.

I think it is fair to state that *The New Dinosaur Dictionary* has required more time to produce than any dinosaur book ever to hit the popular market. This volume came into being only because of Don Glut's devotion to the topic and his patience and intelligence in dealing with a plethora of data.

Robert Allen Long
Museum of Paleontology,
University of California, Berkeley,
April 1981

The ceratopsian dinosaur *Centrosaurus* with its eggs.

INTRODUCTION 2

The dry "winter" of north-central Queensland is sometimes quite hot. We pile out of the ute* with a temperature of over 30 degrees Celsius and keep to the sparse shade of the koala-scarred eucalyptus that form an open woodland on the cattle property southeast of Hughenden. Following the manager and his wife through the tall, dry grasses of the flat paddocks, we come to one of the anthills smaller than usual, rising only about half a meter from the ground, and halt in the shade. In the midst of the anthill lie the broken and eroded remains of an iguanodont, a large plant-eating dinosaur, the bones cleared of the surrounding rock by centuries of the action of plant roots and soil organisms.

I have also worked in areas with a little more relief (both in topography and temperature) than the table-top plains of central Queensland. Even during the summer heat of January, the coast of Victoria is swept by the south wind that comes crisp across the ocean from Antarctica. The green-gray sandstone bluffs have eroded into fanciful forms, exaggerated by the hard cylindrical concretions that project like the muzzles

*Utility vehicle.

of cannon above us, as we scramble along. Other spherical concretions stand partly exposed, small domes along the rock platforms, and one small one stands, hollow inside, on a stem of rock like a sandstone chalice. Here fossils are few but we do find lungfish and theropod remains and the upper jaw of a little hypsilophodont perched on a ledge ten meters above the waves. (You will not find these particular dinosaurs in this book as they have yet to be scientifically described; but you will find others even more interesting.)

Although there is undeniably a charm and an attraction to hunting for dinosaurs, at least during the cool winter evenings of the outback with the deep vibrato call of the brolga and howling of the dingos and the gentle wind blowing across three thousand empty miles (and the day's work done), one has other thoughts in the face of the hot clouds of flies everpresent in the bush, or of prospecting perpendicular cliffs footed by twenty-foot waves washing north from the Antarctic, or of a seemingly endless search of block after hot block of limestone, wondering if anything other than fish ever got preserved in this empty and curious land. Why such effort, and for that matter, why an interest in dinosaurs?

Dinosaurs are, of course, interesting in themselves as all schoolchildren know before becoming contaminated by the "real" world; and this book captures this interest and tells curious gossipy information about each one, much like Suetonius tells about the Caesars. Dinosaurs are

One *Leptoceratops* battles another. Restoration by Robert T. Bakker. Courtesy of the National Museums of Canada.

creatures with which almost everyone is familiar but most, and even some of those who work with them, are familiar with them only at second hand. Recently much that we thought we knew about dinosaurs has proved incorrect. The recent, and continuing, controversy over their body temperature, and, more significantly, over whether the probably elevated body temperatures of some forms were due to elevated metabolic rates (as in birds and mammals) or to their sheer volumes relative to their surface areas, has focused attention on them. But other new and exciting things have been learned about dinosaurs. While some were indeed large in size, this did not mean, as is often said, that their brains were small. In fact their brains were no smaller relative to their body size than are the brains of modern lizards and crocodiles. And in some (*Stenonychosaurus*) the brain was as large in proportion to the body as in many mammals, much larger than in any living reptile. We can even make deductions about their behavior in several ways.

Dinosaur tracks indicate that some forms of herbivores were gregarious and suggest that some sauropods traveled in herds, with the young toward the center. Dinosaur tracks in central Queensland document a stampede of small forms startled by a large theropod. The horns of ceratopsians, domes of pachycephalosaurs and crests, hoods, and horns of hadrosaurs and iguanodonts all suggest competitive contests for mates. We can picture two male *Stegoceras* clashing together like modern mountain sheep, the two *Torosaurus* beak to beak, with horns locked together, in a pushing contest like those of modern deer.

Dinosaur eggs have been known for some time, but recently a scientist from Princeton has found nests of a horned hadrosaur (*Maiasaura*) that indicate some form of parental care for the hatchlings for an extended (but unknown) period after hatching. Nests and babies of a primitive saurischian (*Mussaurus*) have been found in Argentina as well. And restudy of Mongolian material suggests that several different species of dinosaurs may well have nested together, as well as several females of one species, so that one could stand guard while the others went to feed.

But we are learning about more than behavior. Their very size makes dinosaurs of interest. Although some (*Compsognathus*) were quite small, others were large indeed. Several—*Antarctosaurus, Brachiosaurus* and *Diplodocus*—are known or reliably estimated to have been eighty or more feet in length, and the tracks of *Breviparopus* indicate an animal more than half again as long. We can no longer be certain that the famous blue whale is the largest vertebrate, for *Breviparopus* was certainly longer and may have been generally larger as well.

Of more than "academic interest" is the size of these creatures, for an understanding of how the sauropod heart pumped blood up thirty feet of neck (in *Mamenchisaurus*) to the sauropod brain cannot but aid an understanding of how human hearts function. In a culture beset with difficulties of energy supply and distribution, dinosaur fossils are used in the USSR, at least, to determine those geological structures (the stratigraphy) in turn used to help locate oil. And amid the worry over the deterioration of our environment, it is important to remember that the environment recovered from a much more drastic deterioration at the extinction of the dinosaurs. (The environment recovered, but the dinosaurs didn't.)

But the dinosaurs do affect us in a more direct manner, for although almost all did become extinct in those times, one line that had developed feathers and wings did survive, altered into the birds. And the colors and songs of birds add to everyone's life. There may well have been another direct effect, too. At least one respected scientist feels that, had the extinction not intervened in the evolution of the saurornithoidid theropods and had they continued in their development of increased brain size, they would themselves have evolved into creatures with a civilization tens of millions of years ago, and we would have been preempted and have never been.

However, the most important, indeed almost irreplaceable, value to us of the dinosaurs and other such creatures is simply their inherent strangeness and their distance (in time) from us. It is no coincidence that the author of this book was also associated with that story of long-past times and strange places, *The Empire Strikes Back*. For all such curiously different and vastly distant worlds, whether they be largely imaginary as *The Empire* . . . or largely factual as the dinosaurs, react upon our emotions and our thoughts to grant us a perspective on our own small affairs. The old tired platitudes about not being able to run away from problems are just not true, although you may well find new ones in exchange for those you have left. But these, as epic myths from Homer to Tolkien relate, can be of value to us. They allow us some scale by which to distinguish the trivial and petty (although superficially important) from the significant.

Not that this book will weigh you down self-consciously with such considerations, for it is a book to enjoy as well as to inform. These little curiosities of the different dinosaurs allow us to visualize, if not to see, them as living creatures once again after all these millions of years.

R. E. Molnar,
Queensland Museum,
Queensland, 1980

A BACKGROUND

The dinosaurs were the most successful group of terrestrial animals ever to inhabit this planet. For over 150 million years these creatures, some more diminutive in size than the modern-day chicken and others the most gigantic land dwellers of all time, dominated the earth. Their peculiar, often spectacular, appearances and frequently tremendous sizes have rendered them objects of particular fascination.

This volume is, quite obviously, a dictionary of dinosaur genera. It is an alphabetical listing with capsule data and illustration of virtually every genus of dinosaur known to paleontologists at this time. Those new genera which have not yet been formally named have been listed in a special section following the "official" body of the text.

In *The Dinosaur Dictionary*, I do not attempt to trace in detail the evolution of the dinosaurs from their ancestral stock; nor do I speculate on the reasons for their relatively abrupt extinction. For these insights I encourage your perusal of the bibliography at the end of this volume. *The Dinosaur Dictionary* is a reference book, a supplement to the other published works. Hopefully, this volume represents the most complete and up-to-date catalogue of dinosaur genera presently available to the public.

Naturally, a project such as this has presented its share of problems. Paleontology is a speculative and opinionated science. Recently the classification of dinosaurs has been in a state of revamping by specialists. Oftentimes, experts in the field differ drastically as to which dinosaur genera are valid and which are not. Egos have often contributed to the problem of compiling a concise list of dinosaur genera as some workers have ascribed names to virtually every fossil they personally dug from the ground or rock, the result being an excess of synonyms which must eventually be weeded out. Fragmentary specimens and isolated fossil teeth constitute problems in themselves, and it is usually impossible to classify any of these. Consequently, no one has yet been able to define every genus of the known dinosaurs, and not every worker in this field will agree upon the arrangement of this list of dinosaur names.

Though this work is not intended to give a comprehensive history of the dinosaurs, it will prove of value to present a brief and skeletal background of the nature of these extinct creatures.

Traditionally, dinosaurs have been regarded as reptiles, an assumption based upon the similarity between some dinosaur bones and those of modern reptiles. Today, however, paleontologists are seriously re-evaluating these erstwhile rulers of our world. Considerable evidence exists indicating that the dinosaurs may very well have been endothermic creatures, with some physiological characters seen in birds and

Skeletons of the saurischian dinosaur *Allosaurus fragilis* (left) and the ornithischian *Camptosaurus dispar* (right), realistically mounted in the pose of battle. Courtesy of the Los Angeles County Museum of Natural History.

mammals, rather than the cold-blooded reptiles they have been assumed to be for nearly a century. John H. Ostrom of Yale University has determined that the theropod dinosaurs were more closely allied with birds than with reptiles and that *Archaeopteryx*, long designated as the first bird, may actually have been a feathered dinosaur. Robert T. Bakker, a former student of Ostrom, has taken the idea further by proposing that dinosaurs are not extinct at all but are alive in another incarnation, as birds. Furthermore, Bakker suggests that the birds should be placed into an order with the dinosaurs called *Dinosauria*. R. Anthony Thulborn has suggested that the carnivorous dinosaurs be classified as birds. Alan Jack Charig, however, considers it possible that dinosaurs were endothermic, though the evidence for their being such is highly suspect, and he completely rejects the *Dinosauria* as a natural group. The outcome of these controversies will probably not be known for many years.

The dinosaurs reigned over this earth for some 150 million years during the Mesozoic Era, the so-called Age of Reptiles. This era is subdivided into three periods: the Triassic Period (230 to 180 million years ago), the Jurassic Period (180 to 135 million years ago) and the Cretaceous Period (135 to 63 million years ago). Dinosaurs are first known from the Middle Triassic Period, some forms soon attaining gigantic sizes. Following the culmination of the Cretaceous Period, these former earth rulers, who had flourished in such variety and abundance, were extinct.

Though we have been using the term "dinosaur" quite liberally, the word requires some explanation. According to the traditional classification of these fantastic creatures, the term "dinosaur" is a misnomer. Dinosaur bones had been first recorded in the seventeenth century* or earlier; but it was Sir Richard Owen, the famed paleontologist and anatomist, who coined the word *Dinosauria* to represent the fossil remains of several extinct giants. Owen proposed his *Dinosauria*, denoting "a distinct tribe or suborder of Saurian reptiles," to the Geological Society of London on June 30, 1841. The term combined the Greek work *deinos*, meaning "terrible," with *sauros*, meaning "lizard." Surely, Owen probably thought, all these creatures must have been terrible indeed as they stalked and lumbered over the earth. According to Owen, the term *Di-*

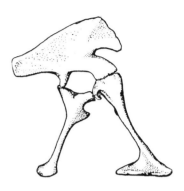

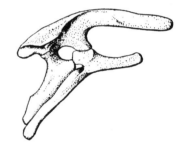

(Top) Pelvis of a typical saurischian dinosaur *Allosaurus*. (Bottom) Pelvis of the ornithischian *Stegosaurus*. (After Gilmore.)

---

*The earliest recorded dinosaur discovery known to date was published in 1677 by Dr. Robert Plot, who described a partial femur apparently that of *Megalosaurus*. Since neither the term *Megalosaurus* nor the more general term *dinosaur* were known in the seventeenth century, Plot assumed the bone to be that of some unknown elephant. In 1763 a picture of the bone was captioned, due to its shape, *Scrotum humanum* by Richard Brookes, and it can be accepted as the first name ever ascribed to a dinosaur specimen. The term, however, was never used again and has been discarded from paleontological literature.

nosauria applied to all dinosaurs, which were to be grouped into a single biological order. Owen (unless we are to adopt Bakker's proposal and reinstate the term *Dinosauria*) was wrong about this, but his error has endured in popular beliefs.

But actually, in the classical sense, there are two orders of dinosaurs, Saurischia and Ornithischia—as different from each other as they are from the Pterosauria (flying reptiles), Crocodilia (alligators and crocodiles) and the ancestors of all four of these orders, the Thecodontia.

Both dinosaurian orders fall under the great class Reptilia. According to Romer, the subclass of Reptilia is Archosauria, which includes all "ruling reptiles" (dinosaurs, pterosaurs, crocodilians and thecodonts). The thecodonts appeared by the end of the Permian Period and were characterized by strong hindlegs and smaller forelimbs. Though some thecodonts had flat, crocodile-like heads, the skulls of others are deep and narrow, looking very much like those of the earliest kinds of dinosaurs. From the order Thecodontia evolved the two great orders of dinosaurs, Saurischia and Ornithischia.

Saurischia is the order of "lizard-hipped" dinosaurs, as derived from the Greek word again because of the more or less reptilian structure of the pelvis. In the saurischian pelvis, the pubis extends down from the ilium, while a third bone, the ischium, extends down from the ilium behind the pubis. Ornithischia, the order of "bird-hipped" dinosaurs, is typified by a pelvis in which the ilium is considerably elongated while the pubis is usually parallel with the ilium.

Teeth in the saurischian skull appear along the front and side margins of the jaws, or only in the front. Contrarily, teeth are usually absent from the front of the ornithischian mouth, though a few genera of this order display premaxillary teeth. In many ornithischian forms there is a horny, birdlike beak, and all have a predentary bone at the front of the lower jaw. Also, the saurischian skull is equipped with openings in front of the orbits, which subtract from the animal's mass; usually such fenestrae are absent in the ornithischian skull. Behind the orbits of the saurischian skull are two large openings that provide attachment areas for the jaw muscles of the animal. In the ornithischian skull, these fenestrae have usually been considerably reduced or eliminated. With one probable exception, all the carnivorous forms are saurischians, and virtually all the armored forms are ornithischians.

The following breakdown of the two dinosaurian orders is the most widely used at this time and corresponds to abbreviations in the text entries in the main body of this volume:

Allosaurus attacks the herbivorous *Camarasaurus* in this early twentieth-century restoration.

Courtesy of the Dinosaur Nature Association.

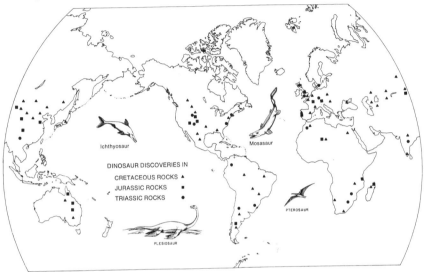

Hypothetical skeleton of *Hadrosaurus foulkii,* as restored in plaster by Waterhouse Hawkins during the 1890s, at the old Field Columbian Museum, Chicago, Illinois. From left to right can also be seen skeletons of the extinct ungulate *Uintatherium,* the "Irish elk" *Megaloceros* and the jaws of a fossil shark *Carcharodon.* Courtesy of the Field Museum of Natural History.

Order SAURISCHIA

Suborder THEROPODA—almost exclusively carnivorous; bipedal, with strong hind legs and small forelimbs equipped with claws used primarily for grasping; flourished during the entirety of the Mesozoic Era.

Families: *

Podokesauridae—small to moderately large; primitive; built for speed; neck of moderate length; forelimbs short and slender, with four digits; hind legs very long; five metatarsals with outer ones greatly reduced; Upper Triassic to Lower Jurassic.

?Archaeopterygidae—theropods or primitive birds; small; skeleton resembling that of small theropods; feathers; Upper Jurassic.

Segisauridae—small; lightly built; relatively long neck; characterized by the persistence of the collarbone; body vertebrae and long body bones solid; resembled thecodonts; Upper Triassic to Lower Jurassic.

Coeluridae—very small, light, with hollow bones; front legs slender and of medium length; femur larger than tibia; Upper Jurassic and Lower Cretaceous.

*R. Barsbold (1976) has proposed that the suborder Theropoda be broken down into the following infraorders: Coelurosauria, Carnosauria, Deinonychosauria, Ornithomimosauria, Deinocheirosauria and Oviraptorosauria. A. Perle has added Segnosauria (1980).

The great horned *Triceratops* as sculpted by Sylvia Massey Czerkas.

Head of the hadrosaur *Corythosaurus*.
Model by Charles Whitney Gilmore.
Courtesy of the Smithsonian
Institution.

Model of the plated dinosaur *Stegosaurus* by
Charles Whitney Gilmore. Courtesy of the
Smithsonian Institution.

egosaurus, a plated dinosaur from the Jurassic Period, as
ulpted by Sylvia Massey Czerkas.

Head of the ceratopsian *Styracosaurus*.
Model by Charles Whitney Gilmore.
Courtesy of the Smithsonian Institution.

A baby *Protoceratops* hatches from its egg in this
sculpture by Sylvia Massey Czerkas.

*Troödontidae**—possibly synonymous with Saurornithoididae or Dromaeosauridae; known only from teeth, slender-crowned, laterally compressed, recurved with very prominent anterior and posterior serrations; apparently animals of small size; Upper Cretaceous.

Compsognathidae—very small; resemble the Coeluridae; moderately long neck; Upper Jurassic.

Ornithomimidae—very light; average height; not hunters; skull very small, with slender, toothless jaws; neck long; forelimbs long with three digits; femur shorter than tibia; long feet with three close digits resembling those of the ostrich; built for running; Upper Cretaceous.

?Gobipterygidae—possibly a junior synonym of Caenagnathidae; theropods or birds; small; known only from skulls, with moderately long jaws, no external mandibular fenestrae and palate said to resemble that of certain avians; lower jaws superficially similar to caenagnathids and oviraptorids; Upper Cretaceous.

Oviraptoridae—possibly a junior synonym of Caenagnathidae; small; bipedal; front limbs very long and similar to that of ornithomimids; skull with very large braincase for a dinosaur; jaws parrot-like, short and toothless; Upper Cretaceous.

Deinocheiridae—gigantic, known only from huge front limbs; resembling in general proportions the ornithomimids but more massive; three-fingered hand; metacarpals of equal length; Upper Cretaceous.

Dromaeosauridae—small; skull large with modestly deep jaw; forelimb half the length of the hind limb; highly specialized foot, with greatly enlarged second claw raised off the ground during locomotion; long, overlapping ossified tendons stiffening most of the tail; Lower to Upper Cretaceous.

Saurornithoididae—similar to dromaeosaurids, but with braincase more specialized; tail not stiffened into a rigid structure; second claw of hind foot not so large or curved; Upper Cretaceous.

*Recently discovered material shows that Troödontidae is probably a family of carnivorous ornithischians.

Itemiridae—known only from a braincase showing similarities with the Dromaeosauridae, but several characters different from all other theropods; Upper Cretaceous.

Caenagnathidae—probably closely related to the oviraptorids; small; known only from lower jaws, without teeth, dentaries fused in a rather large symphysis; large opening in mandible; scooplike anterior termination in lower jaw; Upper Cretaceous.

Megalosauridae—large; skull large, with long jaws; sharp teeth with double edges and usually rounded; forelimbs very short; hind legs powerful and adapted for running; femur longer than tibia; claws large and sharp, curved for tearing; Lower Jurassic to ?Upper Cretaceous.

Allosauridae—large, some giant forms; skull large; long hind legs and short front legs equipped with formidable claws; similar to the megalosaurids, and the two families may be synonymous; Upper Jurassic to Lower Cretaceous.

Ceratosauridae—similar in appearance to the allosaurids, but with horns surmounting the snout and many differences in respect to the vertebrae and girdles; Upper Jurassic.

Spinosauridae—giant; spines of the vertebrae lengthened to form a high sail; Upper Cretaceous.

Tyrannosauridae—large to giant forms; with the general look of the megalosaurids and allosaurids, but more powerful; forelimbs reduced to being virtually useless; possibly scavengers as well as stalkers of prey; Upper Cretaceous.

Therizinosauridae—gigantic; known only from front limbs, with very long and straight claws; bones resemble those of deinocheirids, but are more massive, with metacarpals being of unequal lengths; first metacarpal very short and heavy; Upper and perhaps Lower Cretaceous.

?Teratosauridae—known with certainty only from a single maxilla with teeth; teeth large, recurved, serrated, possibly pertaining to a large thecodont; Upper Triassic.

Herrerasauridae—moderate-sized; carnivorous; head apparently large; teeth probably of typical theropod type; neck apparently short; probably bipedal; pelvis differs from that of other saurischians; exact placement among the Saurischia is not certain; Middle to Upper Triassic.

Staurikosauridae—most primitive and ancient of all known dinosaurs; small and very generalized; Middle Triassic.

Shanshanosauridae—small; small skull; caniniform teeth; relatively long neck; short forelimbs; tibia longer than femur; humerus approximately one-third as long as femur; Upper Cretaceous.

Noasauridae—medium-sized; large claw on the second digit of the foot with different shape than that in dromaeosaurids; Upper Cretaceous.

Segnosauridae—medium to large-sized; skull comparatively small, jaws toothless anteriorly with a horny beak provided during life, and with small "cheek" teeth; opisthopubic pelvis, alti-iliac with widely separated ilia and a cubic projection on the posterior iliac wing's lateral surface; tetradactyl pes with metatarsus short and non-compact; vertebrae elongated and large; possibly amphibiotic and icthyophagous; some superficial resemblances to ornithischians; Upper Cretaceous.

Suborder SAUROPODOMORPHA—large, often gigantic; long neck; small head; flourished from Upper Triassic to Upper Cretaceous.

Infraorder PROSAUROPODA*—possibly ancestors of sauropods; both small and large varieties; carnivorous, herbivorous and perhaps omnivorous forms; skull small with leaf-shaped teeth; bones heavy; stocky hind limbs; bipedal or quadrupedal; Triassic to Lower Jurassic.

Families:

Anchisauridae—extremely primitive; mainly slender-limbed forms; Upper Triassic to Lower Jurassic.

Plateosauridae—heavy and large; mainly stout-limbed forms; Upper Triassic to Lower Jurassic.

Life-sized figure of *Struthiomimus* at the New York World's Fair (1964-65). Courtesy of the Sinclair Oil Corporation.

*Heerden has proposed that the name Prosauropoda be replaced by Palaeopoda.

Juvenile specimen (cast) of an Asian theropod *Tarbosaurus bataar*. Courtesy of the Institute of Paleobiology in Warsaw.

Actual-size model of one of the largest theropods *Tyrannosaurus*, created for the New York World's Fair (1964–65). The model was equipped with a moving lower jaw. Courtesy of the Sinclair Oil Corporation.

Incomplete skeleton of the sauropodomorph *Apatosaurus excelsus*. Courtesy of the Field Museum of Natural History.

The huge sauropodomorph *Apatosaurus* as it appeared at the New York World's Fair (1964-65). Courtesy of the Sinclair Oil Corporation.

Skeleton of the flat-headed hadrosaur *Anatosaurus annectens*.
Courtesy of the South Dakota School of Mines and Technology.

Melanorosauridae—trend toward quadrupedal locomotion; possibly should be placed among the Sauropoda; mainly Upper Triassic with some possible representation in Middle Triassic and at least one Lower Jurassic form.

Infraorder SAUROPODA—usually gigantic, quadrupedal forms; heavy bones; small head and long neck; tail long; feet broad; Upper Triassic to Upper Cretaceous.

*Families:**

Camarasauridae—skull short, light, with very large openings; snout short; nasal openings in front of eyes; teeth heavy; neck vertebrae with short spines; shoulder blade short; Middle Jurassic to Lower Cretaceous.

SUBFAMILIES:
Cetiosaurinae—moderate to large; the most primitive sauropods
Brachiosaurinae—huge; front legs longer than hind legs; tail

*This family breakdown of sauropods is an old one. More recent studies indicate that some sauropod subfamilies should be elevated to familial status. John S. McIntosh (1978) has proposed that the family Diplodocidae embrace the family Mamenchisauridae and the subfamilies Atlantosaurinae, Diplodocinae and Dicraeosaurinae. The subfamily Titanosaurinae, including the only known armored sauropods, will probably be raised to the status of family.

Anatosaurus, a typical flat-headed hadrosaur, portrayed here as an aquatic creature. Courtesy the National Museums of Canada.

short; moderate to large
Euhelopodinae—usually small
Camarasaurinae—large

Diplodocidae–skull long and moderately heavy; snout long; nasal openings high on head; teeth delicate; neck vertebrae with well developed spines; shoulder blade long; ?Lower Jurassic to Upper Cretaceous.

SUBFAMILIES:
?Titanosaurinae—slender to heavy, including forms with armor
Atlantosaurinae—massive
Diplodocinae—slender; extremely long; pencil-shaped teeth
Dicraeosaurinae—similar to Diplodocinae, with shorter neck

Skull of a typical pachycephalosaur, *Stegoceras validus*. Courtesy of the Smithsonian Institution.

The suborder Stegosauria is exemplified by *Stegosaurus*, here depicted as a "Dinoland" exhibit for the New York World's Fair (1964–65). Courtesy of the Sinclair Oil Corporation.

Mamenchisauridae—similar in many characters to Diplodocidae, but with neck much longer; known only from Upper Jurassic of East Asia

?Chubutisauridae—gigantic, heavily constructed; Upper Cretaceous

Order ORNITHISCHIA

Suborder ORNITHOPODA—mostly if not entirely bipedal; usually without armor.

Families:

Fabrosauridae—small; hollow-boned; bipedal; leaf-shaped teeth, the tooth row being continuous with the margin of the outer jaw; cheekless; Upper Triassic to Upper Jurassic.

Heterodontosauridae*—similar to fabrosauridae, except that the tooth row is recessed inward and sharp teeth are present; Upper Triassic to Lower Jurassic.

Scelidosauridae**—armored forms resembling iguanodonts in general appearance; skull of moderate size with antorbital fenestrum present; neck moderately long; limb bones hollow; feet clawed; Lower Jurassic.

Hypsilophodontidae—generally small; feet have claws; Jurassic to Cretaceous.

Iguanodontidae—all sizes; limbs slender to massive; Jurassic to Cretaceous.

Hadrosauridae—large; "duck bills" formed by flat, broad jaws; new teeth replace from below those worn out; adapted for swimming; Cretaceous.

SUBFAMILIES:

Hadrosaurinae—flat-headed or solid-crested
Lambeosaurinae—skulls usually surmounted by hollow crests, possibly for heightening olfactory sense, formed by premaxillary and nasal bones

*Possibly the Heterodontosauridae is not an ornithopod family. It may require its own suborder.

**Possibly the Scelidosauridae is not an ornithopod family. It may require its own suborder.

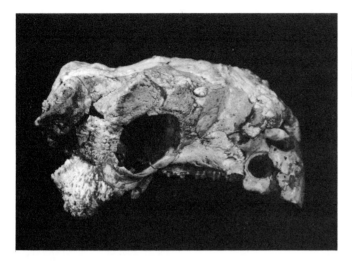

Skull of the ankylosaur *Pinacosaurus grangeri*. The specimen is from a juvenile individual. Courtesy of the Institute of Paleobiology in Warsaw.

The armored dinosaur *Ankylosaurus* strikes a menacing pose in this life-sized exhibit created by the Jonas Studios for the New York World's Fair (1964–65). Courtesy of the Sinclair Oil Corporation.

Skeleton of the small ceratopsian dinosaur *Protoceratops andrewsi*. Courtesy of the Field Museum of Natural History.

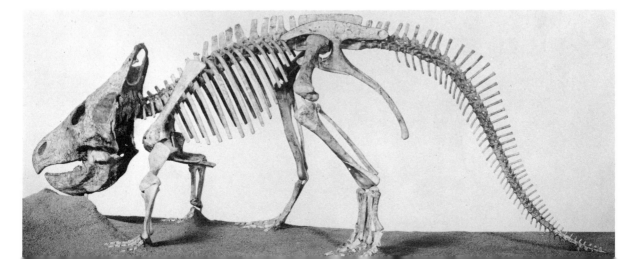

Tracks left by a theropod dinosaur in sandstone. Courtesy of the Field Museum of Natural History.

The large ceratopsian *Chasmosaurus* emerges from a cave in *When Dinosaurs Ruled the Earth*, a Hammer/Warner Brothers motion picture of 1970. The model was sculpted by Jim Danforth and animated by Dave Allen.

Full-sized statue of *Triceratops*, equipped with a moving head for its appearance at the New York World's Fair (1964–65). Courtesy of the Sinclair Oil Corporation.

Broken dinosaur egg discovered in the Gobi Desert of Mongolia. Courtesy of the Field Museum of Natural History.

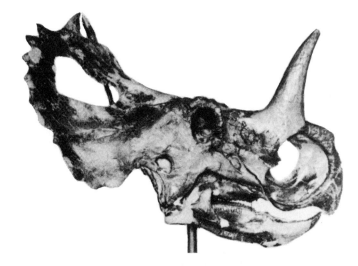

Skull of *Centrosaurus nasicornis*, a large, short-frilled ceratopsian. Courtesy of the Smithsonian Institution.

Suborder PACHYCEPHALOSAURIA*—"bone-headed" dinosaurs, so named because of the domed skull; bipedal; various sizes; probably entirely terrestrial; Cretaceous.

Family:

Pachycephalosauridae—same as above.

Suborder STEGOSAURIA—quadrupedal; forelimbs shorter than hind legs; dorsal region surmounted by two rows of bony plates and/or spines; plates probably used for protection and/or temperature control; Jurassic through Upper Cretaceous.

Family:

Stegosauridae—same as above.

Suborder ANKYLOSAURIA—stocky, armored dinosaurs; short, broad feet; carapace with bony armor; head carried low; Upper Jurassic to Upper Cretaceous.

Families:

Nodosauridae—body upright; no tail club; large lateral spikes often present; skull hornless and pear-shaped, armored with bony plates; lateral temporal openings covered with bone; temporal nostrils; teeth small; possibly somewhat aggressive; Middle Jurassic to Upper Cretaceous.

Ankylosauridae—body squat; triangular head with horns; lateral spikes small if present at all; tail terminates with a heavy club used as a defensive weapon; probably more passive than nodosaurids; Cretaceous.

Suborder CERATOPSIA—varying sizes; skulls large to gigantic, often with horns and large shields of bone; snout beaklike; almost exclusively quadrupedal; Cretaceous.

Families:

*Psittacosauridae***—ancestral ceratopsians; bipedal, with rather large forelimbs; small size; Lower to Upper Cretaceous.

*Not all scientists agree that Pachycephalosauria should be separate from Ornithopoda; Dong (1878) places the flat-headed pachycephalosaurs in their own family, Homalocephaleridae.

** Some paleontologists believe the Psittacosauridae to be a family under the suborder Ornithopoda.

Protoceratopsidae—primitive; hornless or with rudimentary horn; with or without frill; small size; quadrupedal and perhaps bipedal forms; Upper Cretaceous.

Ceratopsidae—large to giant forms; frilled skull enormous; horns of varying sizes; quadrupedal; Upper Cretaceous.

Abbreviations

In order to simplify each text entry and to obviate the repetition of frequently recurring terms, the following abbreviations shall be used:

SUBORDERS—Ank., Ankylosauria; Cer., Ceratopsia; Orn., Ornithopoda; Pach., Pachycephalosauria; Saur., Sauropodomorpha; Steg., Stegosauria; and Ther., Theropoda.

INFRAORDERS—Prosaur., Prosauropoda; and Sauro., Sauropoda.

FAMILIES—Allo., Allosauridae; Anchi., Anchisauridae; Anky., Ankylosauridae; Archae., Archaeopterygidae; Caenag., Caenagnathidae; Camar., Camarasauridae; Cerat., Ceratopsidae; Cerato., Ceratosauridae; Chubut., Chubutisauridae; Coel., Coeluridae; Compsog., Compsognathidae; Deino., Deinocheiridae; Diplod., Diplodocidae; Dromae., Dromaeosauridae; Fabro., Fabrosauridae; Gobi., Gobipterygidae; Hadro., Hadrosauridae; Herrer., Herrerasauridae; Heter., Heterodontosauridae; Hypsil., Hypsilophodontidae; Iguan., Iguanodontidae; Item., Itemiridae; Megal., Megalosauridae; Melan., Melanorosauridae; Noa., Noasauridae; Nodo., Nodosauridae; Ornith., Ornithomimidae; Ovi., Oviraptoridae; Pachy., Pachycephalosauridae; Plate., Plateosauridae; Podok., Podokesauridae; Proto., Protoceratopsidae; Psittac., Psittacosauridae; Saurorn., Saurornithoididae; Scelid., Scelidosauridae; Segi., Segisauridae; Segno., Segnosauridae; Shanshan., Shanshanosauridae; Spino., Spinosauridae; Staurik., Staurikosauridae; Stego., Stegosauridae; Terat., Teratosauridae; Theriz., Therizinosauridae; Troödon., Troödontidae; and Tyrann., Tyrannosauridae.

SUBFAMILIES—Atlanto., Atlantosaurinae; Brachio., Brachiosaurinae; Camara., Camarasaurinae; Cetio., Cetiosaurinae; Dicraeo., Dicraeosaurinae; Diplodo., Diplodocinae; Euhelo., Euhelopodinae; Hadrosaur., Hadrosaurinae; Lambeo., Lambeosaurinae; Mamenchi., Mamenchisaurinae; and Titano., Titanosaurinae.

MESOZOIC PERIODS—Cret., Cretaceous; Jur., Jurassic; Trias., Triassic; also L., Lower; M., Middle; U., Upper.

Fossilized dinosaur skin. Courtesy of the National Museums of Canada.

This life-sized statue of *Apatosaurus* stands on a hilltop in
Dinosaur Park, Rapid City, South Dakota.

Restoration of the armored dinosaur *Acanthopholis* by Neave Parker.
Courtesy of the British Museum (Natural History).

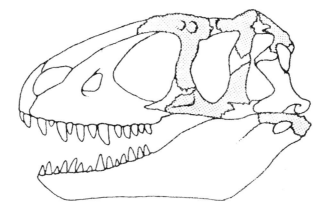

Skull of the theropod *Acrocanthosaurus atokensis*. (After Langston.)

A

Abrictosaurus Hopson, 1975—*Orn., Heter., U. Trias.* (Possibly *Lycorhinus*.) This heterodontosaur from the Stormberg Series of South Africa is known from a presumably female specimen lacking the caniniform teeth.

Acanthopholis Huxley, 1867—*Ank., Nodo., L. Cret.* Known from scattered fossil fragments, including many armor plates, this ankylosaur was discovered in the Chalk Marl of Folkestone and in the Cambridge Greensand near Cambridge, England. Though fossil material pertaining to this genus is poor, artists have created fanciful restorations of the animal with a slender body armed with spines on the shoulders and with dermal plates.

Acrocanthosaurus Stovall and Langston, 1950—*Ther., ?Family, L. Cret.* (Possibly, in part, *Altispinax*.) This giant theropod is probably more closely allied with the allosaurids or tyrannosaurids than the megalosaurids. The skull is large and one of the more unusual aspects of the skeleton is the great height of the vertebral spines. The genus is known from an incomplete skull and two incomplete skeletons from Atoka County, Oklahoma.

Pelvis of the theropod
Adasaurus. (After Barsbold.)

Adasaurus Barsbold, 1978—*Ther., ?Dromae., L. Cret.* Name was given to a picture of a pelvis which is similar to that of *Deinonychus.* The dinosaur itself has not yet been described.

Aegyptosaurus Stromer, 1932—*Saur., Sauro., Diplod., ?Titano., U. Cret.* The genus is imperfectly known from fragments and some good limb bones discovered in Egypt. The material has apparently been destroyed.

Aepisaurus Gervais, 1853—*Saur., Sauro., ?Diplod., ?Titano., L. Cret.* (*Aepyosaurus.*) Known only from a humerus from Monte Ventoux, France, this dinosaur might be a titanosaurid.

Aepyosaurus Huene, 1932—A misspelling of *Aepisaurus.*

Aethyopus E. Hitchcock, 1848—(See *Fulicopus.*)

Aetonychopus Ellenberger, 1974—*U. Trias.* The term has been given to ichnites, possibly made by a prosauropod or a theropod, found in

Restoration of the carnivorous dinosaur *Acrocanthosaurus* prepared for this book by George Olshevsky and Franc Reyes.

1 m

South Africa and in the Upper Stormberg Series of Mokanametsong, in Lesotho.

Aetonyx Broom, 1911—*Saur., Prosaur., Anchi., U. Trias.* (See *Massospondylus.*)

Agathaumas Cope, 1872—*Cer., Cerat., U., Cret.* (Possibly *Triceratops.*) The term *Agathaumas* has been given to an incomplete skeleton, lacking the skull, from the Lance Formation of Sweetwater County, Wyoming. Fragmentary material from Colorado and South Dakota has also been ascribed to *Agathaumas*, though there is no real proof for this assumption. Some of this latter material, called *A. mortuarius*, has been referred to *Polyonax.* Lull felt this genus was transitional between *Monoclonius* and *Triceratops.* Though *Agathaumas* is too poorly known to be restored, artists have in the past created their own imaginative versions of the animal with three horns and a spiked frill.

Aggiosaurus Ambayrac, 1913—*?Ther., ?Megal., U. Jur.* (Possibly *Megalosaurus.*) The genus is known from a lower jaw as large as that of *Tyrannosaurus*, discovered in the Cape d'Aggio–La Turbie of Monaco. It may be a valid genus or, as some paleontologists believe, crocodilian or a plesiosaur.

Agialopous Branson and Mehl, 1933—*U. Trias.* These fossil footprints discovered in Wyoming may have been left by the theropod dinosaur or even a quadrupedal saurischian. Haubold has placed the ichnites in the footprint family Parachirotheriidae.

Agrosaurus Seeley, 1891—*Saur., Prosaur., Anchi.* This genus, discovered on the coast of Queensland, is known only from fragmentary material, including a claw and broken tooth, and a tibia approximately 21 centimeters (8 inches) long. Though the material has previously been referred to the Coeluridae from the Upper Jurassic, recent studies indicate that it belongs to the prosauropod family Anchisauridae and occurs in the Upper Triassic or Lower Jurassic.

Alamosaurus Gilmore, 1922—*Saur., Sauro., Diplod., ?Titano., U. Cret.* From New Mexico, Utah and Texas, this genus is one of the latest known sauropods. *Alamosaurus* is considerably larger than *Titanosaurus* and has extremely long front limbs.

Albertosaurus Osborn, 1905—*Ther., Tyrann., U. Cret.* (*Gorgosaurus*; probably *Deinodon.*) Known from numerous complete skeletons, some immature, *Albertosaurus* was a giant predator approximately 10.5 me-

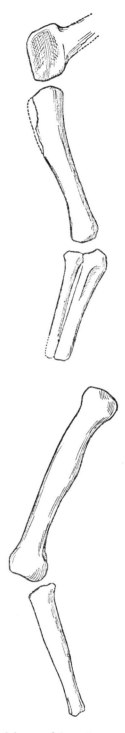

Limb bones of *Aegyptosaurus baharijiensis.* (After Stromer.)

The giant dinosaur *Aegyptosaurus* as restored by George Olshevsky and
John Allison.

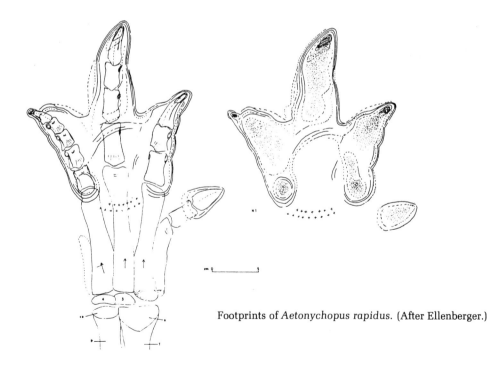

Footprints of *Aetonychopus rapidus*. (After Ellenberger.)

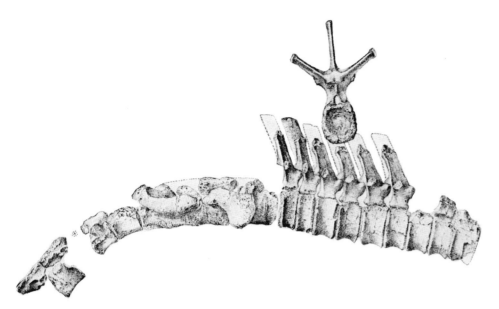

Presacral and sacral vertebrae of the ceratopsian
Agathaumas sylvestris. (After Cope.)

ters (35 feet) long and weighing 2.6 metric tons (3 tons). Superficially, the animal resembles a smaller version of *Tyrannosaurus,* with two sharp claws on each of the almost useless hands. *Albertosaurus* represents one of the last stages in theropod evolution. It stalked the Red Deer River region of Alberta, Canada, and was also present in Montana and Wyoming, and perhaps in other regions. In 1970, Russell proposed that *Albertosaurus* primarily hunted hadrosaurs.

Albisaurus   Frič, 1905—*Ank., ?Family, L. Cret.* Known only from an incomplete tarsal found in Bohemia, *Albisaurus* was once considered to be an ornithopod (*Iguanodon albinus*) but is now accepted by some paleontologists as an ankylosaur. McIntosh believes the specimen to be non-dinosaurian.

Alectrosaurus   Gilmore, 1933—*Ther., Tyrann., U. Cret.* Known from imperfect skeletal remains found in Inner Mongolia and fragmentary material perhaps relating to this genus from Kazakhstan, *Alectrosaurus* is a slender, moderate-sized theropod. Recently discovered specimens indicate that the large humerus referred to *Alectrosaurus* by Gilmore does not belong to that genus, and may be that of a segnosaurid.

Algoasaurus   Broom, 1904—*Saur., Sauro., ?Fam., ?L. Cret.* This dinosaur from the Sunday River Formation of South Africa is known from

A fanciful conception of *Agathaumas* fights *Triceratops*, both models sculpted by Marcel Delgado and animated by Willis O'Brien in *The Lost World* (First National, 1925), a film based on a novel by Sir Arthur Conan Doyle.

poor skeletal material including a femur, phalanx and incomplete scapula and vertebrae. The femur, probably some .4 meters (over 1 foot 4 inches) when complete, and the vertebrae, about .4 meters high when complete, resemble those of *Diplodocus*. Though it has been recorded that the tail was less developed than in most sauropods, this assumption is not based upon evidence. Recent work by paleobotanists indicates that the beds in which *Algoasaurus* was found may be as old as Middle Jurassic.

Alioramus Kurzanov, 1976—*Ther., Tyrann., U. Cret.* From Nogon-Tsav, Mongolia, this modest-sized tyrannosaur is unusual in having six small, jagged crests surmounting the low snout.

Allosaurus Marsh, 1877—*Ther., Allo., U. Jur. (Apatodon, Creosaurus, Epanterias, Labrosaurus, Saurophagus;* in part, *Hypsirophus;* probably *Antrodemus.)* From the Morrison Formation of Colorado, Wyoming, Utah and Shanxi, this theropod was one of the most dangerous predators of the Jurassic Period. As in all the heavily built flesh-eating dinosaurs, the neck is relatively short but strong. The forelimbs terminate with three powerful claws and the taloned feet were capable of efficiently pinning down and rending the flesh of its prey. *Allosaurus* reached an average length of 8.5 meters (approximately 30 feet) but some individuals attained gigantic size. One specimen of *Allosaurus*, informally called *Saurophagus maximus*, may have reached an impressive length of 12.5 meters (42 feet) and could even have outweighed the celebrated *Tyrannosaurus*. Lachrymal horns are present in the skull of *Allosaurus*,

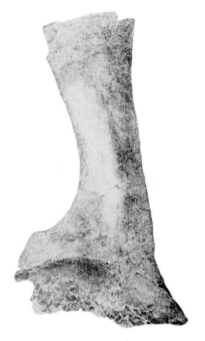

Left sacrum of the sauropod dinosaur *Alamosaurus sanjuanensis*.

Restoration of the sauropod *Alamosaurus* prepared for this book by William Stout.

Skeleton of the giant carnivore *Albertosaurus libratus*. This exhibit, prepared by Orville Gilpin, was the first dinosaur skeleton to be mounted without external supports. Courtesy of the Field Museum of Natural History.

Skull of *Albertosaurus lancensis*.
Courtesy of R. A. Long,
S. P. Welles and the Cleveland
Museum of Natural History.

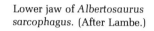

Lower jaw of *Albertosaurus
sarcophagus*. (After Lambe.)

The flesh-eating *Albertosaurus libratus* mounted realistically over the
herbivore *Lambeosaurus lambei*. Courtesy of the Field Museum of Natural
History.

Model of *Albertosaurus* standing over the vanquished *Lambeosaurus* by Maidi Wiebe. Courtesy of the Field Museum of Natural History.

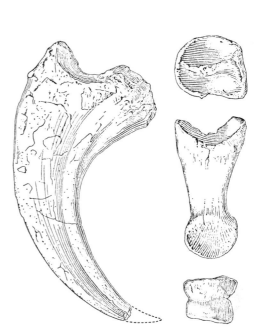

Manus bones of *Alectrosaurus olseni*. (After Gilmore.)

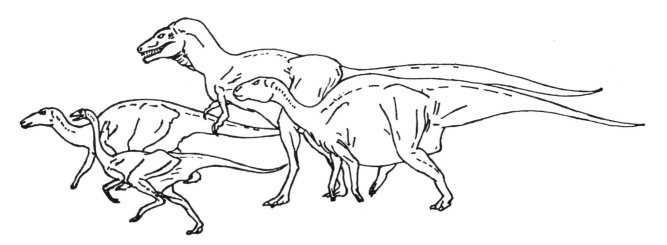

Hypothetical restoration by George Olshevsky of Gilmore's dinosaurs from Iren Dabusu. From left to right are the hadrosaur *Gilmoreosaurus asiaticus*, the theropods *Archeornithomimus asiaticus* and *Alectrosaurus olseni*, and the hadrosaur *Bactrosaurus johnsoni*. From *Mesozoic Vertebrate Life* #1 (1980).

placed slightly in front of the eyes. As a result of Madsen's monograph, based on at least forty-four individuals, *Allosaurus* is now the best known of all theropods.

Alocodon   Thulborn, 1973—*Orn., Fabro., U. Jur.* From Pedrógão, Portugal, this genus is based on teeth. It has been proposed that the predentary, which is not entirely known, is between that of *Fabrosaurus australis* and *Hypsilophodon foxii* in shape.

Altispinax   Huene, 1923—*Ther., ?Family, L. Cret.* (Possibly, in part, *Acrocanthosaurus.*) *Altispinax* cannot be absolutely classified. The type specimen is a single tooth from the Wealden Formation of Germany and named *Megalosaurus dunkeri* by Dames in 1884. More indeterminate teeth and three very high dorsal vertebrae were discovered in the same sediments in England and, with no proof, were referred to *M. dunkeri.* Huene, after examining the material from England, said that it was not attributable to *Megalosaurus* and renamed the material, including the type specimen, *Altispinax dunkeri.* Based on recent studies by Langston and Stovall, *Altispinax* may be synonymous with *Acrocanthosaurus.*

Amblonyx   E. Hitchcock, 1858— (See *Fulicopus.*)

Amblydactylus   Sternberg, 1932—*L. Cret.* These large, tridactyl footprints from British Columbia may have been made by an ornithopod dinosaur.

Ammosaurus   Marsh, 1891—*Saur., Prosaur., Plate., L. Jur.* From Connecticut and Arizona, this moderate-sized prosauropod is quite similar to *Anchisaurus.* The animal was possibly capable of some quadrupedal locomotion. *Ammosaurus* is related to *Massospondylus.*

Amphicoelias   Cope, 1877—*Saur., Sauro., Diplod., Diplodo., U. Jur.* (Possibly *Diplodocus.*) Based on poor skeletal material including a femur, scapula, ulna, coracoid and incomplete vertebrae, this dinosaur is known to be from Colorado and Utah. The animal's limb bones are very slender, as in *Diplodocus,* but the seemingly longer neck indicates that it may be a valid genus. Some material referred by Cope to *Amphicoelias* intimates a truly gigantic dinosaur; unfortunately, this material has been lost.

Amphisaurus   Marsh, 1882— (See *Anchisaurus.*)

Amtosaurus   Kurzanov and Tumanova, 1978—*Ank., Anky., U. Cret.* Known only from a piece of a braincase found in the Bayan-Shireh suite of Mongolia, *Amtosaurus* seems most similar to *Talarurus.*

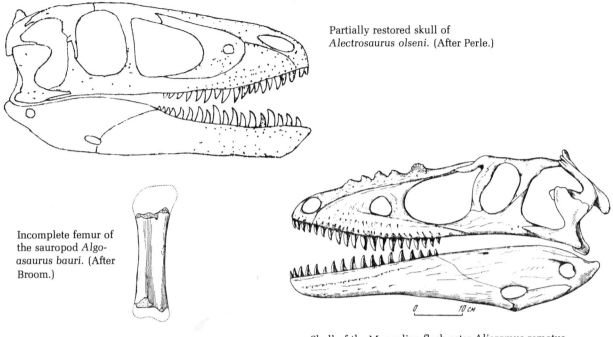

Partially restored skull of *Alectrosaurus olseni.* (After Perle.)

Incomplete femur of the sauropod *Algo-asaurus bauri.* (After Broom.)

Skull of the Mongolian flesh-eater *Alioramus remotus.* (After Kurzanov.)

Amygdalodon   Cabrera, 1947—*Saur., Sauro., Camar., Brachio., M. Jur.* This genus, known from very poor material—including four teeth, an incomplete pubis and scapula, and several vertebrae—was discovered in the Chubut province of Argentina.

Anatopus   de Lapparent and Montenat, 1967—*L. Jur.* The term has been given to webbed footprints, apparently dinosaurian, discovered in Veillon, France. Though de Lapparent and Montenat believe them to be ornithischian, other paleontologists consider them to be possibly saurischian.

Anatosaurus   Lull and Wright, 1942—*Orn., Hadro., Hadrosaur, U. Cret.* (Possibly *Edmontosaurus, Thespesius.*) This huge ornithopod is the classic "duck-billed dinosaur," so called because of the long, low and narrow hadrosaurian skull resembling a duck's bill. The skull of *Anatosaurus* had approximately two thousand teeth in the back of the mouth, with new ones replacing those worn down by the continual chewing of vegetation. The flat, heavy tail served as both a balancing device and as a propulsive organ for swimming. The dinosaur attained a length of more than 9 meters (over 30 feet). Controversy remains among

Two skeletons of *Allosaurus fragilis* with the ornithopod *Camptosaurus dispar* (center). Courtesy of J. H. Madsen, Jr., and the Utah Museum of Natural History, University of Utah.

Restoration of *Alioramus* prepared for this book by William Stout.

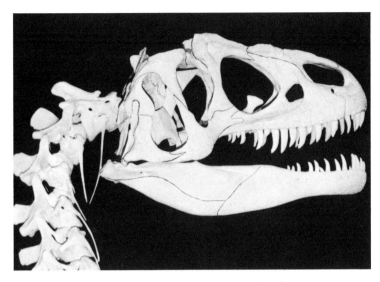

Restored skull and cervical vertebrae of *Allosaurus fragilis*.
Courtesy of J. H. Madsen, Jr.

Endocast of *Allosaurus*. Courtesy of J. H.
Madsen, Jr., and the Utah Museum of
Natural History, University of Utah.

Stegosaurus prepares to use its spiked tail in defense against the approaching
Allosaurus in a diorama of the Jurassic Period. Courtesy of the Milwaukee Public
Museum.

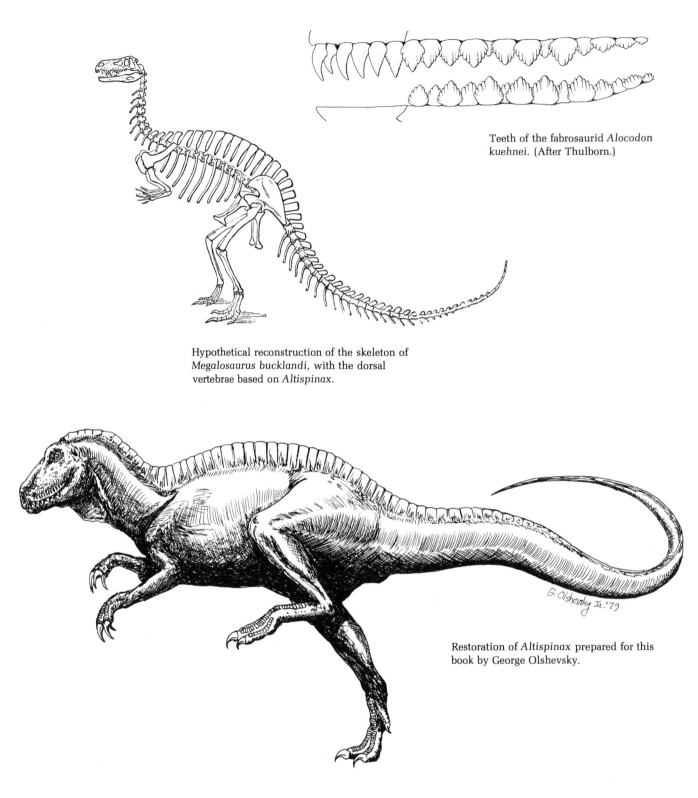

Teeth of the fabrosaurid *Alocodon
kuehnei*. (After Thulborn.)

Hypothetical reconstruction of the skeleton of
Megalosaurus bucklandi, with the dorsal
vertebrae based on *Altispinax*.

Restoration of *Altispinax* prepared for this
book by George Olshevsky.

paleontologists as to whether or not the animal's feet were webbed. Excellent mummified specimens of *Anatosaurus* have provided much information as to the creature's appearance in life. Based on more recent studies, Brett-Surman believes that *Anatosaurus* is really a junior synonym of *Edmontosaurus*, though no formal comparison of the two genera has yet been published, and that *A. copei* should be assigned a new generic name.

Anatrisauropus Ellenberger, 1970—*U. Trias.* From the Keuper of d'Anduze, France, Lesotho and the Lower Stormberg Series of South Africa, these footprints may have been left by a saurischian dinosaur.

Anchiceratops Brown, 1914—*Cer., Cerat., U Cret.* A short-crested giant ceratopsian from the Horseshoe Canyon Formation and Oldman Formation of Alberta, Canada, this genus is not too unlike its ancestor *Chasmosaurus*, though with a somewhat shorter tail and longer body. It has three horns—two relatively large ones above the orbits and a smaller horn above the snout. Since fossils of *Anchiceratops* occur only in coaly beds, it has been suggested that this dinosaur was a swamp dweller.

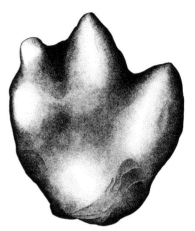

Natural cast of the dinosaur ichnite *Amblydactylus.* Drawing by Elizabeth Garsonnin, Provincial Museum of Alberta.

Anchisauripus Lull, 1904—*U. Trias. and L. Jur.* (Probably *Grallator;* possibly *Jeholosauripus.*) The term has been given to footprints found in New England, New Jersey, New Mexico, Pennsylvania, France, Wales and Argentina. The ichnites are three-toed, with an additional small digit toward the anterior part of the foot. Apparently the animal that left the tracks was a podokesaurid or other small, lightly built theropod.

Anchisaurus Marsh, 1885—*Saur., Prosaur., Anchi., L. Jur. (Amphisaurus, Megadactylus, Yaleosaurus.)* From Massachusetts, this prosauropod was probably an omnivore, though its blunt teeth indicate that *Anchisaurus* was more herbivorous than carnivorous. The dinosaur's limbs are stout, its feet are short and heavy and the small head surmounts a fairly long neck. The thumb sports one large claw. Marsh reported that the limb bones of *Anchisaurus* are hollow. In life the creature grew to a length of 2.1 meters (7 feet) and weighed about 27 kilograms (60 pounds).

Anchylosaurus Sternberg, 1971—A misspelling of *Ankylosaurus.*

Ancylosaurus Huene, 1909—A misspelling of *Ankylosaurus.*

Ankylosaurus Brown, 1908—*Ank., Anky., U. Cret.* This rare North American armored dinosaur exemplifies the suborder Ankylosauria.

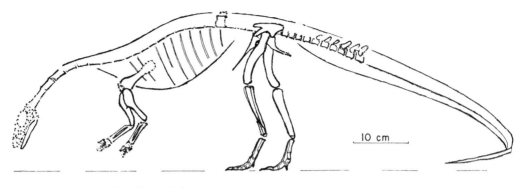

Reconstructed skeleton of the prosauropod
Ammosaurus major. (After Galton.)

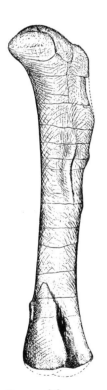

Femur of the sauropod
dinosaur *Amphicoelias
altus.* (After Osborn and
Mook.)

The body is completely protected by a series of bony armor plates. A series of conical dermal scutes protected the sides and back of the animal. The tail, which ended in a heavy club, could be swung as a formidable weapon. The jaws were massive but the teeth were tiny. *Ankylosaurus* was suitably protected against attack by theropod dinosaurs and was virtually invulnerable unless turned on its back. It was discovered in the Hell Creek beds of Montana.

Anodontosaurus   Sternberg, 1929—(See *Euoplocephalus.)*

Anomoepus   E. Hitchcock, 1848—*U. Trias. to L. Jur.* These footprints have been found in the Connecticut Valley, in New Jersey, New Mexico and Lesotho. The tracks are of both hind and front feet, intimating at least a somewhat quadrupedal animal. The manus has five digits and is not equipped with the usual theropod claws. The hind feet are slender with three functional claws. Perhaps the *Anomoepus* tracks were made by an ornithischian dinosaur; Haubold (1971) believes the footprint family Anomoepodidae may be prosauropod in origin.

Anoplosaurus   Seeley, 1879—*Orn., Iguan., L. Cret.* (Possibly *Eucercosaurus.*) This genus, once considered to be an ankylosaur, is now classified with the ornithopods. From the Cambridge Greensand of England, it is known from incomplete material, including part of a lower jaw, a humerus, tibia, femur and fragments.

Antarctosaurus   Huene, 1929—*Saur., Sauro., Diplod., Titano., U. Cret.* (Probably *Argyrosaurus.*) Reportedly from Brazil, Uruguay, Argentina, India and Kazakhstan, *Antarctosaurus* is among the largest of the sauropods. The skull measures over 60 centimeters (almost 2 feet) and one femur is more than 2.2 meters (7 feet, 2 inches) long. *Antarcto-saurus* is relatively slender for a sauropod.

Anticheiropus   E. Hitchcock, 1865—*L. Jur.* These ichnites from Massa-chusetts and southwest Africa may have been left by a giant dinosaur, possibly saurischian. These are the largest of the Newark Group of giant footprints.

Antrodemus   Leidy, 1870—*Ther., Allo., U. Jur.* (Probably *Allosaurus.*) Although *Antrodemus* is commonly referred to *Allosaurus*, their syno-nymity cannot be absolutely proven. *Antrodemus* is based upon half of a sixth caudal vertebra which closely resembles that of *Allosaurus.*

Restoration of *Ammosaurus* prepared for this book by Richard Hescox.

Partial braincase of the
armored dinosaur
Amtosaurus magnus.
(After Kurzanov and
Tumanova.)

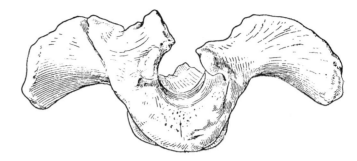

Amphicoelias portrayed as an
aquatic dinosaur by Charles R.
Knight.

Skull of *Anatosaurus
saskatchewanesis.* Courtesy of
the National Museums of
Canada.

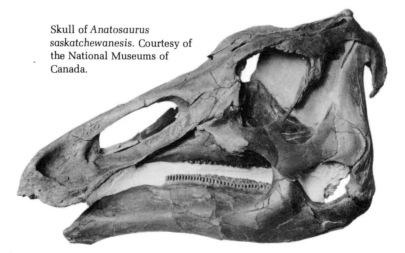

Restoration of *Anatosaurus*, the classic duck-billed dinosaur. From a
painting by Zdeněk Burian.

Skeleton of the hadrosaur *Anatosaurus annectens*. Courtesy of the
Smithsonian Institution.

Rare skull specimen of
Anatosaurus annectens
showing the sclerotic ring and
beak, now in the Senckenburg
Museum, the Netherlands.

Apatichnus   E. Hitchcock, 1858—*L. Jur.* These ichnites from the Connecticut Valley are apparently those of an ornithischian dinosaur; Haubold (1971) believes the tracks were made by prosauropods.

Apatodon   Marsh, 1877—(See *Allosaurus.*)

Apatosaurus   Marsh, 1877—*Saur., Sauro., Diplod., Atlanto., U. Jur.* (*Brontosaurus;* probably *Atlantosaurus;* possibly *Elosaurus.*) This giant dinosaur, known in both North America and Europe, embodies the universal conception of a "dinosaur." Typically sauropod, *Apatosaurus* had the classic massive body, the thick limbs and padded feet, the small head terminating the long neck and the lengthy whiplike tail. *Apatosaurus*, known by most people as the famed *Brontosaurus*, averages 20 meters (70 feet) in length. During life the animal must have weighed approximately 32 metric tons (up to 36 tons). In recent years a skull has finally been attributed to *Apatosaurus*, which is quite large and similar to that of *Diplodocus.* Traditionally, such titans as *Apatosaurus* have been described as spending considerable time in the water, which helped to support their weight and offered protection from the land-roaming theropods; but their aquatic habits are now being seriously questioned by some paleontologists. In 1978, Berman and McIntosh referred *Apatosaurus* to the Diplodocidae.

Aralosaurus   Rozhdestvensky, 1970—*Orn., Hadro., Hadrosaur., U. Cret.* From central Kazakhstan, central Asia, this genus is known from an incomplete skull. *Aralosaurus* is similar to *Kritosaurus* and *Lophorhothon.*

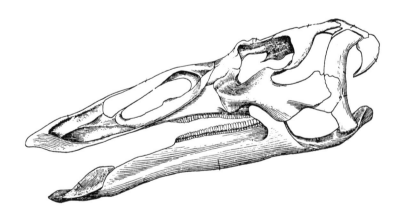

Skull of the ornithopod *Anatosaurus copei.* (After Lull-Wright.)

Archaeopteryx Meyer, 1861—?*Ther., Archae., U. Jur.* (*Archaeornis, Griphornis, Griphosaurus.*) Discovered in Germany, *Archaeopteryx* has traditionally been regarded as the first bird, somewhat reptilian with scales and clawed forelimbs, but definitely avian with imprints of its feathers finely preserved. In 1973 Ostrom proposed that, minus the feathers, *Archaeopteryx* would be taken for a small theropod dinosaur—or "coelurosaur," as they were once described—not unlike *Compsognathus* in skeletal structure. Ostrom postulated that *Archaeopteryx* and all later birds descended directly from theropods. Some other paleontologists have gone a step further to consider *Archaeopteryx* a feathered dinosaur, or at least closer to the dinosaurs than the birds. Ostrom further proposed that *Archaeopteryx* could not fly but used its feathered forelimbs for seizing prey. The feathers could have been used for insulation and/or flight.

Archaeornis Petronievics, 1922—(See *Archaeopteryx.*)

Archaeornithomimus Russell, 1972—*Ther., Ornith., U. Cret.* From Maryland and the Gobi Desert of Mongolia and possibly also from Montana, Wyoming and Arkansas, this genus is known from poor skeletal material including an almost complete manus and various isolated bones. *Archaeornithomimus* resembles a smaller version of *Struthiomimus* with slightly shorter hind legs.

Arctosaurus Adams, 1875—?*Ther., ?Family, U. Trias.* This genus is known only from one cervical vertebra resembling that of *Calamospondylus*, except for its neural spine and free cervical ribs. It may or may not even be dinosaurian; some paleontologists believe it to be a turtle.

Footprints of *Anatrisauropus ginsburgi* (left) and *A. hereroensis* (right). (After Ellenberger.)

Skull of the horned dinosaur *Anchiceratops longirostris.* Courtesy of the University of Wyoming.

Latter portion of the skull of *Anchiceratops ornatus*, including the orbital horns and shield. Courtesy of the Field Museum of Natural History.

Restoration of *Anchiceratops*, prepared for this book by William Stout.

© 1977 Wm Stout

The specimen is from Bathurst Island in the Arctic. In 1976 Galton and Cluver referred *Arctosaurus* to the Theropoda.

Argoides   E. Hitchcock, 1845—*U. Trias. (Argozoum.)* These small footprints, discovered in Massachusetts and Connecticut, may have been left by a theropod.

Argozoum   Hitchcock, 1848—(See *Argoides.*)

Argyrosaurus   Lydekker, 1893—*Saur., Sauro., Diplod., Titan., U. Cret.* (Probably *Antarctosaurus.*) Known from a left front leg and manus, this genus represents one of the largest sauropods. The femur, from the Chubut Province of Argentina, is approximately 2.1 meters (6 feet 6 inches) long.

Aristosaurus   van Hoepen, 1920—*Saur., Prosaur, Plate., U. Trias.* From the Stormberg beds of South Africa, this small prosauropod is known from a nearly complete skeleton lacking the skull. The humerus of this dinosaur is short.

Aristosuchus   Seeley, 1887—*Ther., ?Family, L. Cret. (Calamospondylus* Fox; possibly *Thecocoelurus.)* The genus is known from an incomplete skeleton found on the Isle of Wight, England, with the distal "foot" of the pubis seemingly longer than that in many theropods.

Footprints of *Anchisauripus sillimani.* (After Lull.)

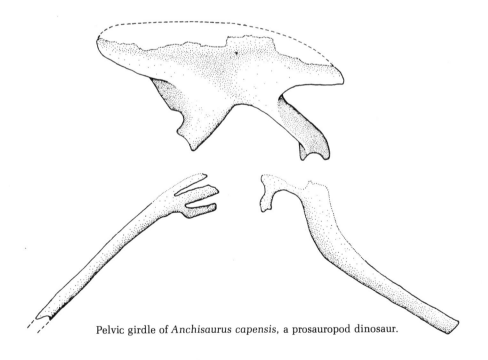

Pelvic girdle of *Anchisaurus capensis,* a prosauropod dinosaur.

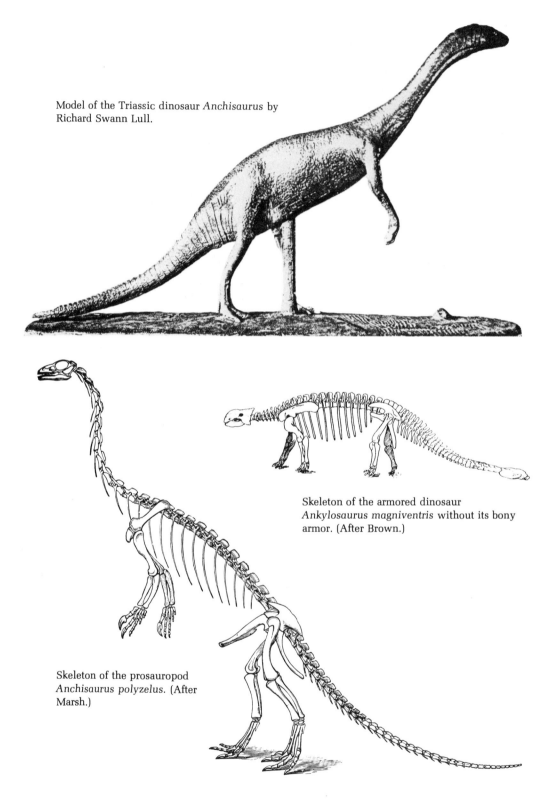

Model of the Triassic dinosaur *Anchisaurus* by Richard Swann Lull.

Skeleton of the armored dinosaur *Ankylosaurus magniventris* without its bony armor. (After Brown.)

Skeleton of the prosauropod *Anchisaurus polyzelus.* (After Marsh.)

Traditional restoration of *Ankylosaurus* incorrectly showing the large lateral
spikes. Courtesy of the Sinclair Oil Corporation.

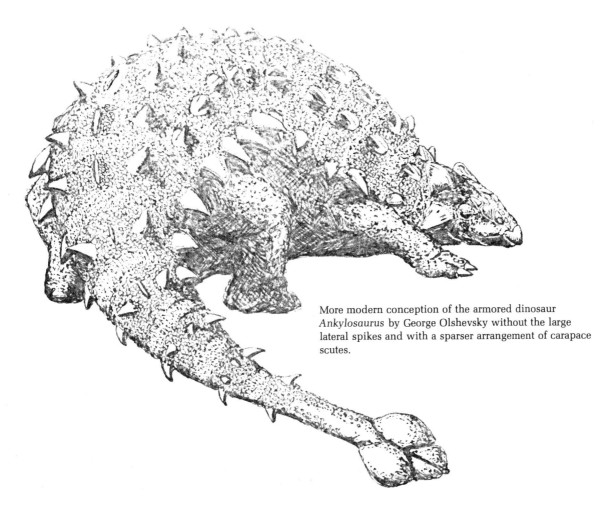

More modern conception of the armored dinosaur
Ankylosaurus by George Olshevsky without the large
lateral spikes and with a sparser arrangement of carapace
scutes.

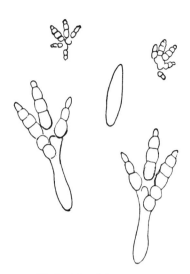

Footprints of *Anomoepus scambus*. (After Lull.)

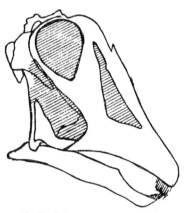

Skull of *Antarctosaurus wichmannianus*. (After Huene.)

Richard Swann Lull's conception of *Anomoepus*.

Arrhinoceratops Parks, 1925—*Cer., Cerat., U. Cret.* From the Horseshoe Canyon Formation of Alberta, Canada, this average-size and very rare ceratopsian vaguely resembles *Anchiceratops* with respect to the appearance of the shield and nasal horn. The shield, with two small fontanelles, may have been equipped with spikes. The snout is short and high. The horns above the orbits are larger than those in *Anchiceratops* and curved forward.

Asiatosaurus Osborn, 1924—*Saur., Sauro., ?Camar., L. Cret.* This genus is known from teeth, possibly indeterminate, found in Mongolia and possibly from vertebrae discovered in Wuerho, China.

Astrodon Johnston, 1865—*Saur., Sauro., Camar., Brachio, U. Jur.* (*Astrodonius;* possibly *Pleurocoelus.*) The dinosaur is known only from teeth from Prince Georges County, Maryland. Though *Astrodon* and *Pleurocoelus* are commonly considered to be synonymous, there is no proof of this.

Astrodonius Kuhn, 1961—(See *Astrodon.*)

Astrodontonius Steel, 1970—A misspelling of *Astrodonius.*

Atlantosaurus Marsh, 1877—*Saur., Sauro., Diplod., Atlanto., U. Jur.* (*Titanosaurus* Marsh; probably *Apatosaurus.*) From Colorado and Wyoming, this giant dinosaur is known from fragmentary material and a femur about 1.75 meters (almost 6 feet) long, indicating that the entire length of the animal would total some 23.5 meters (80 feet). McIntosh says that *Atlantosaurus immanis* is actually an exceptionally large *Apatosaurus.*

Restoration of *Antarctosaurus* by the author.

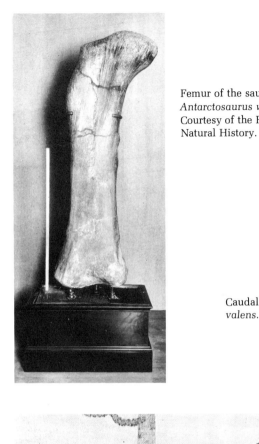

Femur of the sauropod dinosaur *Antarctosaurus wichmannianus.* Courtesy of the Field Museum of Natural History.

Caudal vertebra of *Antrodemus valens.* (After Leidy.)

A scene depicting Jurassic life of the Morrison. The plated dinosaur *Stegosaurus* is in danger of being attacked by the carnivorous *Antrodemus.* Painting by Ernest Untermann. Courtesy of the Dinosaur Nature Association.

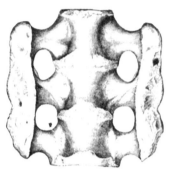

Sacrum of the sauropod
Apatosaurus ajax.

Footprints of *Apatichnus.* (After Lull.)

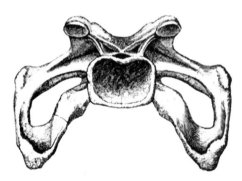

Cervical vertebra of
Apatosaurus laticollis.

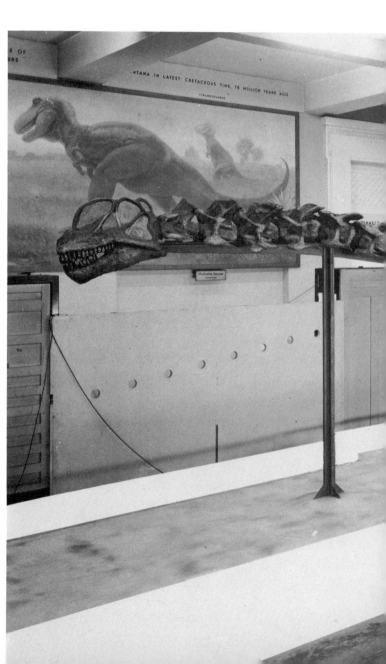

Skeleton of the giant dinosaur *Apatosaurus
excelsus.* The skull on this mount is that of
Camarasaurus. Courtesy of the Field
Museum of Natural History.

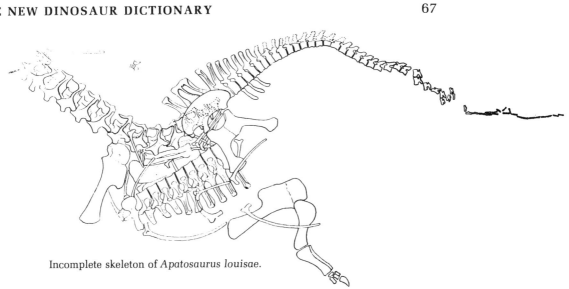

Incomplete skeleton of *Apatosaurus louisae*.

Probable *Apatosaurus* skull,
conforming closely to the skull of
Diplodocus rather than that of
Camarasaurus. (After Berman and
McIntosh.)

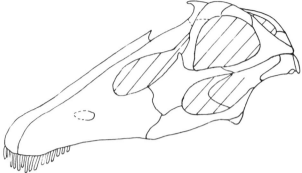

Apatosaurus and Jurassic crocodilians. From a mural by Charles R. Knight. Courtesy of the
Field Museum of Natural History.

Aublysodon   Leidy, 1868—(See *Deinodon.*)

Austrosaurus   Longman, 1933—*Saur., Sauro., ?Family, L. Cret.* This genus is based upon approximately six dorsal centra plus the neural arches and lower portions of the spine, and bits of ribs, from northern Queensland. Portions of five more individuals, including dorsals, caudals, fore and hind material, and parts of both girdles and ribs, found in central Queensland, have also been referred to this genus. The caudal vertebrae are of simple structure, with no struts, buttresses or laminae in the arches. The coracoid has a notch rather than foramen, a characteristic also found in some ornithischians. The metacarpals are exceptional-

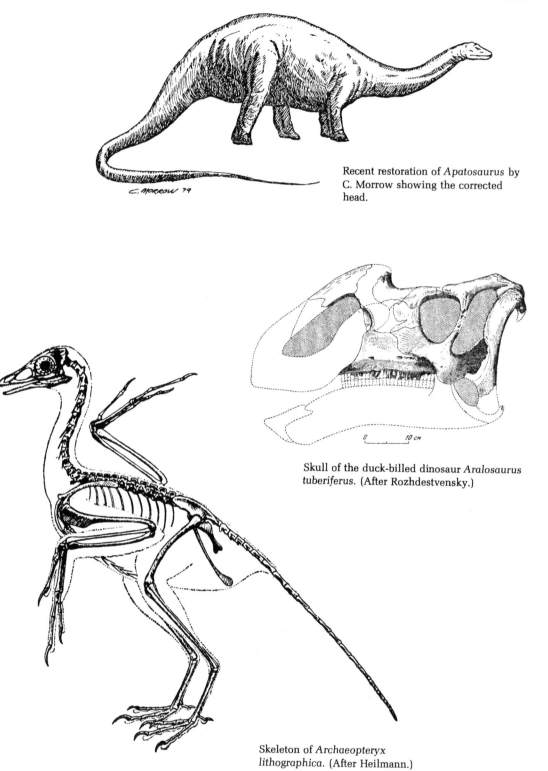

Recent restoration of *Apatosaurus* by
C. Morrow showing the corrected
head.

Skull of the duck-billed dinosaur *Aralosaurus
tuberiferus.* (After Rozhdestvensky.)

Skeleton of *Archaeopteryx
lithographica.* (After Heilmann.)

Model of *Archaeopteryx*, once classified as the first true bird, but now considered by some paleontologists to be a feathered theropod dinosaur. Courtesy of the Field Museum of Natural History.

Metacarpal of the theropod dinosaur *Archaeornithomimus asiaticus*. (After Gilmore.)

J. B. Abbott with the leg bones of the giant sauropod *Argyrosaurus superbus*. In the center background is the femur of *Antarctosaurus wichmannianus*. Courtesy of the Field Museum of Natural History.

Skeleton of the prosauropod
Aristosaurus erectus.

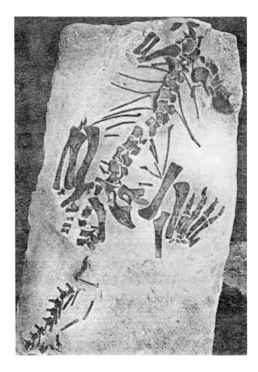

Vertebra of the theropod
Aristosuchus pusillus.

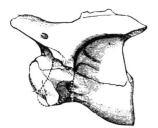

Cervical vertebra of
Arctosaurus osborni.

ly long in relation to the other forelimb elements and to other known sauropods. Presumably the forelimb was quite long, especially distally. *Austrosaurus* has features resembling both cetiosaurs and brachiosaurs, more so the former despite the long forelimb. Though the metacarpals are elongate, the humerus is not, suggesting that the dinosaur is not a brachiosaur but some other type of sauropod paralleling the brachiosaurs; the tooth from Lightning Ridge referred to *Austrosaurus* does, however, appear to be that of a brachiosaur (R. A. Molnar, personal communication).

Avalonia   Seeley, 1898—(See *Avalonianus.*)

Avalonianus   Kuhn, 1958—?*Saur.*, ?*Prosaur.*, ?*Melan.*, U. Trias. (Possibly *Picrodon.*) Known from a single indeterminate tooth from Somerset, England, this genus might be a theropod, prosauropod, or neither. Postcranial elements referred to *Avalonianus* belong to one of the largest known melanorosaurids.

Skull of the horned dinosaur
Arrhinoceratops brachyops. Courtesy
of the Royal Ontario Museum.

Skull of *Arrhinoceratops brachyops*.
Courtesy of the Royal Ontario Museum.

Restoration of *Arrhinoceratops*, prepared for this
book by William Stout.

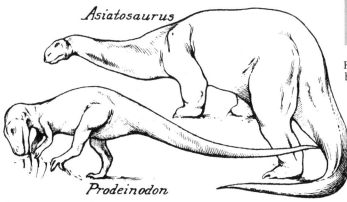

Hypothetical life restorations, prepared under the direction of Osborn, of two
dinosaurs based on teeth, the sauropod *Asiatosaurus* and the theropod
Prodeinodon. Both drawings were published in a 1928 issue of *Natural
History Magazine* and were based upon earlier restorations (of *Diplodocus*
and *Allosaurus*, respectively) by Charles R. Knight.

Avipes Huene, 1932—*?Ther., U. Trias.* This genus was discovered in Thuringia, Germany. It is known from three poorly preserved, incomplete metatarsals. The metatarsals are fused proximally, which is rare in dinosaurs.

Azendohsaurus Dutuit, 1972—*Orn., Fabro., U. Trias.* From Morocco, this moderate-sized dinosaur is known from a jaw fragment with teeth.

Hypothetical contours of *Austrosaurus* showing position of front limb and scapula. Courtesy of Ralph Molnar.

Tooth of the sauropod *Astrodon johnstoni.* (After Leidy.)

Restoration of *Atlantosaurus* prepared for this book by George Olshevsky and Ken Steacy.

Atlantosaurus montanus
Restored as an apatosaurid

Left femur of the giant dinosaur *Atlantosaurus montanus*. (After Marsh.)

Incomplete metatarsal of *Avipes dillstedianus*.

Restoration of *Austrosaurus* as a brachiosaurid by Mark Hallett.

Left femur of a large melanorosaurid
referred to *Avalonianus sanfordi*.

Mandible of the prosauropod
Azendohsaurus larroussii.

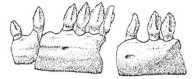

B

Bactrosaurus   Gilmore, 1933—*Orn., Hadro., Lambeo., U. Cret.* From central and western Asia, *Bactrosaurus* is one of the earliest hadrosaurs. The skull is that of a flat-headed hadrosaur while the skeleton is like that of a crested type. In life the animal was approximately 4 meters (13.5 feet) long and about 1.8 meters (6 feet) high at the hips.

Bagaceratops   Osmólska and Maryańska, 1975—*Cer., Proto., U. Cret.* This protoceratopsid was discovered in Mongolia. The skull features a rudimentary horn between the orbits and the snout. The crest is much smaller than that of *Protoceratops*.

Bahariasaurus   Stromer, 1934—*Ther., ?Family, U. Cret.* Known from incomplete material discovered in Egypt and probably destroyed, and recently in Niger, *Bahariasaurus* represents a huge theropod, nearly as large as *Tyrannosaurus*. The femur of this African carnivore measures almost 1.2 meters (4 feet) long.

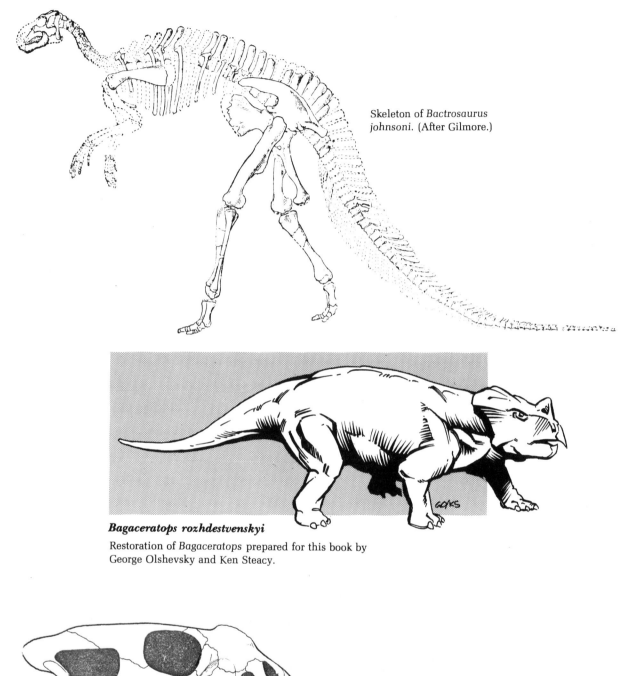

Skeleton of *Bactrosaurus johnsoni.* (After Gilmore.)

Bagaceratops rozhdestvenskyi

Restoration of *Bagaceratops* prepared for this book by George Olshevsky and Ken Steacy.

Skull of *Bagaceratops rozdestvenskyi.* (After Maryańska and Osmólska.)

Barapasaurus Jain, Kutty, Roy-Chowdhury and Chatterjee, 1975—
Saur., Sauro., ?Family, L. Jur. Discovered in the Kota Formation of India, *Barapasaurus* has the distinction of being the earliest known sauropod to date. *Barapasaurus* is a large dinosaur, measuring about 14
meters (47 feet) long and 14.4 meters (15 feet) high. The limbs are slender and the teeth are spoon-shaped.

Barosaurus Marsh, 1890—*Saur., Sauro., Diplod., Diplodo., U. Jur.*
This genus is known from an almost complete skeleton and other fossil
material. The neck is exceedingly long, with powerful vertebrae, and
the tail is relatively short. The caudal vertebrae resemble those in *Diplodocus* but are proportionately shorter and with chevrons lacking the
anterior projections present in the latter genus. *Barosaurus* has been
found in South Dakota, Wyoming, Utah and Tanzania. Bakker suggests
that *Barosaurus* was a terrestrial dinosaur which used its giraffe-like
neck to secure food from treetops.

Basutodon Huene, 1932—*?Ther., U. Trias.* From Lesotho, this genus
is known only from fossil teeth.

Batractosaurus Halstead, 1975—A misspelling of *Bactrosaurus.*

Berninasauropus Ellenberger, 1970—*U. Trias.* These ichnites from
France may have been left by a saurischian dinosaur.

Betasuchus Huene, 1932—*Ther., ?Family, U. Cret.* The genus is based
on a delicate femur discovered in the Netherlands. Though there is no
proof, some workers have believed it to represent an ornithomimid
which, according to D. Russell, it is probably not.

Bosiutrisauropus Ellenberger, 1970—From the Lower Stormberg Series of Phuthiatsan in Lesotho, these fossil footprints may have been
made by a large theropod.

Bothriospondylus Owen, 1875—*Saur., Sauro., Camar., Brachio. U.
Jur. (Marmarospondylus.)* Found in England, France and Madagascar,
this genus is a large sauropod, in life attaining lengths of approximately
14.5 meters (49 feet) to 21 meters (65.5 feet). The teeth are large, from
over 5 to almost 8 centimeters (over 3 inches) in length. The forelimbs of
the animal are as long as the hind limbs. Some of the material assigned
to *Bothriospondylus* may actually refer to one or more other genera. The
best material has come from Madagascar.

Brachiosaurus Riggs, 1903—*Saur., Sauro., Camar., Brachio., U. Jur.*
(Possibly *Caulodon, Chondrosteosaurus, Elosaurus, Eucamerotus, Is-*

Footprints of *Bosiutrisauropus
phuthiatsani.*
(After Ellenberger.)

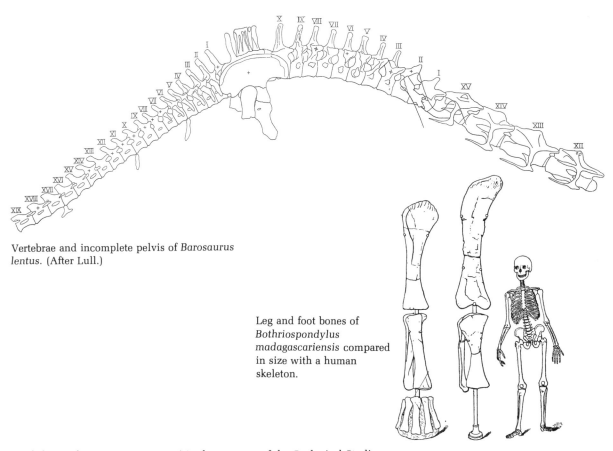

Vertebrae and incomplete pelvis of *Barosaurus lentus*. (After Lull.)

Leg and foot bones of *Bothriospondylus madagascariensis* compared in size with a human skeleton.

Skeleton of *Barapasaurus tagorsi* in the museum of the Geological Studies Unit of the Indian Statistical Institute, Calcutta.

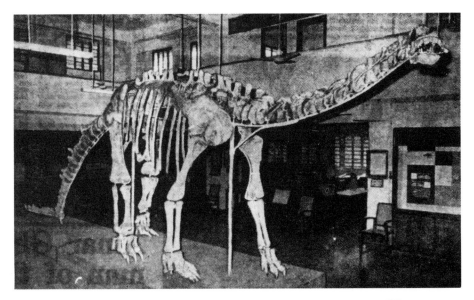

Restoration of *Barapasaurus* prepared for this book by George Olshevsky and the author.

chyrosaurus, Neosodon, Pleurocoelus; probably *Oplosaurus, Ornithopsis, Pelorosaurus.*) The most massive, though not the longest, known terrestrial animal of all time, *Brachiosaurus* weighed an incredible 66 metric tons (80 tons). The creature attained lengths up to approximately 23.5 meters (80 feet) with a height of some 11.75 meters (40 feet). Unlike most sauropods, *Brachiosaurus* has front limbs longer than the hind limbs, so that the body slopes down to the back, terminating in a relatively short tail. The nostrils are located atop a raised mound above the eyes. *Brachiosaurus,* one of the largest dinosaurs, is known from North America, Europe and Africa. Fragments of bone half again as large as those of the 23.5-meter specimen have been informally reported from Tanzania.

Brachyceratops Gilmore, 1914—*Cer., Cerat., U. Cret.* (Possibly *Centrosaurus, Monoclonius.*) From Alberta, Canada, and Montana, this dinosaur is a juvenile ceratopsid, with a modest-sized horn surmounting the snout. The animal is about 1.75 meters (6 feet) in length. Some paleontologists believe it to be a young form of *Centrosaurus* or *Monoclonius.*

Brachylophosaurus Sternberg, 1953—*Orn., Hadro., Hadrosaur., U. Cret.* This duck-billed dinosaur from the Oldman Formation of Alberta, Canada, is known from two skulls and an incomplete skeleton. The skull has a rounded bill and a prominent though relatively small, low and shieldlike crest.

Brachypodosaurus Chakravarti, 1934—*Ornithischia, U. Cret.* Though this short left humerus has often been attributed to the nodosauridae, the material is too poor for any definite classification to be made other than its being ornithischian. The specimen is from the Lameta beds of Jabalpur, Madhya-Pradesh, India.

Brachyrhophus Cope, 1878—*Orn., Iguan., U. Jur.* (Probably *Camptosaurus.*) Known only from centra, the specimen was originally referred to the sauropods, but has the hexagonal cross-section typical of ornithischians.

Brontosaurus Marsh, 1879—(See *Apatosaurus.*)

Brontozoum Hitchcock, 1847—(See *Eubrontes.*)

Bückeburgichnus Kuhn, 1958—*L. Cret.* These fossil footprints from Niedersachsen, Germany, were made by a large theropod dinosaur.

Femur of the theropod dinosaur *Betasuchus bredai.*

H. W. Mencke stands alongside a femur of *Brachiosaurus altithorax*. Courtesy of the Field Museum of Natural History.

Skeleton of the enormous sauropod *Brachiosaurus brancai* in the Berlin Museum.

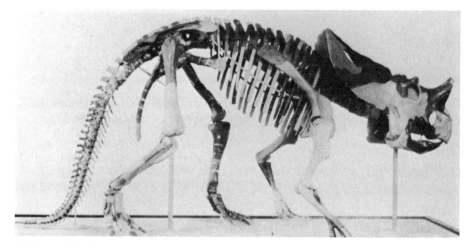

Skeleton of the horned dinosaur *Brachyceratops montanensis*. Courtesy of
the Smithsonian Institution.

Restoration of *Brachiosaurus* supported bouyantly by the water. The notion
of giant sauropods submerged this deep is no longer accepted since the
water pressure would collapse the animal's lungs. From a painting by
Zdeněk Burian.

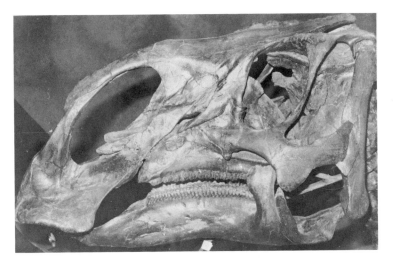

Skull of the duck-billed dinosaur
Brachylophosaurus canadensis. Photograph
courtesy of R. A. Long, S. P. Welles and the
National Museums of Canada.

Humerus of the ornithischian
Brachypodosaurus gravis.

Model of a young *Brachyceratops* by Charles
Whitney Gilmore. Courtesy of the
Smithsonian Institution.

© 1976
Wm
Stout

Brachylophosaurus portrayed as a swamp dweller. Restoration by William Stout.

C

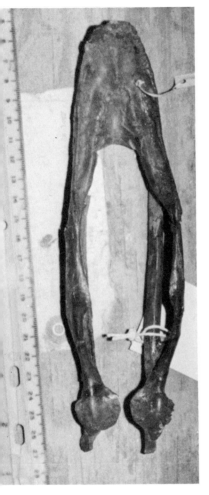

Lower jaw of *Caenagnathus collinsi.* Photograph courtesy of R. A. Long, S. P. Welles and the National Museums of Canada.

Caenagnathus   R. M. Sternberg, 1940—*Ther., Caenag., U. Cret.* Known from two birdlike lower jaws, one of which is 21 centimeters (8 inches) long, found in the Oldman Formation of Alberta, Canada, this genus was originally believed to be a primitive bird. Now, however, *Caenagnathus* is known to be a dinosaur quite similar to *Oviraptor,* though larger.

Calamosaurus   Lydekker, 1891—*Ther., ?Family, L. Cret.* (*Calamospondylus* Lydekker; possibly *Thecocoelurus.*) This small dinosaur is known only from two indeterminate cervical vertebrae and a referred tibia found on the Isle of Wight, England.

Calamospondylus   Fox, 1866—(See *Aristosuchus.*)

Calamospondylus   Lydekker, 1889—(See *Calamosaurus.*)

Calopus   E. Hitchcock, 1845—(See *Platypterna.*)

Camarasaurus   Cope, 1877—*Saur., Sauro., Camar., Camara., U. Jur.* (*Morosaurus, Uintasaurus;* possibly *Caulodon, Elosaurus.*) This sauropod is mostly known from young specimens from the Morrison Formation of Colorado. The adult *Camarasaurus* was quite large. The mature *C. supremus* is approximately 16 meters (56 feet) long and some adults may have grown to a length of about 17.5 meters (60 feet.) The skull, though fenestrated, is heavily built in comparison to that of sauropods like *Diplodocus.* English specimens referred to *Camarasaurus* are not and probably refer to *Titanosaurus. Camarasaurus* is the most commonly found of all sauropods.

Camptonodus   Hoffman, 1880—(Misspelling of *Camptonotus.*)

Camptonotus   Marsh, 1879—(See *Camptosaurus.*)

Camptosaurichnus   Casamiquela, 1968—*L. Cret.* These footprints from Chile were made by a medium-sized ornithopod dinosaur.

Camptosaurus   Marsh, 1885—*Orn., Iguan., U. Jur.* (*Camptonotus;* probably *Brachyrhophus, Cumnoria, Symphyrophus.*) *Camptosaurus* is more primitive than *Iguanodon,* yet more advanced than *Hypsilophodon.* The skull has a horny beak and lizard-like teeth. The manus has

Right foreleg and shoulder blade of
Camarasaurus grandis. Courtesy of the Field
Museum of Natural History.

Scapula and coracoid of *Camarasaurus grandis*
in the rock matrix where they were found.
Courtesy of the Field Museum of Natural History.

Skeleton of *Camarasaurus lentus*. Courtesy of the
Smithsonian Institution.

KRAXBERGER SCHOOL LIBRARY

Young and mature specimens of *Camptosaurus dispar*.
Courtesy of the Smithsonian Institution.

Model of the sauropod dinosaur
Camarasaurus by Charles Whitney
Gilmore. Courtesy of the Smithsonian
Institution.

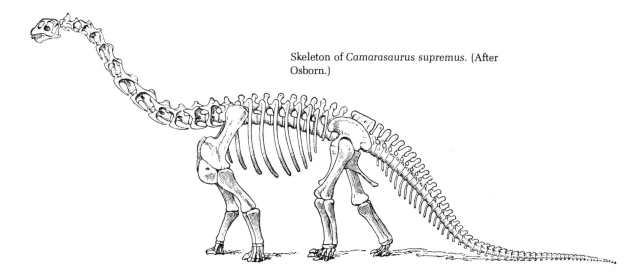

Skeleton of *Camarasaurus supremus*. (After Osborn.)

Restoration of the iguanodont
Camptosaurus prepared for this book by
Jim Danforth.

five fingers, the first three terminating in claws, the first of which forms a low spike. The foot is four-toed with hooflike claws and a hint of a fifth toe. The heavy hind legs of the ornithopod indicate that *Camptosaurus* was essentially a biped, but the broad fingers intimate at least some quadrupedal locomotion. *Camptosaurus* flourished in North America, the greatest abundance of skeletons being found in Wyoming. Specimens of this genus have been found in various sizes and, in the past, have been ascribed to different species. Recently Galton has stated that these supposed species are actually probably growth stages of *C. dispar*. The genus reached an estimated length of 7 meters (25 feet). It is quite unlike other ornithopods in having a low, flattened skull. Possibly this genus belongs to its own family Camptosauridae.

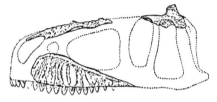

Restored skull of *Carcharodontosaurus saharicus*.

Campylodon   Huene, 1929—(See *Campylodoniscus*.)

Campylodoniscus   Kuhn, 1961—*Saur., Sauro., ?Family, U. Cret.* The genus is known only from a fragmentary, left maxilla with teeth found in Argentina.

Carcharodontosaurus   Stromer, 1931—*Ther., ?Family, U. Cret.* Possibly in a family of its own, this genus, known from the Sahara Desert and probably Iran, was a large dinosaur, attaining lengths exceeding 11.75 meters (40 feet). The animal has uncharacteristically high dorsal vertebrae and the teeth are usually not curved, but sharp and double-ridged.

Cardiodon   Owen, 1841—*Saur., Sauro., Camar., Cetio., M. Jur.* (Probably *Cetiosaurus*.) The only specimens of *Cardiodon* are fossil teeth from Wiltshire, England.

Caudocoelus   Huene, 1932—(See *Teinurosaurus*.)

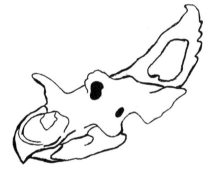

Skull of *Centrosaurus longirostris*. (After Steel.)

Caulodon   Cope, 1877—*Saur., Sauro., Camar., U. Jur.* Known only from teeth, the Colorado specimens of *Caulodon* might actually be *Camarasaurus*, while those from Europe are probably *Brachiosaurus* or *Pelorosaurus*.

Centrosaurus   Lambe, 1904—*Cer., Cerat., U. Cret.* (Possibly *Monoclonius*.) This genus is known from the Oldman Formation of Alberta, Canada, and perhaps from the Judith River Formation of Montana. *Centrosaurus* is a large, short-frilled ceratopsian. The shield, with two large fontanelles, is scalloped around the edges. The back of the frill often curves forward like bony hooks. Above each orbit is a small horn while a long horn, sometimes curving forward, surmounts the snout. At one time generally considered to be synonymous with *Monoclonius*, Cen-

Restoration of *Carcharodontosaurus* prepared for this book by George Olshevsky and the author.

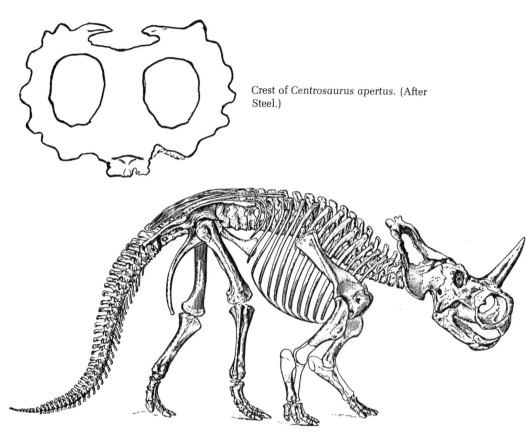

Crest of *Centrosaurus apertus.* (After Steel.)

Skeleton of *Centrosaurus nasicornis.* (After Brown.)

Restoration of the horned dinosaur *Centrosaurus* by the author, based on a model by Lull.

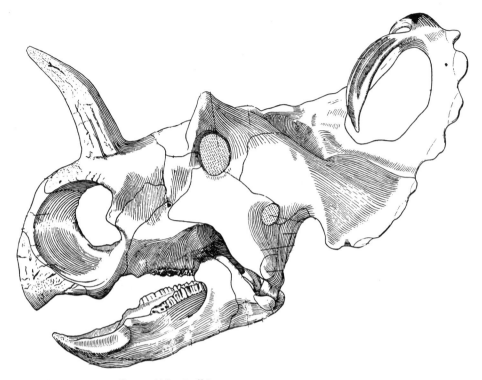

Skull of *Centrosaurus flexus*. (After Lull.)

trosaurus is now regarded by some dinosaur specialists as a distinct genus. The name *Centrosaurus* is actually preoccupied and the genus will be renamed in the future (R. A. Long, personal communication).

Ceratops Marsh, 1888—*Cer., Cerat., U. Cret. (Proceratops).* Known from incomplete skull material from Montana, this dinosaur has three horns, the orbital horns being relatively long. Material found in Alberta, Canada, may also be *Ceratops* while that discovered in Colorado, previously called *Ceratops*, may be another genus altogether.

Ceratosaurus Marsh, 1884—*Ther., Cerato., U. Jur.* From Colorado and Tanzania, this heavily built flesh-eater grew to lengths of approximately 6 meters (20 feet) and some material indicates it grew much larger. Unlike most theropods, *Ceratosaurus* has a more specialized skull, with a bony ridge above each orbit and a horn surmounting the snout. This horn may have been used as a weapon. It has also been suggested that the horn might have been a sexual dimorphism or that it aided the young to hatch from their eggs. A row of bony protuberances surmounted the dorsal region.

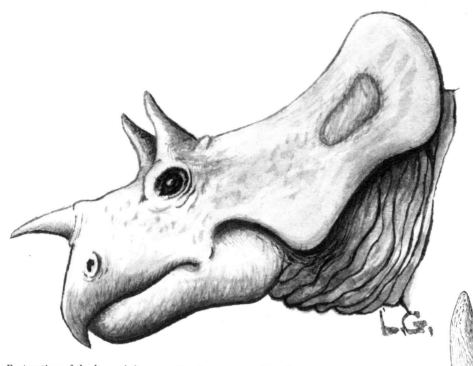

Restoration of the horned dinosaur *Ceratops* prepared for this
book by Linda L. Glut.

Horn cores of *Ceratops montanus*. (After Marsh.)

Skeleton of the theropod dinosaur *Ceratosaurus nasicornis*. Courtesy of the Smithsonian Institution.

Anterior teeth of left dentary of
Ceratosaurus. Courtesy of J. H. Madsen, Jr.

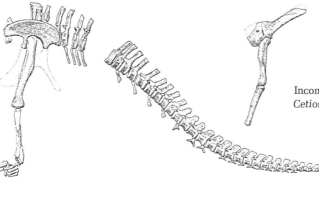

Incomplete skeletal remains of the sauropod
Cetiosauriscus leedsi. (After Huene.)

Model by Charles Whitney Gilmore of *Ceratosaurus* feeding on the
herbivorous dinosaur *Camptosaurus.* Courtesy of the Smithsonian
Institution.

Restoration of the sauropod *Cetiosauriscus* prepared for this book by George Olshevsky.

Cetiosauriscus   Huene, 1927—*Saur., Sauro., Diplod., Diplodo., U. Jur.* Generally considered to be synonymous with *Cetiosaurus*, this genus, based on a pelvis from Oxford Clay of England, is now considered to be a separate genus closely related to *Diplodocus*. A second specimen referred to this genus has been found in Switzerland.

Cetiosaurus   Owen, 1841—*Saur., Sauro., Camar., Cetio., M. Jur. to ?L. Cret.* (Probably *Cardiodon*; possibly *Haplocanthosaurus*.) The only material that may be conclusively ascribed to this genus is that from the Middle Jurassic of Peterborough and Oxfordshire, England, and that from Morocco. All later material is probably another genus altogether. *Cetiosaurus* is a large sauropod ranging in size from almost 15 meters (50 feet) to over 17.5 meters (60 feet). Unlike the later sauropods, the vertebrae of the animal possess a spongy texture. When first described, *Cetiosaurus* was believed to be a giant crocodile and later confused with *Iguanodon*.

Changpeipus   Young, 1960—*M. Jur.* These ichnites found in Queensland and in Liaoning, China, were probably left by a large theropod.

Restoration of the giant
sauropod dinosaur
Cetiosaurus by Neave
Parker. Courtesy of the
British Museum (Natural
History).

Two representatives of the
genus *Chasmosaurus*.
Restoration by Robert T.
Bakker. Courtesy of the
National Museums of
Canada.

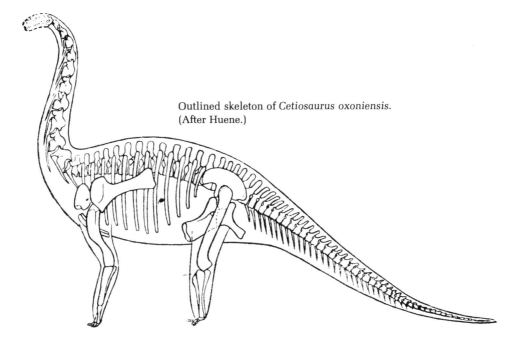

Outlined skeleton of *Cetiosaurus oxoniensis.*
(After Huene.)

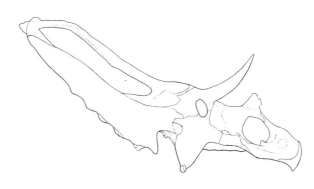

Skull of *Chasmosaurus kaiseni.* (After
Marsh.)

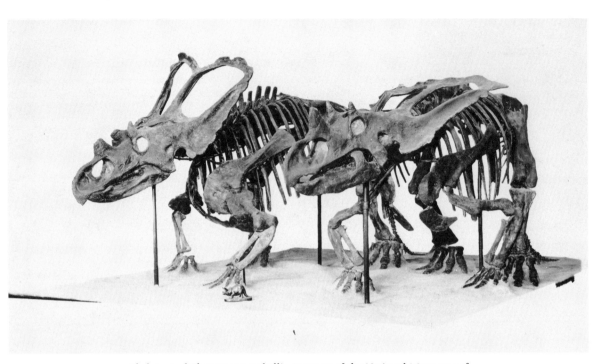

Skeletons of *Chasmosaurus belli*. Courtesy of the National Museums of Canada.

Skull of *Chasmosaurus brevirostris*. (After Steel.)

Skull of *Chasmosaurus russelli*. (After Steel.)

Chasmosaurus Lambe, 1914—*Cer., Cerat., U. Cret. (Protorosaurus.)* From the Oldman beds of Alberta, Canada, this moderate-sized dinosaur may have been the ancestor of many other long-frilled ceratopsians such as *Pentaceratops*. The shield is long with large fontanelles. There are two small- to medium-sized horns above the orbits and a small horn above the snout in some species. *Chasmosaurus* reached a length of 5 meters (17 feet) and weighed about 3.6 metric tons (4 tons).

Cheneosaurus Lambe, 1917—*Orn., Hadro., Hadrosaur, U. Cret.* (Probably *Hypacrosaurus*.) Known only from a skull found in the Horseshoe Canyon beds of Alberta, Canada, *Cheneosaurus* has a crest resembling a bony rise over and slightly in front of the eyes. This hadrosaur of moderate size is probably a juvenile form of *Hypacrosaurus*.

Chialingosaurus Young, 1959—*Steg., Stego., M. or U. Jur.* From Sichuan, China, this relatively slender dinosaur is known from fragmentary material, including a left femur, limb bones, vertebrae and dermal spines. This primitive stegosaur, with its small and platelike spines, seems to have been related to *Kentrosaurus*.

Chiayasaurus Dong, 1977—A misspelling of *Chiayüsaurus*.

Chiayuesaurus Young, 1958—A misspelling of *Chiayüsaurus*.

Chiayüsaurus Bohlin, 1953—*Saur., Sauro., Camar., ?Euhelo., U., Cret.* The term was given to camarsaur-like teeth found in Gansu, Mongolia. The teeth resemble those of *Euhelopus* but are probably too late to be synonymous with that genus.

Chienkosaurus Young, 1942—*Ther., ?Family, M. and ?U. Jur.* The genus is based on four *Ceratosaurus*-like teeth and a fragmentary ulna from Sichuan, China.

Chilantaisaurus Hu, 1964—*Ther., ?Family, L. and U. Cret.* Known from incomplete skeletal material found in Tashuikou, Inner Mongolia, this giant theropod is distinguished by its enormous forelimbs and their powerful, hooked claws, used to rip into its prey, and its remarkably thickly built skull.

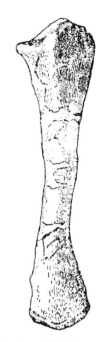

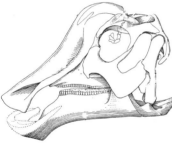

Skull of the hadrosaur *Cheneosaurus tolmanensis*. (After Lull-Wright.)

Right ulna of *Chienkosaurus ceratosauroides*. (After Young.)

Restoration by the author of *Cheneosaurus*.

The theropod *Chilantaisaurus* is about to use its monstrous claws on the ostrich-like dinosaur *Archaeornithomimus*. Restoration prepared for this book by Rick Hoberg.

Right and left manus of *Chirostenotes pergracilis.* Courtesy of the National Museums of Canada.

HOBERG SPT. 1977

Posterior cervical vertebra of *Chondrosteosaurus gigas.* (After Owen.)

Dorsal vertebra of *Chubutisaurus insignis.* (After del Corro.)

Chimaera   E. Hitchcock—(See *Sauropus*.)

Chimaerichnus   E. Hitchcock—(See *Sauropus*.)

Chingkankousaurus   Young, 1958—*?Ther., U. Cret.* Based on a very long and slender piece of bone, possibly a right scapula, found in Shandong, China, this genus is generally included with the Theropoda.

Chirostenotes   Gilmore, 1924—*Ther., ?Dromae., U. Cret.* From the Oldman Formation and Horseshoe Canyon Formation of Alberta, Canada, this genus is primarily known from an almost complete right and left manus and a light mandible. The hands were similar to those of *Oviraptor*. A light mandible referred to this form may actually pertain to a different dromaeosaurid.

Chiryuesaurus   Young, 1958—A misspelling of *Chiayüsaurus*.

Chondrosteosaurus   Owen, 1876—*Saur., Sauro., Camar., Brachio., L. Cret.* This dinosaur is known only from fragmentary large cervical vertebrae found on the Isle of Wight, England.

Chubutisaurus   del Corro, 1974—*Saur., Sauro., ?Chubut., U. Cret.* Known from a humerus, femur, vertebrae and fragments found in Chubut, Argentina, *Chubutisaurus* is a gigantic, heavily constructed sauropod. Apparently the dorsal vertebrae are large with great neural spines. The forelimbs are shorter than the hind limbs and the femur is large and solidly constructed.

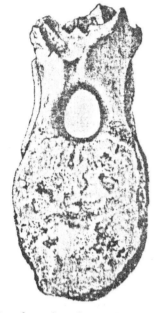

Dorsal vertebra of *Cionodon arctatus*.

Cinodon   Cope, 1874—A misspelling of *Cionodon*.

Cionodon   Cope, 1874—*Orn., Hadro., U. Cret. (Cinodon.)* Known from fragmentary material including an incomplete ulna, metatarsal, right maxilla and two dorsal vertebrae found in Colorado, this genus is of doubtful validity. The maxilla with teeth attributed to *C. stenopsis* is not in the American Museum collection where it was placed and is not listed in their catalogue. Material found in Kazakhstan has also been referred to *Cionodon*, though for no valid reason.

Tooth of *Cladeiodon lloydi*. (After Owen.)

Cladeiodon   Owen, 1841—*?Ther., U. Trias. (Claderodon, Cladyodon, Kladeisteriodon, Kladyodon.)* This genus is imperfectly known from a single tooth found in the Warwickshire Sandstone of England. The specimen has apparently been lost. Possibly *Cladeiodon* is not a dinosaur but a thecodont.

Claderodon   Agassiz, 1846—A misspelling of *Cladeiodon*.

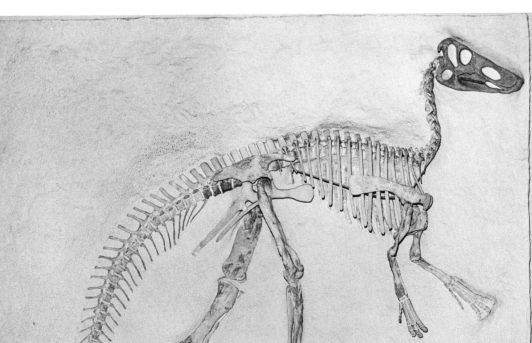

Skeleton of *Claosaurus agilis*. Parts of this specimen, including the skull, have been restored. Courtesy of the Peabody Museum of Natural History, Yale University.

Restoration of *Coelophysis* by R. Freund.

Early restoration of the primitive hadrosaur *Claosaurus*.

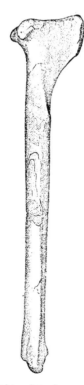

Tibia of *Coelosaurus
antiquus*.

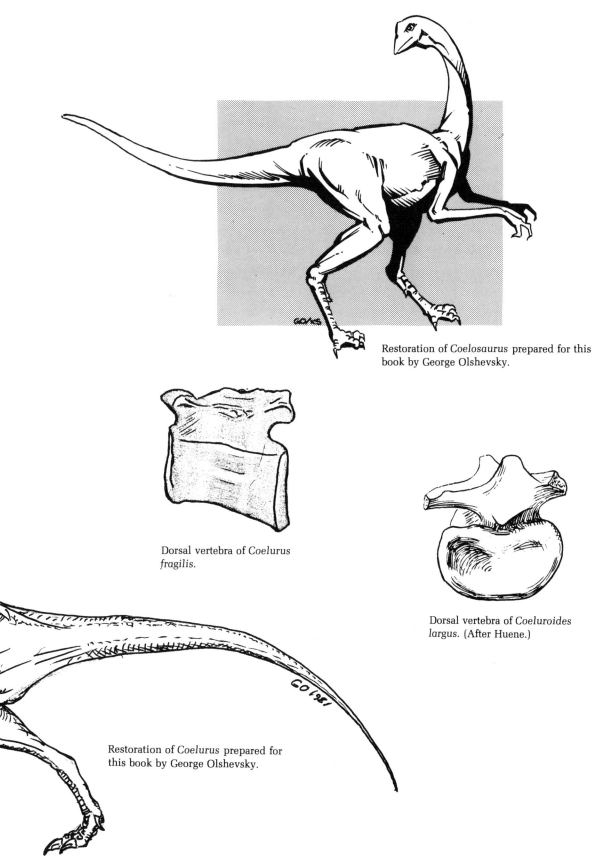

Restoration of *Coelosaurus* prepared for this book by George Olshevsky.

Dorsal vertebra of *Coelurus fragilis.*

Dorsal vertebra of *Coeluroides largus.* (After Huene.)

Restoration of *Coelurus* prepared for this book by George Olshevsky.

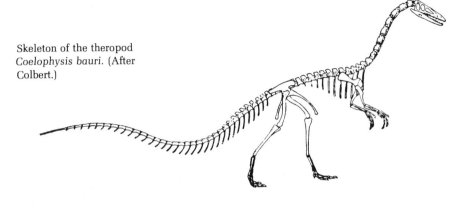

Skeleton of the theropod
Coelophysis bauri. (After
Colbert.)

Cladyodon   Owen, 1842—A misspelling of *Cladeiodon.*

Claorhynchus   Cope, 1892—*Cer., Cerat., U. Cret.* (Possibly *Triceratops.*) The genus is known from fragmentary material, including a tooth
and piece of a frill, from South Dakota. Previously *Claorhynchus* was
ascribed to the hadrosaurs.

Claosaurus   Marsh, 1890—*Orn., Hadro., Hadrosaur., U. Cret. Claosaurus* is one of the oldest known North American hadrosaurs and the most
primitive of which there is currently comparative evidence. The genus
resembles the later noncrested hadrosaurs but is somewhat smaller,
probably some 3.5 meters (12 feet) long. The skull has not been preserved, but jaw fragments indicate the teeth were primitive and somewhat camptosaur-like. The caudals of the tail are poorly known yet
some paleontologists have proposed that the tail was longer than in later hadrosaurs. *Claosaurus* was discovered in the Niobrara Formation of
Kansas.

Clasmodosaurus   Ameghino, 1899—*Saur., Sauro., ?Family, U. Cret.*
Known only from fossil teeth, the genus comes from Santa Cruz, Argentina.

Coelophysis   Cope, 1889—*Ther., Podok., U. Trias.* (Probably *Podokesaurus.*) From New Mexico and the Connecticut Valley, this dinosaur
was a sleek, agile, lightly built predator. The animal grew from lengths
of about 2.4 meters (8 feet) to 2.9 meters (10 feet). In life the animal
weighed approximately 32 kilograms (50 pounds). The bones are hollow and somewhat thin, the hind legs birdlike and designed for running. The legs, neck and tail are long and slender. The animal's jaws are

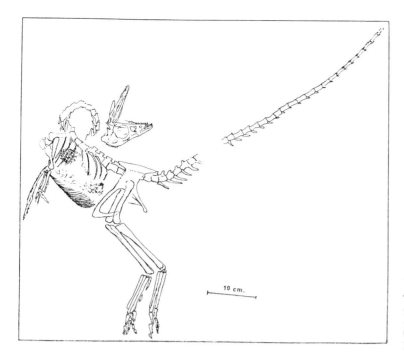

Skeleton of *Compsognathus corallestris* in a death pose caused by a tightening of the neck ligaments. (After Bidar.)

A scene of the Upper Jurassic, depicting the tiny theropod *Compsognathus* (lower left), the feathered *Archaeopteryx* (center) and the pterosaur *Rhamphorhynchus* (above). Now *Compsognathus* is known to have had a two-digit hand. From a mural by Charles R. Knight. Courtesy of the Field Museum of Natural History.

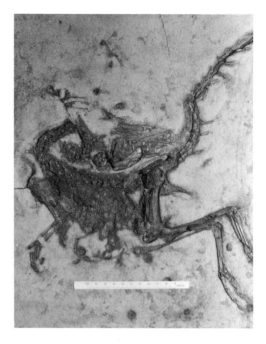

Skeleton of *Compsognathus longipes* in the Institut für Päaontologie und Historische Geologie, Munich. Courtesy of J. H. Ostrom.

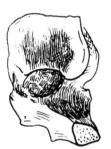

Cervical vertebra of *Composuchus solus.* (After Huene.)

long and filled with numerous small but sharp teeth, suitable for trapping prey. It has been theorized that, unlike most dinosaurs, *Coelophysis* did not lay eggs but bore its young alive. Raath has proposed that *Coelophysis* flourished in upland forests near streams and ponds.

Coelosaurus Leidy, 1865—*Ther., Ornith., U. Cret. (Coelurosaurus.)* The genus is known from a tibia discovered in New Jersey.

Coeluroides Huene and Matley, 1933—*Ther., ?Family, U. Cret.* From the Lameta Formation of India, *Coeluroides* is based on three dorsal vertebrae which indicate a very large theropod about the size of *Allosaurus.* The genus is also, though probably incorrectly, reported from Kazakhstan.

Coelurosaurus White, 1973—A misspelling of *Coelosaurus.*

Coelurosaurichnus Huene, 1941—*U. Trias. to L. Jur.* From Italy, France, England, Germany, Pennsylvania and New Jersey, these fossil tracks were made by a theropod of medium to small size. They have been referred to the footprint family Anchisauripodidae.

Coelurus Marsh, 1879—*Ther., Coel., U. Jur.* Based on a dorsal vertebra from Como Bluff, Wyoming, *Coelurus* has often been considered to be congeneric with *Ornitholestes;* but current work has proven them to be

Skeleton of *Corythosaurus casuarius*. Courtesy of the Academy of Natural Sciences in Philadelphia.

Restoration of the crested dinosaur *Corythosaurus*. Courtesy of the Sinclair Oil Corporation.

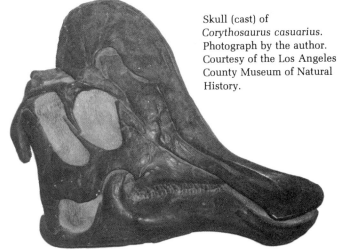

Skull (cast) of *Corythosaurus casuarius*. Photograph by the author. Courtesy of the Los Angeles County Museum of Natural History.

distinct genera. *Coelurus* is small, lightly built, with even the ribs being hollow.

Columbosauripus   Sternberg, 1932—*L. and U. Cret.* (Possibly *Gypsichnites.*) These ichnites, found in British Columbia and Algeria, are very similar to *Irenesauripus.* Apparently they were made by a swiftly moving, medium-sized theropod, possibly an ornithomimid.

Compsognathus   Wagner, 1859—*Ther., Compsog., U. Jur.* From Germany and France, *Compsognathus* has long held the tenuous position of being the smallest dinosaur known from skeletal material. (Fossil footprints and fragmentary bones indicate dinosaurs considerably smaller, however.) *Compsognathus* grew to the approximate size of a chicken, about 74 centimeters (2.5 feet) in length and weighed about 6.8 kilograms (15 pounds). The animal was probably quite swift and graceful. The skull measures about 8 centimeters (3 inches) long and has numerous sharp teeth. Within the type specimen from Germany were found what was once thought to be an infant specimen, intimating that *Compsognathus* either bore its young alive or cannibalized them, but Ostrom has recently shown that this is a lizard. Generally the animal's diet probably consisted of small reptiles and mammals. Possibly *Compsognathus* represents an immature dinosaur though it probably is an adult. The suggestion that the French *Compsognathus* had flippers instead of forelimbs has not been generally accepted.

Compsosuchus   Huene and Matley, 1933—*Ther., ?Family, U. Cret.* From the Lameta Formation of Jabalpur, India, this dinosaur is known only from an axis.

Corythosaurus   Brown, 1914—*Orn., Hadro., Lambeo., U. Cret.* (In part, *Procheneosaurus, Tetragonosaurus*; probably *Pteropelyx.*) This large hadrosaur grew to an approximate length of 8.4 meters (30 feet). The dinosaur has a high, helmet-shaped crest occupying the upper cranial region. The crest is hollow and formed by the premaxillary and nasal bones. Variations in the size of the crests, earlier assigning different species to the genus, are now considered to represent growth stages of *C. casuarius.* Excellent skeletons of *Corythosaurus* have been found, some with impressions of the animal's skin. The dinosaur is known from the Oldman beds of Alberta, Canada, and perhaps from the Judith River beds of Montana.

Craspedodon   Dollo, 1883—*Orn., Iguan., U. Cret.* From Namur, Bel-

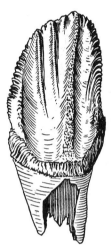

Tooth of *Craspedodon lonzeensis.* (After Dollo.)

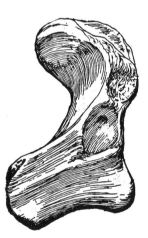

Neural arch of a vertebra of *Craterosaurus pottonensis.* (After Nopcsa.)

gium, the genus is based on two teeth which are similar to those of *Iguanodon.* The teeth are five-ridged, laterally compressed and better suited to chewing than those of *Iguanodon.*

Crataeomus Seeley, 1881—*Ank., Nodo., U. Cret.* (Possibly *Struthiosaurus.*) Usually considered to be a junior synonym of *Struthiosaurus,* this dinosaur is known from imperfect skeletal material from the Gosau Formation of Austria. Seeley, however, described two scapulae of *Crataeomus,* a smaller one resembling that of *Struthiosaurus* and a larger specimen quite different, intimating a valid genus.

Craterosaurus Seeley, 1874—*Steg., Stego., L. Cret.* This dinosaur is known from an incomplete dorsal neural arch discovered in Bedfordshire, England. Originally this specimen was described as part of a skull. Galton has recently determined that the specimen is stegosaurian.

Creosaurus Marsh, 1878—(See *Allosaurus.*)

Cridotrisauropus Ellenberger, 1970—*U. Trias. and L. Jur.* These footprints from the Upper Stormberg Series of Ornozomong, in Lesotho, and from the Lower Lias of de Sanarg, France, were possibly made by a small theropod.

Cryptodraco Lydekker, 1889—*Ank., Nodo., U. Jur.* (*Cryptosaurus.*) The genus is known only from a right femur discovered in Great Gransden, England. Long regarded as an ornithopod of uncertain standing, Cryptodraco was recently determined by Galton as being a Jurassic nodosaurid.

Cryptosaurus Seeley, 1875—(See *Cryptodraco.*)

Cumnoria Seeley, 1888—*Orn., Iguan., U. Jur.* (*Cumnovia.*) Sometimes considered to be distinct from *Camptosaurus,* this genus seems to be congeneric on the basis of recent studies. The genus is known in England, France and possibly Portugal and is based on an incomplete skeleton and incomplete skull. (See *Camptosaurus.*)

Cumnovia Carus, 1888—A misspelling of *Cumnoria.*

Cunichnoides Hitchcock, 1858—*U. Trias.* These fossil tracks from Massachusetts and Connecticut indicate a quadrupedal animal that apparently walked on the tips of its toes. The creature may have been a dinosaur, though there is no proof of this.

Femur of *Cryptodraco eumerus.* (After Seeley.)

D

Dacentrurus Lucas, 1902—*Steg., Stego., U. Jur. (Omosaurus.)* From Wiltshire, England, and from France and Portugal, this dinosaur superficially resembles the American *Stegosaurus*. But *Dacentrurus* has no plates but, rather, a series of erect and paired spikes running along the neck, back and tail. The pelvic regions of *Dacentrurus* and *Stegosaurus* also differ. The posterior of the ilium in *Dacentrurus* is shorter and then deepened, which gives some paleontologists reason to believe that the animal and *Stegosaurus* are congeneric, the differences being sexual. Also, the neural arches of the dorsal vertebrae in *Dacentrurus* are not as elevated as those in *Stegosaurus* and the front legs are longer. In life *Dacentrurus* reached a length of about 4.4 meters (15 feet). Eggs believed to be those of this dinosaur have been found in Portugal.

Dakotasaurus Branson and Mehl, 1932—*U. Cret.* These footprints from the Dakota Formation of Fremont County, Wyoming, may have been made by an ornithopod, but are probably not dinosaurian.

Danubiosaurus Bunzel, 1871—(See *Struthiosaurus*.)

Daspletosaurus D. Russell, 1970—*Ther., Tyrann., U. Cret.* (Possibly *Deinodon*.) This giant, heavy theropod, similar to *Albertosaurus*, reached a length of approximately 8.4 meters (30 feet) and in life weighed about 2.2 metric tons (2.5 tons). Russell has suggested that *Daspletosaurus* was primarily a hunter of ceratopsians.

Deinocheirus Osmólska and Roniewicz, 1967—*Ther., Deino., U. Cret.* This giant theropod is known only from a set of enormous forelimbs and some small ribs found in the Nemegt Basin of Mongolia's Gobi Desert. The hands, which show some similarity to the ornithomimids, have claws about .3 meters (1 foot) in length which, in life, were probably fortified by a horny sheath. Rozhdestvensky once suggested that *Deinocheirus* had a slothlike appearance and used its forelimbs to hang upside-down from trees.

Deinodon Leidy, 1856—*Ther., Tyrann., U. Cret. (Aublysodon, Dinodon;* probably *Albertosaurus*, possibly *Daspletosaurus*.) The genus is known only from teeth from the Judith River Formation of Montana. In the past century numerous fossils have been referred to *Deinodon*, but without any real proof.

Restoration of the stegosaur *Dacentrurus* prepared for this book by Linda L. Glut.

Spine of *Dacentrurus armatus*. (After Owen.)

Deinonychus Ostrom, 1969—*Ther., Dromae., L. Cret.* Found in Montana and Wyoming, *Deinonychus* is a rather slender theropod and only of modest size, reaching a length of about 2.4 meters (slightly over 8 feet) and weighing 45 kilograms (100 pounds). But the animal was probably a cunning hunter and was possessed of highly developed sensory apparatus. Most remarkable about the animal are the long tail and the claws. The tail vertebrae are encased in bony rods as long as 45.6 centimeters (17½ inches), which kept the tail rigid and worked as a counterbalance as the animal was literally forced into a bipedal gait. The forelimbs are long and equipped with three huge claws. The feet are three-clawed, with the second toe an enormous 13-centimeter (5-inch) bladelike claw that was raised off the ground. Balanced by the tail, *Deinonychus* would hold its prey with its front claws, then stand upon one leg and use its lifted hind limb for tearing into its victim's flesh.

Delatorrichnus Casamiquela, 1964—*?Cret.* From Argentina, these quadrupedal ichnites may have been made by a small theropod.

Deuterosauropodopus Ellenberger, 1970—*U. Trias.* These fossil tracks may possibly represent the earliest sauropod records. They are from the Lower Stormberg Series of Maphutseng and Subeng, in Lesotho.

Deuterotetrapous Nopcsa, 1923—*Trias.* These dinosaur footprints were discovered in England.

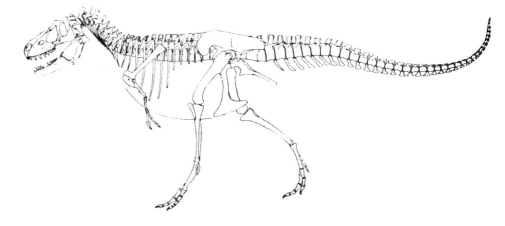

Skeleton of *Daspletosaurus torosus*. (After Russell.)

Incomplete caudal spine of
Dacentrurus lennieri.

Deuterotrisauropus   Ellenberger, 1970—*U. Trias.* From the Keuper of d'Anduze, France, and the Lower Stormberg Series of Subeng and Maphutseng, in Lesotho, these ichnites may have been left by a prosauropod.

Diceratops   Lull, 1905—(See *Triceratops.*)

Diclonius   Cope, 1876—*Orn., Hadro., Hadrosaur, U. Cret.* The term has been given to a number of presumably hadrosaurian teeth discovered in Montana's Judith River Formation. One species, *D. perangulatus,* is probably a ceratopsian tooth, although it has mistakenly been considered to be synonymous with *Trachodon mirabilis.*

Dicraeosaurus   Janensch, 1914—*Saur., Sauro., Diplod., Dicraeo., U. Jur. and U. Cret.* From the Tendaguru Formation of Tanzania and from the Baharia Formation of Egypt, this dinosaur superficially resembles a smaller version of *Diplodocus.* The animal is relatively slender with a very long tail and a relatively short neck. The vertebrae lack lateral pits and are not as cavernous as those in *Camarasaurus.* The neural spines in *Dicraeosaurus* are relatively high and forked. In life the animal reached a length of approximately 12.5 meters (43 feet) and weighed about 5.3 metric tons (6.5 tons). Coombs has suggested that a dinosaur like *Dicraeosaurus* might have been equipped with a well developed snout terminating in a trunk.

Didamodon   Huene, 1956—A misspelling of *Didanodon.*

Didanodon   Osborn, 1902—(See *Procheneosaurus.*)

Closeup of the skull of a mounted skeleton of *Daspletosaurus torosus*.
Courtesy of the National Museums of Canada.

One *Daspletosaurus* challenges another for the carcass of a slain *Monoclonius*. Restoration by Robert T. Bakker. Courtesy of the National Museums of Canada.

Zofia Kielan-Jaworowska stands before the forelimbs and shoulder girdle of the gigantic theropod *Deinocheirus mirificus*. Courtesy of the Institute of Paleobiology in Warsaw.

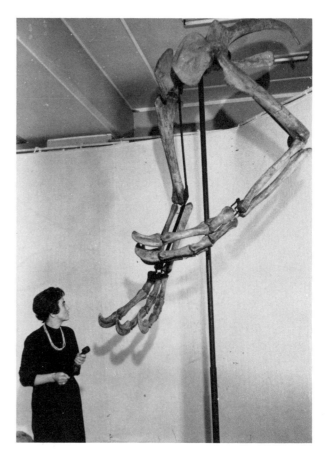

Dilophosauripus Welles, 1971—*U. Trias. or L. Jur.* These theropod tracks were found in Arizona.

Dilophosaurus Welles, 1970—*Ther., Coel., L. Jur.* From Coconino County, Arizona, *Dilophosaurus* is unlike most theropods in that the head is surmounted by an ornate double crest and the skull is delicately constructed with weak jaws. Because of these jaws, the animal probably used its birdlike, taloned feet to attack its victims. In life the creature grew to a length of 5.8 meters (20 feet).

Dimodosaurus Pidancet and Chopard, 1863—(See *Plateosaurus.*)

Dinodocus Owen, 1884—*Saur., Sauro., Camar., ?Brachio., L. Cret.* (Possibly *Ornithopsis, Pelorosaurus.*) The dinosaur was probably quite large with slender forelimbs. The genus is known from fragments, including a partial humerus and broken limb and pelvic bones, found in Kent, England.

Dinodon Cope, 1866—A misspelling of *Deinodon.*

Tooth of *Deinodon horridus.*

An Upper Cretaceous scene. The carnivorous *Deinodon* stalks toward the water as the bone-headed dinosaur *Stegoceras* flees. The armored *Panoplosaurus* waits on land along with the crested hadrosaur *Corythosaurus.* Gliding overhead is the pterosaur *Pteranodon.* Courtesy of the Los Angeles County Museum of Natural History.

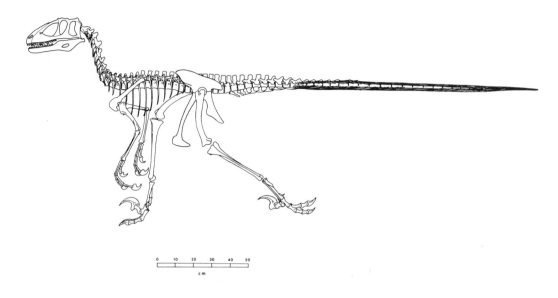

Skeleton of *Deinonychus antirrhopus*. (After Ostrom.)

The remarkable theropod *Deinonychus* as restored by Robert T. Bakker.
Courtesy of John H. Ostrom.

Dinosaurichnium   Rehnelt, 1950—(See *Parachirotherium.*)

Dinosauripus   Rehnelt, ?date—?*U. Trias.* These European fossil tracks may have been made by a theropod.

Dinosauropodes   Strevell, 1932—?*U. Cret.* The term has no scientific standing. It refers to gigantic tridactyl footprints from the Mesauerde Group of Utah and Colorado, including both theropod and ornithopod tracks.

Dinosaurus   Rütimeyer, 1856—(See *Gresslyosaurus.*)

Dioplosaurus   Hay, 1929—A misspelling of *Dyoplosaurus.*

Diplodocus   Marsh, 1878—*Saur., Sauro., Diplod., Diplodo., U. Jur.* to *L. Cret.* (Possibly *Amphicoelias.*) Although relatively lightweight (about 10.5 metric tons or less than 12 tons, according to Colbert [1962]), when compared with *Apatosaurus* and *Brachiosaurus*, this slender creature has the distinction of being one of the longest dinosaurs, its length nearly 28 meters (87 feet). Much of this fantastic length may be attributed to the serpentine neck and the long, whiplike tail. The head of *Diplodocus* is almost ridiculously small with the nostrils set high on the skull. The teeth are peglike and delicate. Some specimens of *Diplodocus* had arthritis in the tail. The dinosaur is known from Colorado, Utah, Wyoming, Montana and perhaps Oklahoma. Though previously known only from the Upper Jurassic, in 1975 *Diplodocus* caudal vertebrae were discovered in the Lower Cretaceous of the Isle of Wight.

Diplotomodon   Leidy, 1868—?*Ther., U. Cret.* (*Tomodon.*) From Greensand, New Jersey, these teeth, though sometimes considered to belong to a mosasaur or crocodile, are apparently theropod. Similar teeth have been found in Egypt and Italy.

Diracodon   Marsh, 1881—(See *Stegosaurus.*)

Dolichosuchus   Huene, 1932—?*Ther., U. Trias.* Known only from a left fibula found in Würtemberg, Germany, this genus may not even be a dinosaur.

Doryphorosaurus   Nopcsa, 1916—(See *Kentrosaurus.*)

Dromaeosaurus   Matthew and Brown, 1922—*Ther., Dromae., U. Cret.* From the Red Deer River of Alberta, Canada, this possible descendant of *Deinonychus* is known from an incomplete skull and some bone fragments. The jaws are long, but not massive, with well developed teeth.

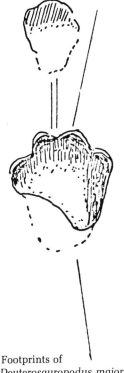

Footprints of *Deuterosauropodus major.* (After Ellenberger.)

Footprint of *Deuterotrisauropus socialis.* (After Ellenberger.)

KRAXBERGER SCHOOL LIBRARY

Restoration of *Dicraeosaurus* prepared for this book by Linda L. Glut.

Skeleton of the sauropod dinosaur *Dicraeosaurus hansemanni*. (After Janensch.)

The skull, of which the top is fragmentary, is slightly smaller than that of *Struthiomimus* and is of the general proportions of the larger theropods. The brain cavity is broad, indicating that the animal's brain was quite large for a dinosaur. In life the animal must have been cunning and a skillful hunter, its formidableness increased by its agile body, sharp teeth and recurved hind claws. Russell has suggested that *Dromaeosaurus* was a hunter of small ornithischians.

Dromiceiomimus Russell, 1972—*Ther., Ornith., U. Cret.* Known from incomplete material from the Oldman and Horseshoe Canyon Formations of the Red Deer River locality in Alberta, Canada, the genus was a swiftly moving, large-brained ornithomimid. The eyes were large and Russell speculates that the retina was larger than that in any other terrestrial animal. The size of the brain, states Russell, intimates that *Dromiceiomimus* may have been capable of caring for its young. The dinosaur grew to a length of 2.9 meters (10 feet) and weighed about 80 kilograms (175 pounds).

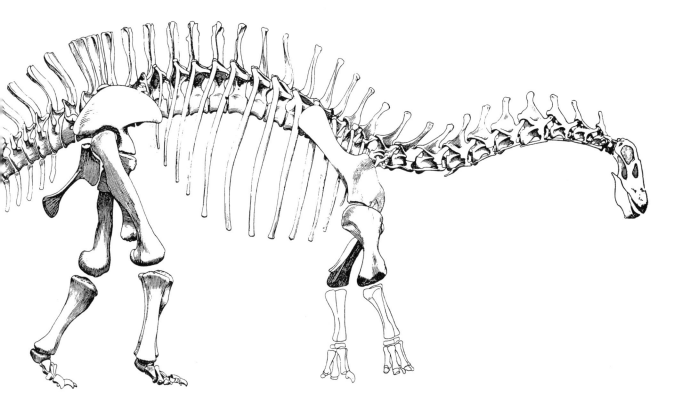

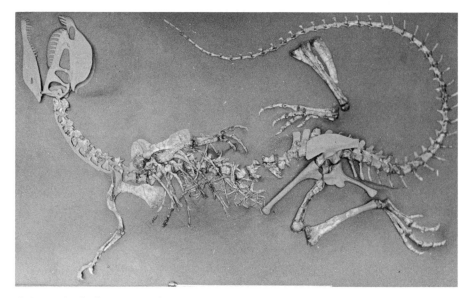

Skeleton of *Dilophosaurus wetherilli*. Courtesy of the University of
California, Berkeley.

Restoration of the crested theropod
Dilophosaurus prepared for this book by
Rick Hoberg.

Dromicosaurus Hoepen, 1920—(See *Massospondylus*.)

Dryosaurus Marsh, 1894—*Orn., Hypsil., U. Jur. and ?L. Cret.* (Probably *Dysalotosaurus*.) This slender, graceful dinosaur resembles *Hypsilophodon*. The forelimbs are small, each manus having five digits. The metatarsals are long and hollow. The head has a slim snout with large eyes. The hindlimbs are lengthy and strong. In life the animal attained a length of from 2.9 meters (10 feet) to 3.5 meters (12 feet). One specimen has a malformation of the vertebrae which is probably congenital. *Dryosaurus* is known from Como Bluff, Wyoming, and perhaps from New South Wales and the Isle of Wight. *Dysalotosaurus* from Tanzania has been synonymized with the American *Dryosaurus* by Galton.

Dryptosauroides Huene and Matley, 1933—*Ther., ?Family, U. Cret.* This large theropod is known from six dorsal vertebrae found in the Lameta Formation of Jabalpur, India. Some paleontologists believe the genus to belong to the family Megalosauridae.

Dryptosaurus Marsh, 1877—*Ther., ?Family, U. Cret. (Laelaps.)* The genus is known from fragments, including caudal vertebrae, teeth, pieces of a jaw, metatarsals, phalanges, an astragalus and two tibiae discovered in Barsborough, New Jersey. The animal apparently had very large front limbs and foreclaws. *Dryptosaurus* has traditionally been classified with the Megalosauridae but is probably in a family of its own. Early restorations have depicted the animal as capable of taking tremendous leaps. Huene suggested that the huge manual claw of *Dryptosaurus* was a useful tool in cutting blood vessels and prying between an ankylosaur's armor plates.

Dynamosaurus Osborn, 1905—(See *Tyrannosaurus*.)

Dyoplosaurus Parks, 1924—(See *Euoplocephalus*.)

Dysalotosaurus Virchow, 1919.—*Orn., Hypsil., U. Jur.* (Probably *Dryosaurus*.) This dinosaur, about 2.35 meters (8 feet) in length, is known from incomplete skulls and numerous bones found in Tanzania. The animal closely resembles *Dryosaurus*. The head has a slim snout and the eyes are large. The animal walked on hind limbs that were both lengthy and strong. One specimen has a malformation of the vertebrae which is probably congenital. (See *Dryosaurus*.)

Dysganus Cope, 1876—*Ornithischia, U. Cret.* This genus is based on a number of detached teeth from the Judith River Formation of Montana. Most of this material is now considered to be other than hadrosaurian

Humerus of *Dinodocus mackesoni*. (After Woodward.)

Skeleton of *Diplodocus longus*.
Courtesy of the Smithsonian
Institution.

Skeleton of *Diplodocus carnegii*. (After Holland.)

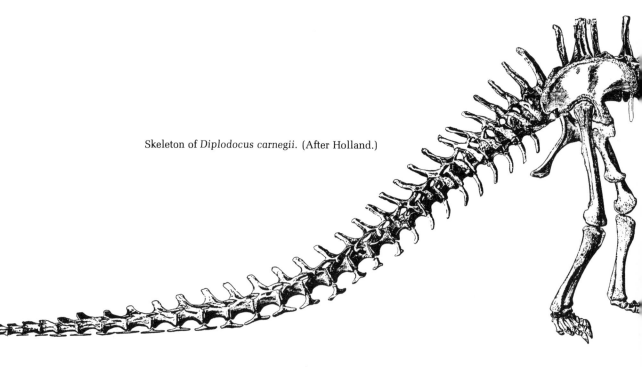

Skeleton of *Diplodocus hayi*.
Courtesy of the Houston
Museum of Natural Science.

Restoration of the incredibly long sauropod *Diplodocus*. From a painting by Zdeněk Burian.

while the remaining specimens are yet questionable. *D. peiganus* resembles the teeth in *Hypsilophodon* and may belong to a thescelosaur or ankylosaur. *D. haydenianus* is probably really *Ceratops* or *Monoclonius*.

Dystrophaeus   Cope, 1877—*Saur., Sauro., ?Family, ?U. Jur.* The genus is known from extremely poor material, including metacarpals, an ulna, radius and partial pubis, from the Morrison Formation of Painted Canyon, Utah.

Restoration of *Dromiceiomimus* prepared for this book by William Stout.

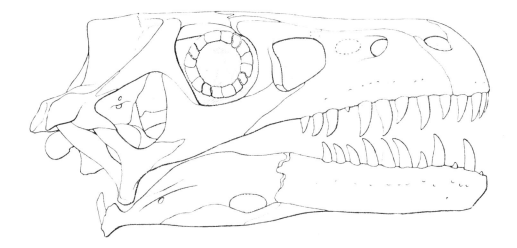

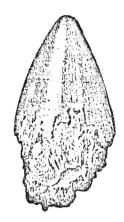

Tooth of *Diplotomodon horrificus.*

Skull of the theropod
Dromaeosaurus albertensis.

Restoration of *Dromaeosaurus* prepared for this book by William Stout.

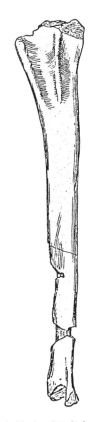

Left fibula of *Dolichosuchus cristatus.* (After Huene.)

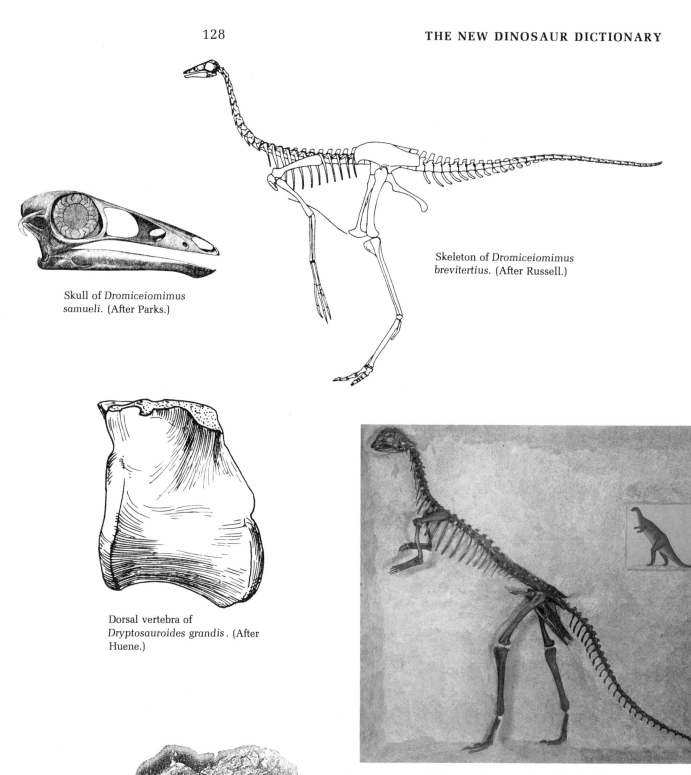

Skeleton of *Dromiceiomimus
brevitertius*. (After Russell.)

Skull of *Dromiceiomimus
samueli*. (After Parks.)

Dorsal vertebra of
Dryptosauroides grandis. (After
Huene.)

Skeleton and restoration of the birdlike dinosaur
Dryosaurus altus. Courtesy of the Carnegie
Museum.

Caudal vertebra of
?*Dryptosaurus medius*.

A lively Cretaceous scene as one *Dryptosaurus* leaps upon another. The claws of the hind feet were actually based upon the large claw now known to belong to the manus. From a painting by Charles R. Knight. Courtesy of the American Museum of Natural History.

Manual claw and jaw fragment of *Dryptosaurus aquilunguis*.

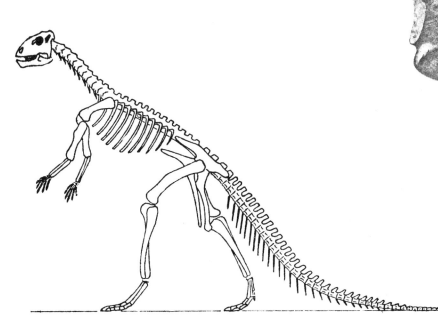

Skeleton of *Dysalotosaurus lettowvorbecki*. (After Steel.)

Pubis of *Dystrophaeus viaemalae*.

E

Maxilla of *Echinodon becklessii*.
(After Owen.)

Echinodon Owen, 1861—*Orn., ?Fabro., U. Jur.* (*Echinosaurus, Sauraechinodon.*) This genus is based on fragments of maxillae and two incomplete dentaries from the Isle of Purbeck, England. The teeth are similar to those in *Scelidosaurus, Fabrosaurus* and many other ornithischians, but with well developed canines like those of the heterodontosaurs.

Echinosaurus Morris, 1976—A misspelling of *Echinodon.*

Edmontonia Sternberg, 1928—(See *Panoplosaurus.*)

Edmontosaurus Lambe, 1917—*Orn., Hadro., Hadrosaur, U. Cret.,* (probably *Anatosaurus.*) From the Horseshoe Canyon Formation of Alberta, Canada, and possibly from the Hell Creek Formation of Montana, this large duck-billed dinosaur reached a length of 10.1 meters (35 feet) and weighed about 5.4 metric tons (6 tons). The animal resembles *Anatosaurus*, which Brett-Surman proposes is a junior synonym of *Edmontosaurus*, though no formal comparison of the two genera has yet been published. One specimen of *Edmontosaurus* displays a crest along the back and tail, a characteristic which may have been present in all hadrosaurs. Stomach contents show that at least one individual fed on conifers. Russell has suggested that this dinosaur lived in forested regions.

Efraasia Galton, 1973—*Saur., Prosaur, Anchi, U. Trias.* (Previously *Palaeosauriscus diagnosticus, Palaeosaurus diagnosticus.*) This German prosauropod is lightly built and approximately 2.9 meters (10 feet) long. The fourth and fifth digits of the manus are smaller than the other digits. The animal's main weapons were the strong claws. The skeleton usually referred to in paleontological literature as *Palaeosaurus* is actually *Efraasia.*

Elaphrosaurus Janensch, 1920—*Ther., ?Orinth., U. Jur. to L. Cret.* Known in Tanzania, Tunisia, Niger and possibly in Morocco, Egypt, France and the United States (the U.S. record being highly questionable), the genus is based on an incomplete skeleton lacking the skull. The hind limbs are relatively short, with the tibia about two and one half times as long as the femur. The length of the animal is about 5.8 meters (nearly 20 feet). The form of the metatarsus suggests that this dinosaur may have been ancestral to the ornithomimids. Without proof, ichnites from Israel have been referred to *Elaphrosaurus.*

Restoration of *Echinodon* prepared for this book by George Olshevsky and Ken Steacy.

Echinodon becklessii
Restored as a fabrosaurid

Skull of *Edmontosaurus regalis*. Courtesy of the Field Museum of Natural History.

Skeleton of the prosauropod *Efraasia diagnostica*. (After Galton.)

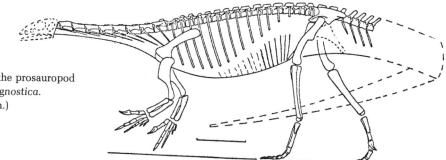

Dinosaurs of the Upper Cretaceous. *Edmontosaurus* (right) pauses before the armored *Palaeoscincus* (center), whose life restoration was actually based upon specimens now known to be *Panoplosaurus*. *Corythosaurus* (left) feeds in the water, while a herd of *Parasaurolophus* (left background) look for food. Two *Struthiomimus* stand in the center background. From a mural by Charles R. Knight. Courtesy of the Field Museum of Natural History.

Skeleton of *Elaphrosaurus bambergi*. (After Janensch.)

Elongatoolithus, the eggs apparently laid by the dinosaur *Protoceratops*. Courtesy of the Field Museum of Natural History.

Protoceratops, in a bipedal pose, stands before a nest of its eggs, given the name *Elongatoolithus*. From a painting by Maidi Wiebe. Courtesy of the Field Museum of Natural History.

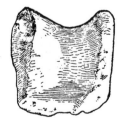

Vertebra of the theropod *Embasaurus minax*.

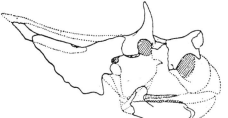

Restored skull of *Eoceratops canadensis.*

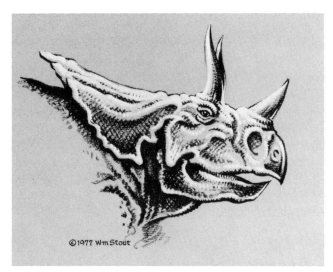

Restoration of the horned dinosaur *Eoceratops* prepared for this book by William Stout.

Restoration of *Elaphrosaurus* prepared for this book by Pete von Sholly.

Femur of *Erectopus sauvagei.*

Footprints of *Eubrontes giganteus*. (After Marsh.)

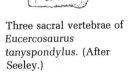

Three sacral vertebrae of *Eucercosaurus tanyspondylus*. (After Seeley.)

Elephantopoides Kaever and de Lapparent, 1974—*U. Jur.* The term has been given to sauropod ichnites from Barkhausen, Lower Saxony, Germany. The tracks show that a herd of sauropods were being pursued by a megalosaur which left the footprints called *Megalosauropus.*

Elongatoolithus Zhao, 1975—*U. Cret.* This genus of fossil eggs is from the Gobi Desert, Mongolia, and Gwangdong, China. The eggs were apparently laid by *Protoceratops.*

Elosaurus Peterson and Gilmore, 1902—*Saur., Sauro., Diplod., U. Jur.* (Possibly *Apatosaurus, Camarasaurus* or *Brachiosaurus.*) The genus is represented by a juvenile specimen, possibly of some other known genus of sauropod, from Wyoming. The dinosaur is imperfectly known from fossil remains, including a humerus, limb bones, ribs and a scapula. The pubis differs from that in most sauropods in its extended backward projection. McIntosh believes (personal communication) that *Elosaurus* is a juvenile *Apatosaurus.*

Embasaurus Riabinin, 1931—*Ther., ?Family, ?L. to U. Cret.* This dinosaur is known only from two vertebrae found in the Transcaspian Steppes of Mount Koi-Kara in Kazakhstan.

Empaterius White, 1973—A misspelling of *Epanterias.*

Eoceratops Lambe, 1915—*Cer., Cerat., U. Cret.* Known from incomplete specimens, this genus has been found in the Oldman Formation of the Red Deer River in Alberta, Canada. The skull is short and deep and measures over .9 meters (nearly 3 feet) long. There are three horns, one small horn over each orbit and curving slightly backward and a small horn above the snout pointing forward.

Epanterias Cope, 1878—(See *Allosaurus.*)

Erectopus Huene, 1923—*Ther., ?Family, L. and U. Cret.* Known from poor material including a tibia, femur and some metatarsals, this moderate-sized genus may be a primitive tyrannosaurid. The femur is very specialized for a theropod, having an erect posture. The fingers have small claws, the second being elongated. The animal is known from Ardennes, France, and from Egypt and Romania.

Erroplocephalus Nopsca, 1928—A misspelling of *Euoplocephalus.*

Eubrontes E. Hitchcock, 1845—*U. Trias and L. Jur.* (In part, *Brontozoum.*) The term has been given to numerous three-toed footprints made by a large theropod like *Dilophosaurus.* These ichnites are known from

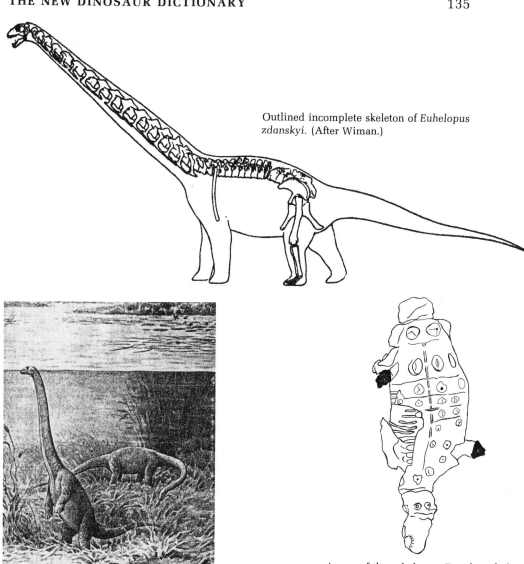

Outlined incomplete skeleton of *Euhelopus zdanskyi.* (After Wiman.)

Restoration of the sauropod *Euhelopus* assuming a bipedal pose underwater. (After Wiman.)

Armor of the ankylosaur *Euoplocephalus tutus.* (After Steel.)

Right tibia of the prosauropod *Eucnemesaurus fortis.*

the United States (Massachusetts, Connecticut, New Jersey), France, Lesotho, Niger, Morocco, Queensland and Russia. Some post-Triassic tracks referred to *Eubrontes* are actually *Megalosauropus*. *Eubrontes* has been placed in the footprint family Eubrontidae.

Eucamerotus   Hulke, 1872—(See *Pelorosaurus*.)

Eucercosaurus   Seeley, 1879—*Orn., Iguan., L. Cret.* (Possibly *Anoplosaurus*.) The genus is based on a neural arch and some imperfect vertebrae from Cambridge, England.

Skull of *Euoplocephalus tutus.* Courtesy of R. A. Long, S. P. Welles and the American Museum of Natural History.

Club tail of *Euoplocephalus tutus.* (After Parks.)

Reconstruction of the skeleton of *Euoplocephalus tutus.* (After Carpenter.)

Restoration of *Euoplocephalus* by Ken Carpenter. This is, to date, the most accurate and current life restoration of an ankylosaur. (After Carpenter.)

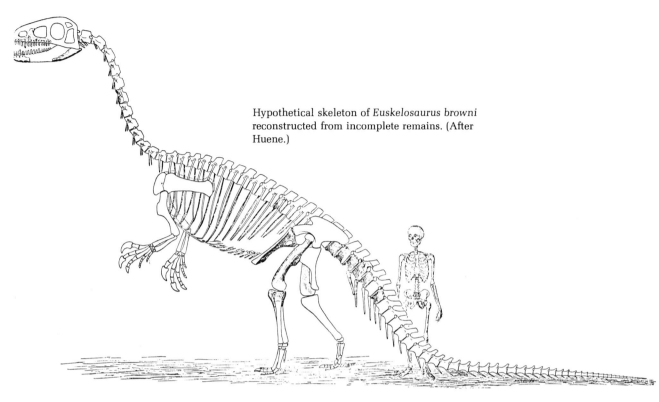

Hypothetical skeleton of *Euskelosaurus browni* reconstructed from incomplete remains. (After Huene.)

Eucnemesaurus Hoepen, 1920—*Saur., Prosaur, Melan., U. Trias.* (Probably *Euskelosaurus.*) From the Red beds of Orange Free State, South Africa, this prosauropod is known from fragments including dorsal and caudal vertebrae, a tibia and incomplete pubis and femur.

Euhelopus Romer, 1956—*Saur., Sauro., Camar., Euhelo., L. Cret. (Helopus.)* This dinosaur is known primarily from a vertebral column almost 8.3 meters (29 feet) long and a skull, discovered in Shandong, China. The neck is extremely long and in life the animal reached a length of about 17.5 meters (60 feet). The skull, for which the precise position of the teeth is not known, resembles that of *Camarasaurus*, but the vertebrae and the pelvis differ. Some restorations have erroneously depicted *Euhelopus* as a biped, based on a drawing showing the animal's forelimbs lifted under water. The dinosaur weighed about 22 metric tons (25 tons).

Euoploasurus Huene, 1956—A misspelling of *Euoplocephalus.*

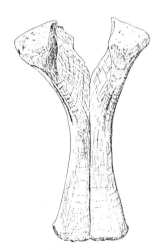

Ischia of *Euskelosaurus africanus.*

Euoplocephalus Lambe, 1910—*Ank., Anky., U. Cret. (Anodonto-saurus, Dyoplosaurus, Scolosaurus, Stereocephalus.)* This genus is the best known ankylosaur, with numerous skulls and much skeletal material from the Oldman and Horseshoe Canyon Formations of Alberta, Canada. The body is squat, the carapace protected by numerous keeled and oval scutes, getting larger toward the tail and the belly with small armor processes. The tail has a club. The snout is large and rounded, curved in front and along the sides, and with large nasal openings and a

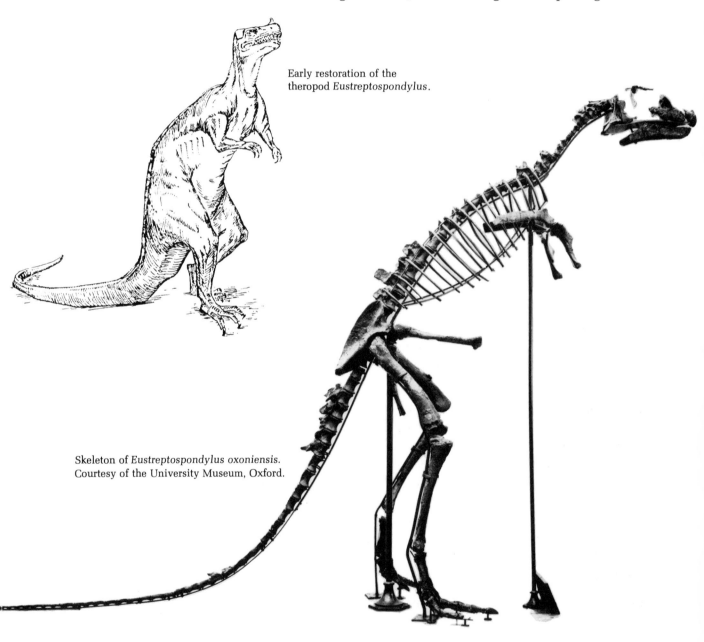

Early restoration of the theropod *Eustreptospondylus*.

Skeleton of *Eustreptospondylus oxoniensis*.
Courtesy of the University Museum, Oxford.

horny beak. The palpebral bone could be lowered to cover and protect the eyes completely. *Euoplocephalus*, about two-thirds as large as *Ankylosaurus*, reached about 5.25 meters (18 feet) in length and weighed some 2.7 metric tons (3 tons).

Euoplology Hou, 1977—A misspelling of *Euoplocephalus*.

Eupaiamopus Hay, 1902—*U. Trias.* From Massachusetts, these fossil footprints may have been made by a theropod.

Euplocephalus Lambe, 1920—A misspelling of *Euoplocephalus*.

Europlocephalus Sternberg, 1915—A misspelling of *Euoplocephalus*.

Europocephalus Nopcsa, 1923—A misspelling of *Euoplocephalus*.

Euscelesaurus Lydekker, 1890—A misspelling of *Euskelosaurus*.

Euscellosaurus Lydekker, 1890—A misspelling of *Euskelosaurus*.

Euscelosaurus Zittel, 1890—A misspelling of *Euskelosaurus*.

Euskelesaurus Huxley, 1867—A misspelling of *Euskelosaurus*.

Euskelosaurus Huxley, 1866—*Saur., Prosaur, Melan., U. Trias.* (*Euscelesaurus, Euscellosaurus, Euscelosaurus, Euskelesaurus;* possibly *Eucnemesaurus, Gigantoscelis, Melanorosaurus, Orinosaurus, Plateosauravus.*) Known from imperfect remains including a tibia, fibula, femur, pubis and pieces of vertebrae from the Stormberg Series of South Africa, this genus is probably similar to *Melanorosaurus*. Van Heerden has proposed that *E. africanus* is synonymous with *E. browni* and that *Euskelosaurus* is a senior synonym for *Eucnemesaurus fortis, Gigantoscelis molengraaffi, Melanorosaurus readi, Orinosaurus capensis* and *Plateosauravus stormbergensis*.

Eustreptospondylus Walker, 1964—*Ther., ?Family, U. Jur.* ("*Streptospondylus.*") From the Middle Oxford Clay of England, this dinosaur has traditionally been described as a "small, elegant and light" (Huene) megalosaur and has been depicted in restorations as a horned theropod resembling *Proceratosaurus*. But, on the basis of recent studies, the genus possibly belongs to a family of its own. The material from Madagascar and South America referred to this dinosaur is not *Eustreptospondylus*.

Eutynichnium Nopcsa, 1923—*U. Jur.* These fossil footprints from Cap Mondego, Portugal, were left by a large theropod, possibly *Megalosaurus*.

Fragmentary right mandible of
Fabrosaurus australis. (After
Ginsburg.)

Partial femur of *Fulgurotherium
australe.*

F

Fabrosaurus   Ginsburg, 1964—*Orn., Fabro., U. Trias.* Based on a fragmentary right mandible with teeth from the Stormberg Series, Red beds, of South Africa, this genus, once believed to be a scelidosaur, is now referred to the ornithopods as the type of the family Fabrosauridae.

Faveoloolithus   Zhao and Ding, 1976—The term has been given to dinosaur eggs discovered in Ningxia, China.

Fenestrosaurus   Osborn, 1924—See *Oviraptor.*

Fulgurotherium   Huene, 1932—*Orn., Hypsil., L. Cret.* Based on a worn femur fragment discovered in New South Wales, this genus was once thought to be a coelurosaurid.

Fulicopus   E. Hitchcock, 1845—*(Aethyopus, Amblonyx; see Sauropus.)*

G

Restoration of the English
sauropod *Gigantosaurus* from
*The Book of Prehistoric
Animals* (1935), by Raymond L.
Ditmars. Courtesy of Charles
Scribner's Sons.

Gallimimus   Osmólska, Roniewicz and Barsbold, 1972—*Ther., Ornith., U. Cret.* From the Gobi Desert in Mongolia, *Gallimimus* is the largest complete ornithomimid known, some specimens having a length of approximately 8.8 meters (30 feet). The skull is toothless and is notable for having chambers below the region of the brain. The animal was not only capable of delivering a fatal kick with its taloned hind feet but was also one of the fastest running dinosaurs.

Genyodectes   Woodward, 1901—*Ther., ?Family, U. Cret.* (Possibly *Loncosaurus.*) This genus is imperfectly known from specimens including a fragment and a jaw with teeth found in Chubut, Argentina. Sometimes *Genyodectes* is referred to the Tyrannosauridae, but the form of the teeth indicate that it is probably not a tyrannosaurid. Reference to a complete skull is apparently in error.

Geranosaurus   Broom, 1911—*Orn., Heter., U. Trias.* From Cape Province, South Africa, *Geranosaurus* is known from incomplete material, including a fibula, tibia, partial foot, mandible and pieces of a skull.

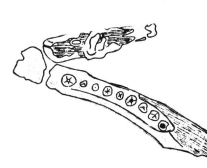

Imperfect lower jaw of
Geranosaurus atavus. (After
Brown.)

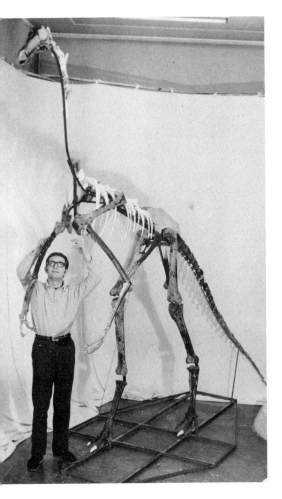

Restoration of the probable
appearance of *Fulgurotherium* by
Mark Hallett.

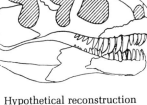

Hypothetical reconstruction
of the skull of *Genyodectes
scrus*, based on incomplete
jaws. (After Bonaparte.)

Skeleton of *Gallimimus bullatus*. Courtesy
of the Institute of Paleobiology in Warsaw.

Incomplete skeletal remains, including skull, pelvic girdle, hind limbs and tail,
and restoration of *Gallimimus bullatus*. Courtesy of the Institute of Paleobiology in
Warsaw.

Right tibia and right femur
of *Gilmoreosaurus
mongoliensis.* (After Gilmore.)

Footprints of *Grallator
cursorius.* (After Lull.)

Differences in the upper jaw distinguish the dinosaur from *Heterodontosaurus.*

Gigandipus   E. Hitchcock, 1855—*L. Jur. (Gigantotherium.)* The term has been given to ichnites found in the Connecticut Valley. The animal that left them probably resembled a large theropod. *Gigandipus* has been placed in the footprint family Gigandipodidae.

Gigantosaurus   Seeley, 1869—*Saur., Sauro., Camar., Brachio., U. Jur.* (Possibly *Brachiosaurus, Ischyrosaurus, Pelorosaurus.*) This genus is based on a terminal phalanx and fibula from the Kimmeridge Clay of Cambridgeshire, England.

Gigantosaurus   Fraas, 1908—(See *Tornieria.*)

Gigantoscelis   Huene, 1932—A misspelling of *Gigantoscelus.*

Gigantoscelus   Hoepen, 1916—*Saur., Prosaur, Melan., U. Trias.* (*Gigantoscelis;* possibly *Euskelosaurus.*) From the Stormberg Series of the Transvaal, this genus is based on the distal end of a femur. It is very similar to or congeneric with *Euskelosaurus.*

Gigantotherium   E. Hitchcock, 1858—(See *Gigandipus.*)

Gilmoreosaurus   Brett-Surman, 1979—*Orn., Hadro., Hadrosaur., U. Cret.* This large duck-billed dinosaur, once believed to be a new species of *Mandschurosaurus,* has many iguanodont and hadrosaurine features and is the earliest known Asian representative of the Hadrosaurinae family. The dinosaur was discovered in the Iren Debasu Formation, Mongolia.

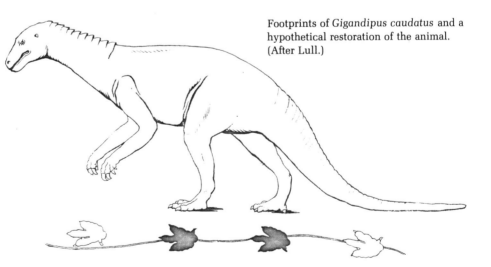

Footprints of *Gigandipus caudatus* and a
hypothetical restoration of the animal.
(After Lull.)

Gobipteryx Elzanowski, 1974—?*Ther.*, *Gobi.*, *U. Cret.* From the Barun Goyot Formation of Mongolia, this genus is represented by at least two incomplete skulls. Though generally considered to be avian, this genus may be a theropod related to the caenagnathids. The skulls have moderately long jaws, no external mandibular fenestrae and birdlike palates, while the lower jaws superficially resemble those of the caenagnathids and oviraptorids.

Gorgosaurus Lambe, 1914—(See *Albertosaurus*.)

Grallator E. Hitchcock, 1858—*U. Trias.* (Probably *Anchisauripus*.) These theropod ichnites are known from the United States (Massachusetts, Connecticut, New Jersey), France and Lesotho. They were left by podokesaurids of various sizes. *Grallator* has been placed in the footprint family Anchisauripodidae.

Gresslyosaurus Rütimeyer, 1857—*Saur.*, *Prosaur*, *Plate.*, *U. Trias.* (*Dinosaurus*; possibly *Pachysaurops*, *Picrodon*, *Plateosaurus*.) This prosauropod is based on fragmentary material including four vertebrae, an incomplete foot, a sacrum and the distal end of a tibia. The upper arm is twice the size of the lower arm. The type specimen is from Switzerland; the genus has also been reported from Germany and North Africa.

Manus of the prosauropod *Gresslyosaurus*. (After Huene.)

Griphornis Woodward, 1902—(See *Archaeopteryx*.)

Griphosaurus Wagner, 1861—(See *Archaeopteryx*.)

Gryphornis Owen, 1862, Lambrecht, 1933—A misspelling of *Griphornis*.

Gryphosaurus Marschall, 1873—A misspelling of *Griphosaurus*.

Gryponyx Broom, 1911—(See *Massospondylus*.)

Gryposaurus Lambe, 1914—(See *Hadrosaurus*.)

Gyposaurus Broom, 1911—*Saur.*, *Prosaur.*, *Anchi.*, *U. Trias.* Based on an incomplete skeleton found on a slab of sandstone in the Stormberg beds of Orange Free State, South Africa, and material found in China, *Gyposaurus* reached a length of almost 1.5 meters (5 feet). Rozhdestvensky and Galton believe that the Chinese material is probably not *Gyposaurus* and could be a young *Lufengosaurus*. The material from Africa is a junior synonym of *Anchisaurus*.

Gypsichnites Sternberg, 1932—*L. Cret.* From British Columbia and Texas, these tracks were made by a large ornithopod, possibly an iguanodont, about the size of *Iguanodon*.

Gyrotriasauropus Ellenberger, 1970—*L. Jur.* These apparently ornith-opod footprints were discovered in the uppermost Stormberg Series of Kolo in Lesotho.

H

Hadrosaurus Leidy, 1858—*Orn., Hadro., Hadrosaur., U. Cret.* (Proba-bly *Kritosaurus;* possibly, in part, *Hypsibema.*) This genus has the dis-tinction of being the first dinosaur known in North America from good skeletal material, found in New Jersey two years after the discovery of the first fragmentary dinosaur remains in Montana and South Dakota. It is based on imperfect material including teeth, vertebrae, matatarsals, a femur, fibula, tibia, ulna, radius, ischium and ilium. Though the skull is not known, the teeth indicate a flat-headed hadrosaur. *Hadrosaurus* grew to a length of about 8.75 meters (30 feet). Traditionally the animal has been portrayed as similar in appearance to *Anatosaurus.* However, recent studies by Baird and Horner indicate that *Hadrosaurus* could be a senior synonym of *Kritosaurus,* though no formal comparison of the two genera has yet been published. Some hadrosaur material, especially

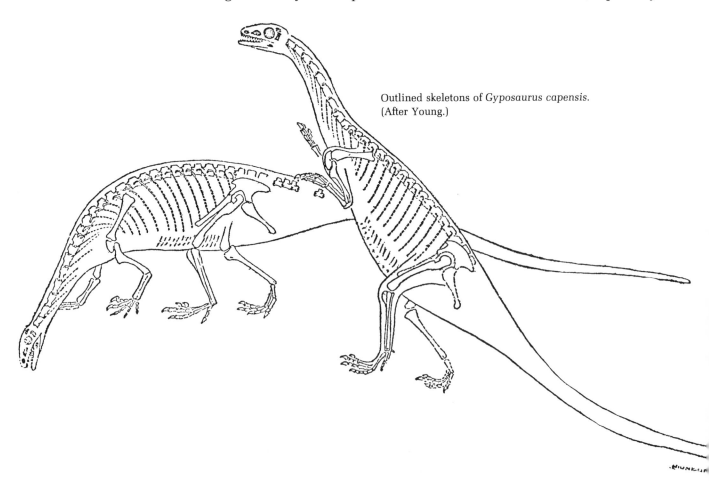

Outlined skeletons of *Gyposaurus capensis.*
(After Young.)

that from the western United States, has incorrectly been referred to *Hadrosaurus*.

Halticosaurus   Huene, 1908—*Ther., Podok., U. Trias.* This genus, known from a rather well preserved skeleton plus several incomplete specimens discovered in Halberstadt, Germany, and from material found in France, has a large skull and relatively short hind legs. Each manus probably has a maximum of four digits, the first and fourth being small. In life *Halticosaurus* reached a length of approximately 5.3 meters (18 feet).

Haplocanthosaurus   Hatcher, 1903—*Saur., Sauro., Camar., Cetio., U. Jur.* (*Haplocanthus*; possibly *Cetiosaurus*.) This large sauropod, discovered in Oil Creek, Canyon City, Colorado, is quite similar to *Cetiosaurus*. The two genera differ primarily with respect to the vertebrae. The Cleveland skeleton referred to *Haplocanthosaurus*, measuring over 21 meters (72 feet), may actually be another genus altogether, possibly related to *Cetiosaurus*.

Haplocanthus   Hatcher, 1903—(See *Haplocanthosaurus*.)

Hecatasaurus   Brown, 1910—(See *Telmatosaurus*.)

Heishansaurus   Bohlin, 1953—*Ank., ?Family, U. Cret.* This armored dinosaur from Chia-yü-kuan, in northwest China, is known imperfectly from material including a damaged skull, fragmentary vertebrae, ribs and some dermal plates. The skull roof is quite thick as in the pachycephalosaurs.

Helopus   Wiman, 1929—(See *Euhelopus*.)

Herrerasaurus   Reig, 1963—*Saurischia, ?Suborder, Herrer., M. or U. Trias.* This primitive carnivorous dinosaur is known from incomplete remains discovered in San Juan and La Rioja, Argentina. *Herrerasaurus* might be a prosauropod.

Heterodontosaurus   Crompton and Charig, 1962—*Orn., Heter., U. Trias.* Discovered in Cape Province, South Africa, this early, specialized ornithischian was mostly bipedal, coming down on all fours during slow locomotion and using the forelimbs primarily for grasping. The structure of the skeleton implies that *Heterodontosaurus* was capable of running. The skull has a short face, with sharp canine-like teeth and cheek teeth with elongated crowns, more specialized than the teeth in *Hypsilophodon*. The animal grew to an approximate length of 85 centimeters (2 feet 8 inches). *Heterodontosaurus* probably left no descendants.

Vertebrae of *Hadrosaurus foulkii*, the first North American dinosaur to be described. (After Leidy.)

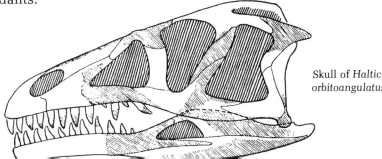

Skull of *Halticosaurus orbitoangulatus*. (After Huene.)

Femur of *Haplocanthosaurus utterbacki*. (After Hatcher.)

Scapula of *Haplocanthosaurus priscus*. (After Hatcher.)

Skeleton of *Halticosaurus liliensterni* mounted on the wall of a German castle.

Skeleton referred to *Haplocanthosaurus* which is either the only representative of this genus mounted for display or is another genus altogether, possibly related to *Cetiosaurus*. In the background is a life-sized model of *Ceratosaurus*. Courtesy of the Cleveland Museum.

Hind foot of the saurischian *Herrerasaurus ischigualastensis*. (After Reig.)

Restoration of *Haplocanthosaurus* prepared for this book by George Olshevsky and the author.

Restoration of *Herrerasaurus* by Mark Hallett.

Skeleton of *Herrerasaurus ischigualastensis*. Courtesy of J. F. Bonaparte.

Restoration of the small ornithopod dinosaur *Heterodontosaurus* prepared for this book by George Olshevsky and Franc Reyes.

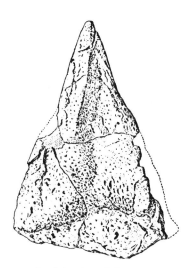

Caudal spine of the ankylosaur *Hierosaurus sternbergii.*

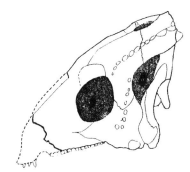

Skull of *Homalocephale calathocercos.* (After Maryańska and Osmólska.)

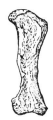

Femur of the armored dinosaur *Hoplitosaurus marshi.*

Life restoration of *Hoplitosaurus* drawn before the animal was named.

Heterosaurus   Cornuel, 1850—(See *Iguanodon.*)

Hierosaurus   Wieland, 1909—*Ank., Nodo., U. Trias.* The type specimen of this dinosaur, *H. sternbergii* from Logan County, Kansas, is indeterminate but considered to be a junior synonym of *Nodosaurus textilis* (W. P. Coombs, personal communication). *Hierosaurus* has been described as possibly being covered with plates, having lateral spikes and a long, slender and flexible tail. Because its remains were found in a marine formation, *Hierosaurus* was once believed to be somewhat aquatic.

Hikanodon   Keferstein, 1825—(See *Iguanodon.*)

Homalocephale   Maryańska and Osmólska, 1974—*Orn., Pachy., U. Cret.* From the Nemegt Formation of Mongolia, this stocky, bone-headed dinosaur is approximately the size of a large dog, about .9 meters (3 feet) long. The cranial dome of *Homalocephale* is only slightly developed, nowhere near the size of that in other pachycephalosaurs.

Hopiichnus   Welles, 1971—*U. Trias, or L. Jur.* These theropod tracks were discovered in Arizona.

Hoplitosaurus   Lucas, 1902—*Ank., Nodo., L. Cret.* This armored dinosaur from Custer County, South Dakota, and probably southern Utah is known from indeterminate vertebrae, some limb bones, rib fragments and pieces of dermal armor. The plates are flattened, rounded, triangular, keeled and spined. When first discovered, these remains were believed to be from a new species of *Stegosaurus* or related to *Scelidosaurus.* It has been suggested that *Hoplitosaurus* was similar to *Hylaeosaurus.*

Hoplosaurus   Seeley, 1881—(See *Struthiosaurus.*)

Hoplosaurus   Lydekker, 1890—A misspelling of *Oplosaurus.*

Hortalotarsus   Seeley, 1894—*Saur. Prosaur., Anchi., U. Trias.* (Possibly *Thecodontosaurus.*) From the Stormberg beds of Cape Province, South Africa, this prosauropod is based on part of a hind limb. Later material referred to this genus is actually *Anchisaurus*, which *Hortalotarsus* resembles.

Hyaelosaurus   Huene, 1956—A misspelling of *Hylaeosaurus.*

Hylaeosaurus   Mantell, 1833—*Ank., Nodo., L. Cret.* (*Hylosaurus, Polacanthus;* possibly *Polacanthoides.*) Known from France, Germany and the Isle of Wight, England, *Hylaeosaurus* was the third dinosaur to be described. Two rows of spikes surmount the dorsal region of the hips and tail and there are large lateral spikes and bony scutes in the pectoral region. Early restorations based upon the original material depicted *Hylaeosaurus* as a fanciful creature with a large lizardlike head and one row of sharp dorsal spikes. Later restorations based upon material called *Polacanthus* incorrectly portrayed *Hylaeosaurus* as having a shield of bone over the hips, actually a geological artifact, and two rows of large spikes over the neck and shoulder region. In life *Hylaeosaurus* reached an approximate length of 4.1 meters (14 feet).

Right ilium of *Hortalotarsus skirtopodus*. (After Seeley.)

Hylosaurus   Fitzinger, 1843—A misspelling of *Hylaeosaurus*.

Hypacrosaurus   Brown, 1913—*Orn., Hadro., Lambeo., U. Cret.* (Probably *Cheneosaurus*.) From the Horseshoe Canyon sediments of Alberta, Canada, and perhaps the Two Medicine Formation of Montana, this duck-billed dinosaur displays a high helmet-shaped crest, formed by the premaxillary and nasal bones, somewhat resembling the crest in *Corythosaurus*. In *Hypacrosaurus*, however, the crest is less expanded and rounded. This genus is quite large, the skull measuring approximately 58 centimeters (22 inches) high, and it has long spines on the vertebrae. These spines probably supported a web of flesh which served as a heat regulator.

Skeleton of *Hylaeosaurus armatus*. (After Huene.)

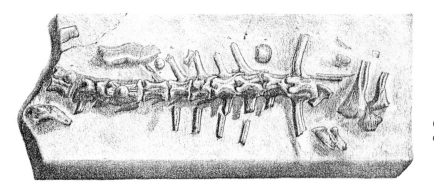

Caudal vertebrae of *Hylaeosaurus armatus*. (After Owen.)

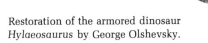

Restoration of the armored dinosaur *Hylaeosaurus* by George Olshevsky.

Tracks of *Hyphepus fieldi* and a
hypothetical depiction of the
animal, its proportions based on
the thecodont *Saltoposuchus*.
(After Lull.)

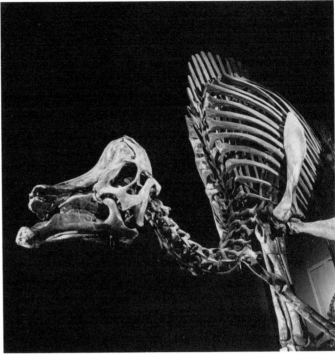

Skeleton of *Hypacrosaurus altispinus*. Courtesy of the National
Museums of Canada.

Restoration of *Hypacrosaurus altispinus*
prepared for this book by George Olshevsky.

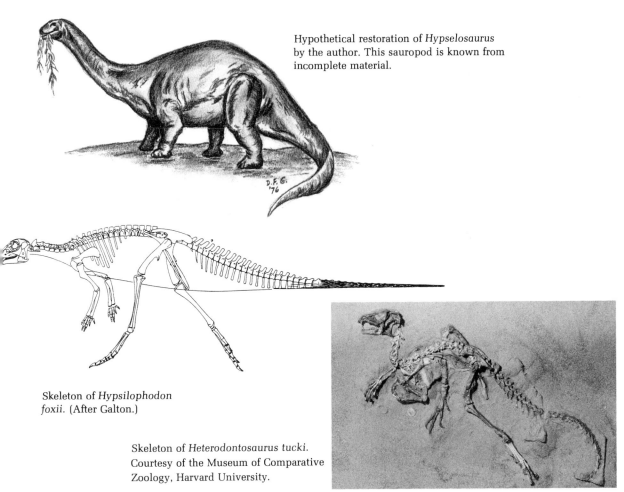

Hypothetical restoration of *Hypselosaurus* by the author. This sauropod is known from incomplete material.

Skeleton of *Hypsilophodon foxii*. (After Galton.)

Skeleton of *Heterodontosaurus tucki*. Courtesy of the Museum of Comparative Zoology, Harvard University.

Hyphepus   E. Hitchcock, 1858—*L. Jur.* The term has been given to theropod tracks found in the Connecticut Valley. The tracks are poor and not really distinguishable from *Grallator*. However, Haubold and others have placed *Hyphepus* in the footprint family Gigandipodidae.

Hypselosaurus   Matheron, 1869—*Saur., Sauro., Diplod., Titano., U. Cret.* (Possibly *Magyarosaurus*.) This large sauropod is based on a femur from Provence, France. Though some material from Transylvania and Spain has been called *Hypselosaurus*, there is no proof to support this. The dinosaur was probably 11.75 meters (40 feet) long. Among the French *Hypselosaurus* remains were numerous fossil eggshells which were identified as either belonging to this dinosaur or to a large bird. A complete egg was discovered in 1930 and it is assumed, though not proven, that this and other egg specimens from France belong to *Hypselosaurus*.

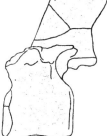

Mid-dorsal vertebra of *Iguanodon dawsoni*. (After Owen.)

Maxilla of *Iguanodon orientalis*. (After Rozhdestvensky.)

Restoration of the ornithopod dinosaur *Iguanodon* by Neave Parker. Courtesy of the British Museum (Natural History).

Hypsibema   Cope, 1870—*Orn., Hadro., Hadrosaur., U. Cret.* (Possibly, in part, *Hadrosaurus, Parrosaurus.*) This dinosaur is based on incomplete material, including a partial humerus and tibia, a metatarsal and caudal centrum, found in Sampson County, North Carolina. The vertebrae are similar to those of *Hadrosaurus* and are significant in indicating that large hadrosaurs lived in that area. Recent studies by Baird indicate that the *Hypsibema* material is not all from the same animal and also includes specimens of theropod and a sauropod like *Parrosaurus* (D. Baird, personal communication).

Hypsilophodon   Huxley, 1870—*Orn., Hypsil., U. Jur. and L. Cret.* (Possibly *Laosaurus.*) This genus is a primitive ornithopod, with teeth present in the front of the mouth and four toes on each hind foot. The animal is small, about 2.35 meters (8 feet) in length and weighing about 68 kilograms (150 pounds). Its posture was such that the head was carried no more than .6 meters (2 feet) off the ground. Because of the long fingers and toes, *Hypsilophodon* has traditionally been depicted as a tree-dweller, but this conception has been disproven on the basis of recent studies. Also, though this dinosaur has been described as having two rows of small armor scutes along the back as in the thecodonts, implying a relationship with ancestral armored dinosaurs, recent studies have shown that such scutes were not present. *Hypsilophodon* is known from the Isle of Wight, England, the late Kimmeridgian rocks of Porto Pinheiro, Portugal, and perhaps from the Lakota Formation of South Dakota.

Hypsirhophus   Cope, 1879—A misspelling of *Hypsirophus.*

Hypsirophus   Cope, 1878—(*Hypsirhophus;* see *Allosaurus, Stegosaurus.*)

I

Ignotornis   Mehl, 1931—*?U. Cret.* These small ichnites from Colorado may have been left by a small or young theropod or even a bird.

Iguanodon   Mantell, 1825—*Orn., Iguan., L. Cret.* (*Heterosaurus, Hikanodon, Iguanosaurus, Sphenospondylus, Therosaurus.*) From Europe, Asia, Africa and North America, *Iguanodon* was originally named for some fossil teeth, roughly resembling those of the modern-day iguana lizard, found in Kent, England. Consequently, early restorations depicted the dinosaur as a giant, horned and quadrupedal iguana somewhat resembling a rhinoceros. With the later discovery of complete skeletons, *Iguanodon* is known to be a biped and the "horn" is identified as a spiked thumb. These thumbs were once believed to have been weapons used in combat; but a more modern theory is that the thumbs were actually used by males to attract females during mating. *Iguanodon* was strong and bulky, probably weighing about 6.2 metric tons (7 tons) and reaching a length of about 8.9 meters (30 feet) and a height of 4.7 meters (16 feet).

Iguanodonichnus   Casamiquela, 1968—*L. Cret.* These ichnites found in Chile are those of a large ornithopod dinosaur.

Iguanosaurus   Ritgen, 1828—(See *Iguanodon.*)

Iliosuchus   Huene, 1932—*Ther., ?Family, U. Jur.* This genus is based on an ilium from Stonesfield, England.

Indosaurus   Huene and Matley, 1933—*Ther., Megal., U. Cret.* (Possibly, in part, *Lametasaurus.*) This dinosaur is based on a braincase from the Lameta Formation of Jabalpur, India. The braincase is heavily built for a theropod. *Indosaurus* was probably a massive carnivore and reportedly had lachrymal horns present behind the orbits. In many respects the animal shares characters with *Allosaurus.* Since the discovery of the braincase, much other material has been referred to *Indosaurus.*

Indosuchus   Huene and Matley, 1933—*Ther., Tyrann., U. Cret.* A primitive, medium-sized tyrannosaurid, this genus is based on the frontal region of a skull from the Lameta Formation of Jabalpur, India. Other material, including a pair of premaxillae, a left maxilla and a right dentary, have since been referred to this dinosaur. There are 4 premaxillary and 14 (as in *Daspletosaurus* and *Albertosaurus*) maxillary teeth with low tooth crowns.

Inosaurus   Lapparent, 1960—*Ther., ?Family, L. to U. Cret.* From the central Sahara of Algeria and Egypt, this dinosaur is based on poor material including vertebrae and an incomplete tibia.

Iranosaurus   Lapparent and Sadat, 1975—*M. Trias.* These "coelurosaur" tracks were discovered in Kerman, Iran.

Irenesauripus   Sternberg, 1932—*L. Cret.* These ichnites from the Peace River area of British Columbia and also from Texas were made by a large theropod the size of *Allosaurus.* The tracks average 37 centimeters (14 inches) in length. The stride averages about .9 meters (3 feet).

Restoration by Neave Parker of *Hypsilophodon* as a tree-climber, a conception that has been disproven in recent years. Courtesy of the British Museum (Natural History).

Ilium of *Iliosuchus incognitus.*
(After Huene.)

Incomplete skull of *Indosaurus matleyi.* (After Huene and Matley.)

Skeleton of *Iguanodon mantelli.*

Skeleton of *Iguanodon anglicum*, one of the first dinosaurs to be described. (After Dollo.)

Hypothetical restoration of the theropod *Indosaurus* prepared for this book by Pete von Sholly. Most of the dinosaur's skull is unknown.

Restored skull of the primitive tyrannosaurid *Indosuchus raptorius.*

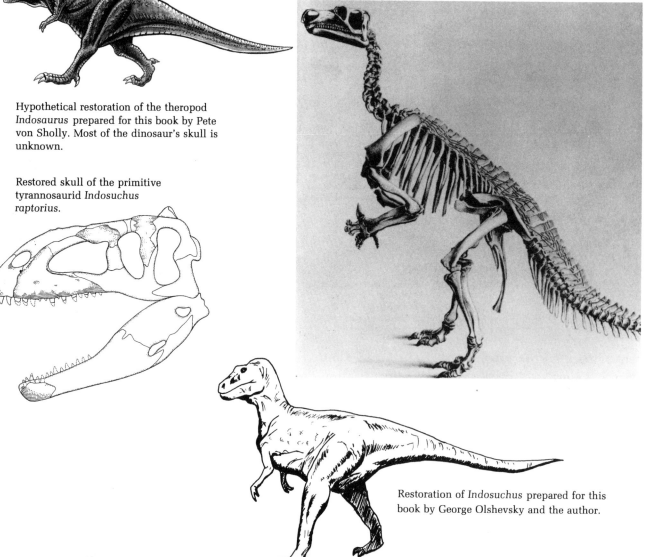

Restoration of *Indosuchus* prepared for this book by George Olshevsky and the author.

Irenichnites Sternberg, 1932—*L. Cret.* (Probably *Ornithomimipus.*) From British Columbia, these tracks were probably made by either a medium-sized ornithopod or theropod.

Ischisaurus Reig, 1963—*Ther., Herrer., M. or U. Trias.* Based on fragmentary material—including parts of a skull and jaws, vertebrae, limbs and girdle—this genus from Argentina may be a prosauropod.

Itemirus Kurzanov, 1976—*Ther., Item., U. Cret.* From Itemir (Dzhara-Kuduk), Mongolia, this dinosaur is based on a short, high braincase unlike that of most theropods. The animal is small, perhaps smaller than *Dromaeosaurus*, with well developed optic lobes. Apparently the dinosaur is close to the ancestry of the dromaeosaurids and tyrannosaurids. Kurzanov suggests that the inner ear indicates the animal to have had a good sense of balance but not acute hearing.

Femur of *Ischisaurus cattoi.* (After Reig.)

Restoration of the probable appearance of *Ischisaurus* by Mark Hallett.

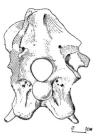

Braincase of *Itemirus medullaris.* (After Kurzanov.)

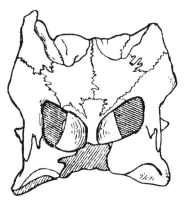

Braincase with frontals (top view) of *Jaxartosaurus aralensis*.

Dorsal vertebra of *Jubbulpuria tenuis*. (After Huene.)

Right femur of *Kangnasaurus coetzei*. (After Haughton.)

J

Jaxartosaurus　Riabinin, 1939—*Orn., Hadro., Lambeo. (Yaxartosaurus;* possibly *Nipponosaurus.*) From Kazakhstan and Sinkiang, China, this hadrosaur is known from various limb bones, vertebrae and the posterior region of the skull.

Jeholosauripus　Yabe, Inai and Shikama, 1940—*U. Trias. to L. Jur.* (Possibly *Anchisauripus.*) These ichnites from Manchuria were possibly made by a small theropod. They have been placed in the footprint family Anchisauripodidae.

Jubbulpuria　Huene and Matley, 1933—*Ther., ?Family, U. Cret.* This small dinosaur from the Lameta Formation of Jabalpur, India, is known only from two dorsal vertebrae and fragments.

K

Kainomoyenisauropus　Ellenberger, 1970—*L. Jur.* These fossil tracks, made by a small theropod, are known from the uppermost Stormberg Series of Li Khoele, in Lesotho.

Kainotrisauropus　Ellenberger, 1970—*L. Jur.* These large, tridactyl footprints, from the uppermost Stormberg Series of several locations in Lesotho and from the Lower Lias of France, may have been left by a large theropod.

Kalosauropus　Ellenberger, 1970—*U. Trias.* These ichnites from the Upper Stormberg Series of Leribe, in Lesotho, may have been made by a possible ornithischian, with delicate toes.

Kangnasaurus　Haughton, 1915—*Orn., Iguan., M. Jur. or U. Cret.* This iguanodont is known from a right femur, right maxillary tooth and possibly other material found in Namagualand, South Africa. The genus is sometimes regarded as an hypsilophodont.

Katosauropus　Ellenberger, 1970—*U. Trias. or L. Jur.* The term has been given to footprints from the Upper Stormberg beds of Masitisi, in Lesotho. They may have been made by a small theropod.

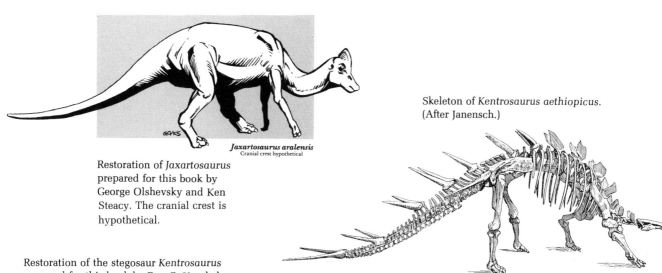

Jaxartosaurus aralensis
Cranial crest hypothetical

Restoration of *Jaxartosaurus*
prepared for this book by
George Olshevsky and Ken
Steacy. The cranial crest is
hypothetical.

Skeleton of *Kentrosaurus aethiopicus.*
(After Janensch.)

Restoration of the stegosaur *Kentrosaurus*
prepared for this book by Roy G. Krenkel.
The pterosaurs actually lived sometime later.

Skeleton of *Kritosaurus
notabilis.* Courtesy of the Royal
Ontario Museum.

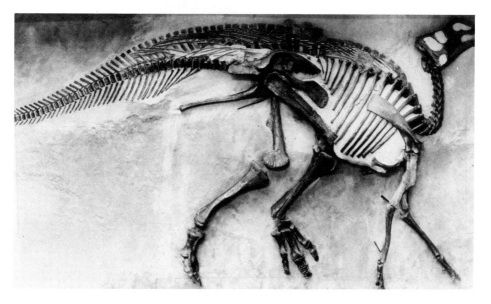

Kayentapus Welles, 1971—*U. Trias. or L. Jur.* These ichnites from Arizona were made by a large theropod.

Kelmayisaurus Dong, 1973—*Ther., ?Megal., L. Cret.* This genus is known from a maxilla and jaw discovered in the Dzungar basin, Dzungaria, China.

Kentrosaurus Hennig, 1915—*Steg., Stego., U. Jur.* (*Doryphorosaurus, Kentrurosaurus.*) From the Tendaguru Formation of Tanzania, this genus resembles *Stegosaurus*, except that the plates are smaller, fewer in number and surmount only the neck and the anterior part of the back, while the rest of the back and tail are protected by sharp spines. Some of these spines are more than .6 meters (2 feet) long. Two additional spines protrude from the hips. The tail ends with a pair of spines. *Kentrosaurus* reached an approximate length of 4.75 meters (16 feet).

Kentrurosaurus Hennig, 1917—(See *Kentrosaurus.*)

Kladeisteriodon Plieninger, 1846—A misspelling of *Cladeiodon.*

Kladyodon Plieninger, 1846—A misspelling of *Cladeiodon.*

Kleitotrisauropus Ellenberger, ?1972—*L. Jur.* These fossil footprints were made by a large theropod. They are known from various localities in the uppermost Stormberg Series of Lesotho.

Kritosaurus Brown, 1910—*Orn., Hadro., Hadrosaur., U. Cret.* (*Gryposaurus*; in part, *Stephanosaurus*; probably *Hadrosaurus.*) The genus is known from the Oldman sediments of Alberta, the Kirkland beds of New Mexico and perhaps the Judith River Formation of Montana and other formations. This flat-headed hadrosaur has a primitive crestlike growth, an upward expansion of the nasal bone, resembling a large bump set directly in front of the orbits. Some paleontologists believe that this growth was used as a horn in battling rivals for mates. *Kritosaurus* is a large duck-billed dinosaur about the size of *Anatosaurus.* Recent studies made by Baird and Horner indicate that *Kritosaurus* could be a junior synonym of *Hadrosaurus*, though at present no formal comparison between the two genera has been published.

Kuangyuanpus Young, 1943—*?M. Jur.* From Kuangyuan, Sichuan, China, these footprints were apparently made by a quadrupedal dinosaur. Young says that the tracks are theropod, but other paleontologists believe them to have been made by a small sauropod. The specimen is too poor for an exact identification.

Skull of *Kritosaurus notabilis*. (After Lambe.)

Left maxilla of *Labocania
anomala*. Photograph courtesy
of R. E. Molnar.

Model of the head of *Kritosaurus*
sculpted by Charles Whitney Gilmore.
Courtesy of the Smithsonian
Institution.

L

Labocania   Molnar, 1974—*Ther., ?Tyrann., U. Cret.* This theropod is
known only from a maxilla, quadrate and other remains found in Baja
California, Mexico. The skull, with the exception of the maxilla, was
apparently more massive than in most tyrannosaurids. The dentary resembles that of *Majungasaurus*. The postcranial elements are similar to
those of *Albertosaurus* and other typical tyrannosaurids. Based on the
relatively large ischial muscle scar and the stout metatarsal, *Labocania*
may have been more massive than the typical members of the family
Tyrannosauridae.

Labrosaurus   Marsh, 1879—(See *Allosaurus*.)

Laelaps   Cope, 1866—(See *Dryptosaurus*.)

Vertebra of *Laevisuchus
indicus*. (After Huene.)

Illustration by Rod Ruth of
Lambeosaurus, a crested
dinosaur. From *Album of
Dinosaurs* by Tom McGowen.
Copyright 1972 by Rand
McNally & Company.

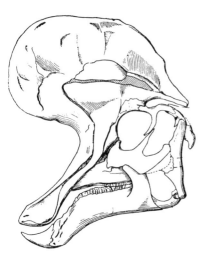

Skull of *Lambeosaurus magnicristatus*. (After Lull-Wright.)

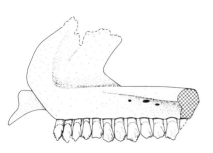

Left maxilla of *Lanasaurus scalpridens*. (After Gow.)

Sacral centrum of *Laplatasaurus madagascariensis*. (After Huene.)

Laevisuchus   Huene and Matley, 1933—*Ther., ?Family, U. Cret.* This theropod is based on three cervical vertebrae found in the Lameta Formation of Jabalpur, India.

Laiyangpus   Young, 1960—*U. Jur.* From Shandong, China, these fossil footprints were made by a small theropod.

Lambeosaurus   Parks, 1923—*Orn., Hadro., Lambeo., U. Cret.* (In part, *Procheneosaurus, Stephanosaurus, Tetragonosaurus.*) This large duck-billed dinosaur was discovered in the Oldman beds of Alberta, Canada. More recently giant specimens, probably of *Lambeosaurus*, have been found in Baja, with an estimated length of 16.5 meters (56 feet). The skull of one species has a hatchet-shaped crest, formed by the premaxillary and nasal bones, which varied in size and shape according to the individual's age, or sex. Some specimens of what was once referred to *Procheneosaurus* are now known to be juvenile forms of *Lambeosaurus*.

Lametasaurus   Matley, 1923—*?Ank., ?Nodo., U. Cret.* (Possibly *Indosaurus.*) This genus is known from the Lameta Formation of Jabalpur, India. Only the armor plating and possibly a tail club are that of an ankylosaur; the other material referred to this genus, including a sacrum, pelvis and tibia, are actually those of a theropod. The recent discovery of an armored sauropod (*Saltasaurus*) has raised the possibility that the *Lametasaurus*'s armor was sauropod, not ankylosaur.

Lanasaurus   Gow, 1975—*Orn., Heter., U. Trias.* Known only from a left maxilla from the Red beds of South Africa, *Lanasaurus* was probably slightly larger than *Heterodontosaurus*.

Laosaurus   Marsh, 1878—*Orn., ?Hypsil., U. Jur.* (Possibly *Dryosaurus, Hypsilophodon* or *Nanosaurus*.) This indeterminate form is based on nine half centra and two complete vertebral centra, found in the Morrison Formation of Como Bluff, Wyoming.

Laplatasaurus   Huene, 1928—*Saur., Sauro., Diplod., Titano., U. Cret.* Reported from Argentina, India and Madagascar, this slender sauropod is apparently similar to *Titanosaurus*.

Lapparentichnus   Haubold, 1971—*U. Jur.* from Ile d'Oleror, France, these ichnites were made by a small theropod.

Leipsanosaurus   Nopcsa, 1918—(See *Struthiosaurus*.)

Lepanosaurus   Romer, 1962—A misspelling of *Leipsanosaurus*.

Model of *Lambeosaurus*, killed by
the carnivorous *Albertosaurus*,
sculpted by Maidi Wiebe. Courtesy
of the Field Museum of Natural
History.

Skull of *Lambeosaurus
lambei*. Courtesy of the
Field Museum of Natural
History.

Skull of *Leptoceratops gracilis*.
Courtesy of the National Museums of
Canada.

Skeleton of *Lambeosaurus
lambei*. Courtesy of the Field
Museum of Natural History.

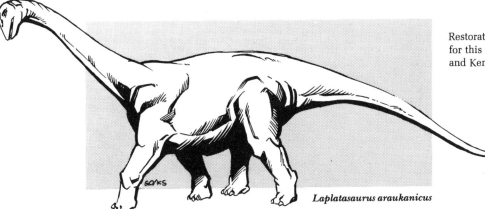

Restoration of *Laplatasaurus* prepared
for this book by George Olshevsky
and Ken Steacy.

Laplatasaurus araukanicus

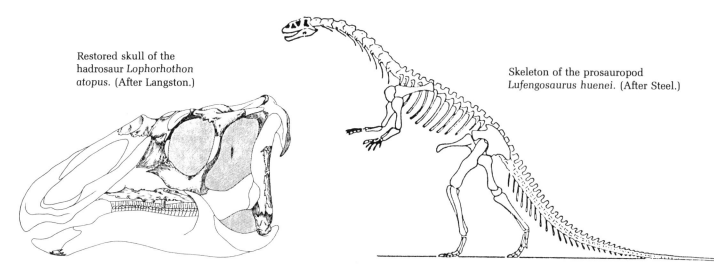

Restored skull of the hadrosaur *Lophorhothon atopus*. (After Langston.)

Skeleton of the prosauropod *Lufengosaurus huenei*. (After Steel.)

Leptoceratops   Brown, 1914—*Cer., Proto., U. Cret.* This genus represents an evolutionary step between *Psittacosaurus* and *Protoceratops*. The bones are long and slender and the toes clawed. The animal was probably capable of either quadrupedal or bipedal ambulation. The flat crest at the back of the skull shows a definite trend toward ceratopsian development. The fontanelles in the crest are smaller than those of *Protoceratops*. The beak at the front of the deep skull is similar to that in *Psittacosaurus*. While coexisting with the larger, more advanced ceratopsians, *Leptoceratops* was small, reaching a length of about 2.1 meters (7 feet) and weighing approximately 54 kilograms (120 pounds). The dinosaur is known from the lower Pascapoo sediments of Alberta, Canada, and from Wyoming, and is also reported in Gwangdong and Mongolia, though the Asian reports are vague and questionable. *Leptoceratops* teeth are among the latest known dinosaur fossils.

Leptonyx   E. Hitchcock, 1865—(See *Stenonyx*.)

Leptospondylus   Owen, 1853—(See *Massospondylus*.)

Lesothosaurus   Galton, 1978—*Orn., Fabro., U. Trias.* Known from the Red Beds of Lesotho, this genus, based on a specimen originally referred to as *Fabrosaurus australis*, probably grew to a length of .88 meters (3 feet), had light bones and leaf-shaped teeth that were continuous with the outer jaw margin, and was cheekless and a biped.

Lexousaurus   Dong, Li, Zhou and Chang, 1978—A misspelling of *Lexovisaurus*.

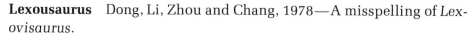

Restoration of *Lufengosaurus* by the author.

Lexovisaurus Hoffstetter, 1957—*Steg., Stego., U. Jur.* From England and northern France, this genus is one of the most primitive stegosaurs, closely related to *Kentrosaurus* but with more varied armor. The genus has plates and spines, with two large spines at the hips. *Lexovisaurus* may be the direct ancestor of all later stegosaurs.

Likhoelesaurus Ellenberger, 1970—*Ther., ?Family, U. Trias.* These reportedly theropod-type teeth are 70 mm. (2.7 inches) long and similar to those of *Basutodon*. Bones might also be among the material. *Likhoelesaurus* is known from Li Khoele in Lesotho. The dinosaur has not yet been formally described.

Limnosaurus Nopcsa, 1900—(See *Telmatosaurus*.)

Loncosaurus Ameghino, 1899—*Ther., ?Family, U. Cret.* (Possibly *Genyodectes*.) This genus is known from teeth and a femur from Argentina. Molnar believes that the femur, incorrectly associated with the teeth, may possibly be that of an hypsilophodont or turtle, while the teeth may actually be crocodilian.

Skull of *Lukousaurus yini* showing the lacrimal "horns." (After Young.)

Lophorhothon Langston, 1960—*Orn., Hadro., Hadrosaur., U. Cret.* From Dallas County, Alabama, this duck-billed dinosaur is known from an incomplete skeleton that is probably a juvenile. The skull has a bump above the snout in front of the orbits. The skeleton of an adult is estimated to measure approximately 14.5 meters (49 feet) long.

Loricosaurus Huene, 1929—*?Saur., ?Sauro., ?Diplod., ?Titano., U. Cret.* (Probably *Titanosaurus*.) This indeterminate genus, known only from armor and bone fragments, was discovered in Argentina. The armor plates strongly resemble those of the sauropod *Saltasaurus*, and it is now thought that they are the armor plates of *Titanosaurus*.

Lufengosaurus Young, 1941—*Saur., Prosaur., Plate., U. Trias.* (Probably *Yünnanosaurus*; possibly *Gyposaurus, Plateosaurus*.) Similar to or congeneric with *Plateosaurus*, this prosauropod is based on a number of skeletons found in Yünnan Province, China.

Lukousaurus Young, 1948—*Ther., ?Podok., U. Trias.* Known from jaws and the anterior part of the skull, this small theropod was discovered in Yünnan Province, China. The skull has five premaxillary teeth and lachrymal "horns" as in *Allosaurus*.

Lusitanosaurus Lapparent and Zbyszewski, 1957—*Ornithischia, ?Scelid., L. Jur.* Based on a left maxilla and teeth from Portugal, this primitive ornithischian may be related to *Scelidosaurus*.

Restoration of *Lukousaurus* by the author.

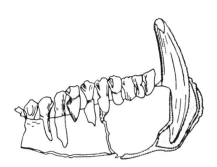

Imperfect mandible of
Lycorhinus angustidens.
(After Haughton.)

Lycorhinus Haughton, 1924—*Orn., Heter., U. Trias.* (Possibly *Abrictosaurus.*) From the Red beds of Cape Province, South Africa, this genus is based on a partial lower jaw with seven teeth; it was originally described as a mammal-like reptile. Apparently this is an early ornithischian related to *Heterodontosaurus.* Other material referred to *Lycorhinus* is probably some other genus.

M

Left maxilla of
Lusitanosaurus liasicus.

Macrodontophion Zborzewski, 1834—*Ther., ?Family, Jur.* This genus is known only from a large fossil tooth discovered in Volhynia-Podolia, Russia. The tooth is slightly recurved and almost as thick at the tip as at the base.

Macroolithus Zhao, 1975—*Cret.* The term has been given to dinosaur eggs discovered in Gwangdong, China.

Macrophalangia Sternberg, 1932—*Ther., ?Dromaes., U. Cret.* This theropod is known only from a right foot with the first digit, discovered in the Oldman Formation of Alberta, Canada.

Macropodosaurus Zacharov, 1964—*U. Cret.* These ichnites from the early Upper Cretaceous of Tadzhikistan, U.S.S.R. were possibly made by a bipedal dinosaur. The tracks are tetradactyl with claws, apparently webbing between the toes, with one toe considerably smaller than the others. The validity of this genus is uncertain.

Macrourosaurus Sauvage, 1879—A misspelling of *Macrurosaurus.*

Macrurosaurus Seeley, 1869—*Saur., Sauro., Diplod., Titano., U. Cret.* From Cambridge, England, this sauropod is known only from forty caudal vertebrae and a foot. *Macrurosaurus* may also appear in France and Argentina, though these references are uncertain.

Mafatrisauropus Ellenberger, 1970—*U. Trias.* The term has been given to dinosaur tracks, possibly those of a small theropod, from the Lower Stormberg Series of Subeng and Maphutseng, in Lesotho, and also from the Keuper of d'Anduze, France.

Maggiarosaurus Huene, 1956—A misspelling of *Magyarosaurus.*

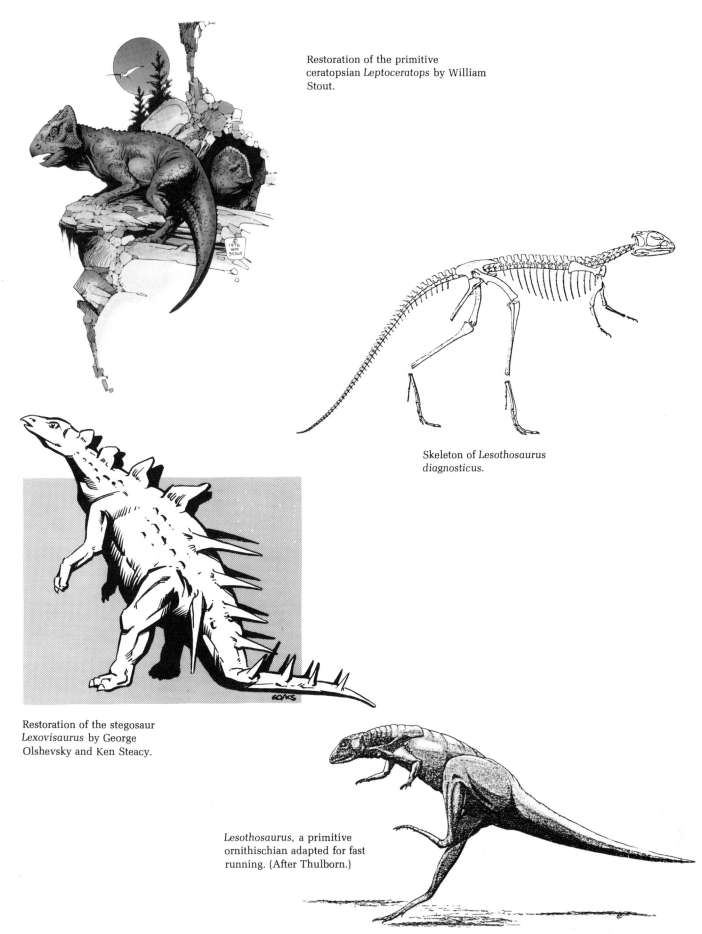

Restoration of the primitive
ceratopsian *Leptoceratops* by William
Stout.

Skeleton of *Lesothosaurus
diagnosticus.*

Restoration of the stegosaur
Lexovisaurus by George
Olshevsky and Ken Steacy.

Lesothosaurus, a primitive
ornithischian adapted for fast
running. (After Thulborn.)

Right foot with first digit
of *Macrophalangia
canadensis.* (After Parks.)

Trackway of
Macropodosaurus gravis.
(After Zacharov.)

Magnosaurus Huene, 1932—*Ther., Megal., L. Jur.* (Possibly *Megalosaurus.*) Known from fragments including vertebrae, pubes, a mandible, two tibiae approximately 48 centimeters long and jaws with teeth, this genus was discovered in Dorsetshire, England.

Magyarosaurus Huene, 1932—*Saur., Sauro., Diplod., Titano., U. Cret.* (*Maggiarosaurus;* possibly *Hypselosaurus, Titanosaurus.*) This genus is based on caudal vertebrae, a right humerus, right ulna, left fibula and dorsal centrum from Transylvania and is also found in Hungary. The entire animal was probably less than 5.25 meters (18 feet) long.

Majungasaurus Lavocat, 1955—*Ther., ?Family, U. Cret.* Based on incomplete right dentary teeth plus vertebrae, this theropod was discovered in the Berivotro Formation of Madagascar. Later, an almost complete right dentary·was described and referred to *Majungasaurus.*

Malutitrisauropus Ellenberger, ?1972—*U. Trias.* These small three-toed footprints from South Africa may have been made by a dinosaur.

Mamenchisaurus Young, 1954—*Saur., Sauro., Diplod., Mamenchi., U. Jur.* This remarkable dinosaur, discovered in Sichuan, China, is that country's largest known sauropod. A skeleton of one species of this dinosaur, with an incomplete tail, measures more than 18.5 meters (62 feet) and a complete skeleton would probably total some 23.5 meters (80 feet). The truly spectacular aspect of *Mamenchisaurus* is the incredibly long neck, with its nineteen elongated vertebrae stretching 9.8 meters (33 feet). In life this sauropod weighed approximately 36 metric tons (40 tons).

Mandschurosaurus Riabinin, 1930—*Orn., Hadro., Hadrosaur., U. Cret.* This genus is one of the largest known hadrosaurs, resembling *Anatosaurus.* Its remains were discovered in Belye Kruchi, Manchuria. Almost certainly this dinosaur is a flat-headed hadrosaur. Other material has been found in Laos, though its reference to *Mandschurosaurus* is highly questionable.

Manospondylus Cope, 1892—(See *Tyrannosaurus.*)

Marmarospondylus Owen, 1875—(See *Bothriospondylus.*)

Marshosaurus Madsen, 1976—*Ther., ?Family, U. Jur.* From the Morrison Formation of Utah, this is a small- to medium-sized dinosaur known from various bones including a pelvic girdle and the tooth-bearing elements of the skull. The skull has interdental plates separate from

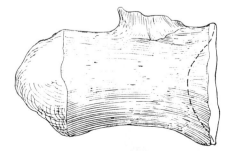

Caudal vertebra of
Macrurosaurus semnus. (After
Nopcsa.)

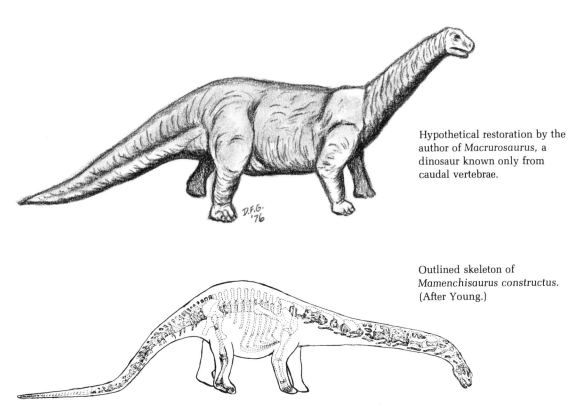

Hypothetical restoration by the author of *Macrurosaurus*, a dinosaur known only from caudal vertebrae.

Outlined skeleton of *Mamenchisaurus constructus*. (After Young.)

one another. In life the animal probably reached a maximum length of 5 meters (17 feet).

Masitisisauropezus   Ellenberger, 1974—*U. Trias. or L. Jur.* From the Upper Stormberg Series of Mokanametsong, Lesotho, these tracks were made by a very small birdlike theropod. Ellenberger believes this animal to be related to the ancestry of birds.

Masitisisauropodiscus   Ellenberger, 1974—*U. Trias. or L. Jur.* These dinosaur ichnites, similar to *Masitisisauropezus*, were found in the Upper Stormberg Series of Mokanametsong, in Lesotho.

Masitisisauropus   Ellenberger, 1974—*U. Trias. or L. Jur.* Similar to *Masitisisauropezus*, these dinosaur tracks show the imprints of feathers or feather-like structures with the manus. Ellenberger has restored the animal as a feathered theropod. The prints are from the Upper Stormberg Series of Mokanametsong, South Africa.

Restoration of *Mamenchisaurus* prepared for this book by William Stout.

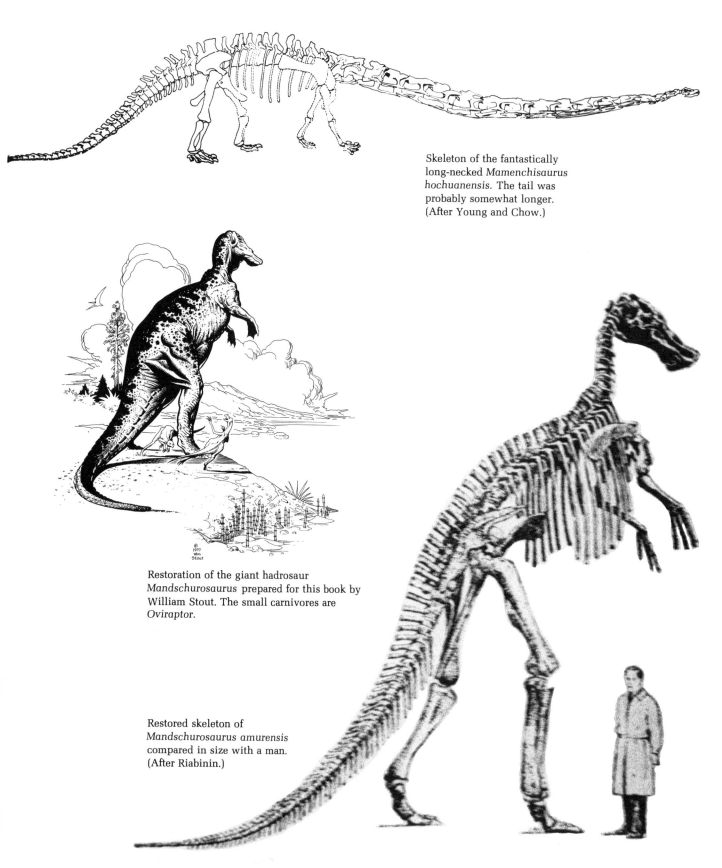

Skeleton of the fantastically
long-necked *Mamenchisaurus
hochuanensis*. The tail was
probably somewhat longer.
(After Young and Chow.)

Restoration of the giant hadrosaur
Mandschurosaurus prepared for this book by
William Stout. The small carnivores are
Oviraptor.

Restored skeleton of
Mandschurosaurus amurensis
compared in size with a man.
(After Riabinin.)

Massospondylus Owen, 1854—*Saur., Prosaur., Plate., U. Trias.* (*Aetonyx, Dromicosaurus, Gryponyx, Leptospondylus, Pachyspondylus.*) From the Stormberg beds of South Africa and Rhodesia, this prosauropod is smaller and less massive than the melanorosaurids. The humerus of one individual is over 23 centimeters (9 inches) long, the radius about 13 centimeters (5 inches), the femur over 37 centimeters (14.5 inches) and the tibia about 30 centimeters (11.5 inches). Some teeth are sharp and strong but others are spatulate, intimating an omnivorous diet. The animal has a very formidable claw which Broom suggested was used to groom elongated scales on the skin, though we have no evidence of such scales. The pelvis figured in Raath's *Vulcanodon* paper is probably *Massospondylus*. Some material from India referred to *Massospondylus* might actually be theropod.

Right ilium of
*Mandschurosaurus
laosensis.* (After Hoffet.)

Megadactylus Hitchcock, 1865—(See *Anchisaurus.*)

Megalosauropus Colbert and Merrilees, 1967—*L. Cret.* These ichnites from west Australia, Texas, Germany and the island of Brioni, Yugoslavia, were made by large theropods. Most post-Triassic tracks referred to *Eubrontes* are actually *Megalosauropus.*

Megalosaurus Parkinson, 1824—*Ther., Megal., M. Jur.* (Possibly *Aggiosaurus, Magnosaurus, Nuthetes.*) This was the second dinosaur to be described, based on a right dentary with teeth from Oxford, England. From this type specimen, Buckland assumed *Megalosaurus* to be a giant more than 11.75 meters (40 feet) long. Actually, this dinosaur attained a length of about 5.8 meters (20 feet) to 8.8 meters (30 feet). *Megalosaurus* is heavily built, with a large skull over .3 meters (over 1 foot) long, with large orbits and laterally compressed, recurved, serrated teeth. The neck is short and thick, the tail flattened at the sides. In life the creature weighed approximately .9 metric tons (1 ton). *Megalosaurus* is well represented in England. But bones attributed to this genus from Tanzania, Australia, France, Portugal, India, North America and Madagascar may be some other genera altogether. *Megalosaurus*, over a period of over 150 years, has had more species referred to it than any other genus of dinosaur. *Megalosaurus* eggs have been reported from France.

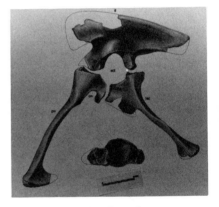

Pelvic girdle of *Marshosaurus
bicentesimus.* Courtesy of J. H.
Madsen, Jr.

Megatrisauropus Ellenberger, 1970—*U. Trias.* These ichnites were discovered in the uppermost Stormberg Series of Quthing-Mokae, Lesotho. They were made by a large theropod dinosaur.

Melanorosaurus Haughton, 1924—*Saur., Prosaur., Melan., U. Trias.* (Possibly *Euskelosaurus, Plateosauravus.*) This genus, which may have

Left dentary of *Marshosaurus
bicentesimus.* Courtesy of J. H.
Madsen, Jr.

Restoration of the prosauropod
Massospondylus prepared for this
book by William Stout. The pterosaurs
actually lived somewhat later.

Footprints of the manus, with feather-
like impressions, and pes of
Masitisisauropus palmipes. (After
Ellenberger.)

Footprints and possible
foot bones of *Masitisi-
sauropodiscus.* (After
Ellenberger.)

Hypothetical reconstruction of the skeleton of *Masitisisauropus palmipes* and the way it may have appeared in life. (After Ellenberger.)

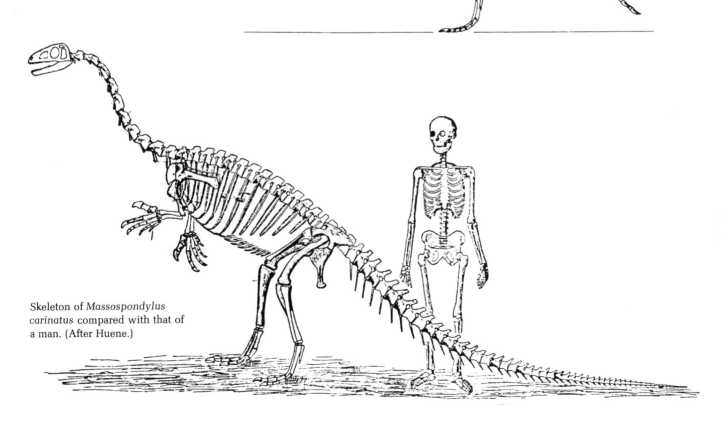

Skeleton of *Massospondylus harriesi* modified from *Thecodontosaurus browni*. (After Galton.)

Skeleton of *Massospondylus carinatus* compared with that of a man. (After Huene.)

Tooth of *Megalosaurus insignis.*

exceeded 11.75 meters (40 feet) in length, was discovered in the Stormberg beds of South Africa. Recent studies indicate that *Melanorosaurus* may actually be a sauropod rather than a prosauropod. In life the dinosaur weighed about 1.8 metric tons (2 tons). Van Heerden has proposed that *Melanorosaurus* be referred to *Euskelosaurus.*

Melanosaurus   Huene, 1954—A misspelling of *Melanorosaurus.*

Metatetrapous   Nopcsa, 1923—*L. Cret.* These fossil footprints, found in Niedersachsen, Germany, were left by a quadrupedal animal, possibly a sauropod dinosaur or an ornithischian.

Restoration of the great theropod dinosaur *Megalosaurus* by Neave Parker. Courtesy of the British Museum (Natural History).

Reconstructed skeleton of *Megalosaurus bucklandi.* (After Huene.)

Metriacanthosaurus Walker, 1964—*Ther., Megal., U. Jur.* This genus is known from a right femur, pelvis and vertebral column found in the Oxford Clay of Dorset, England. The large neural spines, as high as 26 centimeters (10 inches), and the structure of the pelvis distinguish this dinosaur from *Megalosaurus.*

Microceratops Bohlin, 1953—*Cer., Procer., U. Cret.* From Kansu and Shanxi, China, this early protoceratopsid is possibly bipedal and very lightly built. Apparently the animal was capable of rapid locomotion.

Tooth of *Megalosaurus pombali.*

Restoration of *Melanorosaurus* by William Stout.

Left tibia of *Melanorosaurus readi.* (After Haughton.)

Tooth of *Microceratops suicidens.* (After Bohlin.)

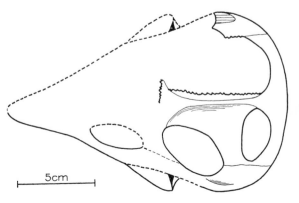

5cm

Dorsal view of the skull of *Microceratops gobiensis.* (After Maryańska and Osmólska.)

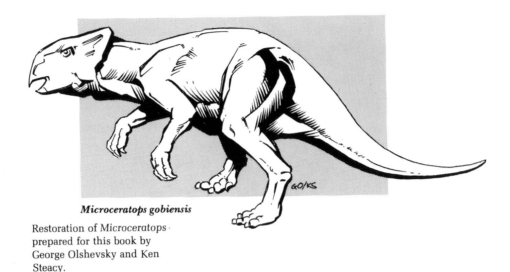

Microceratops gobiensis

Restoration of *Microceratops*
prepared for this book by
George Olshevsky and Ken
Steacy.

Left femur of *Microvenator
celer*. (After Ostrom.)

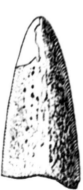

Tooth crown of *Mongolosaurus
haplodon*. (After Gilmore.)

Microcoelus Lydekker, 1894—*Saur., Sauro., Diplod., ?Titano, U.
Cret. (Microsaurops.)* Known only from a humerus and anterior dorsal
and caudal vertebrae, this moderate-sized genus was discovered in
Neuquen, Argentina.

Microsaurops Kuhn, 1964—(See *Microcoelus*.)

Microsaurus Lull, 1910—A misspelling of *Microcoelus*.

Microvenator Ostrom, 1970—*Ther., Coel., L. Cret.* The genus is
known from an incomplete skeleton without a skull, found in
Wheatland County, Montana. *Microvenator* is a small, lightly built
theropod, similar in skeletal structure to *Archaeopteryx*. The limb
bones and vertebrae are hollow and thin walled. In life the dinosaur was
probably a swift runner.

Mochlodon Seeley, 1881—(See *Rhabdodon*.)

Mongolosaurus Gilmore, 1933—*Saur., Sauro., ?Family, L. Cret.* This
genus is known from poor material, including a third cervical vertebra,
fragmentary teeth, axis, atlas and basioccipital, found in Mongolia.

Monoclonius Cope. 1876—*Cer., Cerat., U. Cret.* (Possibly *Centrosaurus*.) From the Judith River sediments of Montana, and also from the
Oldman Formation of Alberta, Canada, *Monoclonius* is known only
from incomplete skull and postcranial material. Apparently the dino-

Restoration of the lightly built flesh-eater *Microvenator* prepared for this book by Scott Shaw!

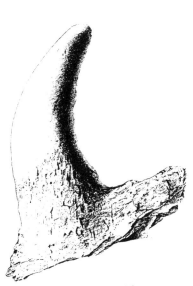

Indeterminate nasal horn core called *Monoclonius dawsoni.* (After Lambe.)

saur is a short-frilled ceratopsian, with one long horn above the snout and two small horns over the eyes. In life the creature may have reached an approximate length of 5.3 meters (18 feet). Most restorations of *Monoclonius* have actually been based on *Centrosaurus* skeletal material.

Montanoceratops   Sternberg, 1951—*Cer., Proto., U. Cret.* This small dinosaur from the St. Mary's River Formation of Glacier County, Montana, shows a considerable degree of ceratopsian development over the related *Protoceratops.* The feet in *Montanoceratops* are more developed and, more significantly, there is a modest yet well developed horn surmounting the snout.

Morinosaurus   Sauvage, 1874—*Saur., ?Family, Brachio., U. Jur.* (Possibly *Pelorosaurus.*) This genus is known only from teeth found in Boulogne-sur-Mer, France.

Morosaurus   Marsh, 1878—(See *Camarasaurus.*)

Moyenisauropezus   Ellenberger, 1972—*U. Trias.* These dinosaur ichnites were discovered in Lesotho.

Moyenisauropodiscus   Ellenberger, 1970—*U. Trias.* From Lesotho, these fossil tracks may have been made by an ornithopod dinosaur.

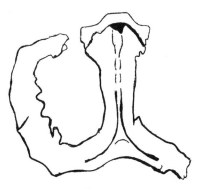

Incomplete crest of *Monoclonius crassus.* (After Steel.)

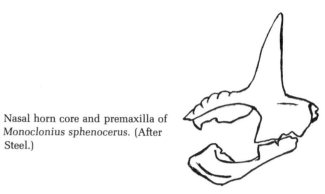

Nasal horn core and premaxilla of
Monoclonius sphenocerus. (After
Steel.)

Restoration of the horned dinosaur *Monoclonius*. From a
painting by Zdeněk Burian.

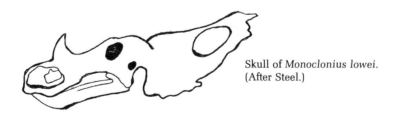

Skull of *Monoclonius lowei*.
(After Steel.)

Skeleton of *Montanoceratops
cerorhynchus.* Courtesy of R. A.
Long, S. P. Welles and the
American Museum of Natural
History.

Restoration of *Montanoceratops* prepared
for this book by William Stout. The
notion of galloping ceratopsians was
recently considered and then discarded
by Bakker.

Tooth of *Morinosaurus typus.*

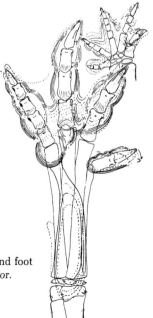

Footprints and possible hand and foot
bones of *Moyenisauropus natator.*
(After Ellenberger.)

Moyenisauropus Ellenberger, 1970—*U. Trias. or L. Jur.* These ich-nites from the Upper Stormberg Series of Moyeni, in Lesotho, may have been made by an ornithopod or small theropod.

N

Nanhsiungoolithus Zhao, 1975—The term has been given to dinosaur eggs found in Gwangdong, China.

Nanosaurus Marsh, 1877—*Orn., ?Fabro., U. Jur.* From the Morrison Formation of Canyon City, Colorado, this small dinosaur is based on incomplete material including one humerus, two tibiae, two femora, a lower jaw and pelvic bones. It is the smallest known ornithopod. One species, *N. rex*, is actually *Othnielia*.

Lower jaw of *Nanosaurus agilis*. (After Marsh.)

Nemegtosaurus Nowiński, 1971—*Saur., Sauro., Diplod., ?Dicraeo., U. Cret.* This genus is known from a skull with jaws rather like the skulls of *Diplodocus* and *Dicraeosaurus*, from the Nemegt Basin of Mongolia.

Neosauropus Antunes, 1976—*L. Cret.* The term has been given to a great trackway of sauropod tracks on the coast of de Lagosteiros, near Espichel Cape, Portugal. It is probably the longest single trackway of dinosaur ichnites ever discovered. The estimated length of the animal that made the tracks is 15.5 meters (52 feet).

Neosaurus Gilmore, 1945—(See *Parrosaurus*.)

Neosodon Moussaye, 1885—*Saur., Sauro., Camar., Brachio., U. Jur.* (Possibly *Brachiosaurus, Pelorosaurus*.) This genus is known only from teeth found in Boulogne, France.

Neotripodiscus Ellenberger, 1970—*U. Trias. or L. Jur.* These birdlike dinosaur ichnites were discovered in the Upper Stormberg beds of Maphutseng, in Lesotho.

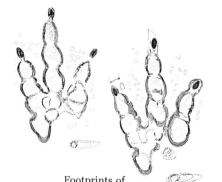

Footprints of *Neotrisauropus deambulator*. (After Ellenberger.)

Neotrisauropus Ellenberger, 1970—*U. Trias. or L. Jur.* The term has been given to fossil tracks, possibly made by a theropod, from the Upper Stormberg Series of several localities in Lesotho.

Ninghsiasaurus Young, 1965—(Error; see *Pinacosaurus*.)

Restoration of various Triassic dinosaurs, including *Podokesaurus* (foreground), *Nanosaurus* (background) and creatures of the *Anomoepus* or *Sauropus* type. By G. Heilmann for his book *The Origin of Birds,* published by D. Appleton-Century Company.

Skull of the sauropod *Nemegtosaurus mongoliensis.* Courtesy of the Institute of Paleobiology in Warsaw.

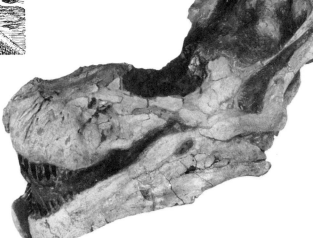

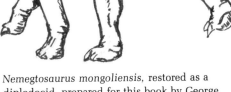

Nemegtosaurus mongoliensis, restored as a diplodocid, prepared for this book by George Olshevsky.

Femur of *Nodosaurus coleii*. (After Mehl.)

Nipponosaurus Nagao, 1936—*Orn., Hadro., Lambeo., U. Cret.* (Possibly *Jaxartosaurus*.) Known from incomplete skeletal material, including a partial skull, some vertebrae, pelvic bones, a fragmentary femur and two humeri, *Nipponosaurus* may be a juvenile of some other lambeosaurine. The genus is known from Sakhalin, Japan.

Noasaurus Bonaparte and Powell, 1980—*Ther., Noa., U. Cret.* This dinosaur, establishing the new family Noasauridae, is known from a left maxilla, right squamosal, right quadrate, cervical rib, second right metatarsal, claw phalanx of the foot and a foot phalanx, discovered in the Lecho formation in El Brete, the southern Salta province of Northwestern Argentina. *Noasaurus*, the first "coelurosaur" from South America's Upper Cretaceous, is medium-sized and advanced. The neural arches have spinous processes and on the second digit of the foot is a large claw, probably used for preying upon birds, young sauropods and other small animals.

Nodosaurus Marsh, 1889—*Ank., Nodo., L. or U. Cret.* (*Hierosaurus, Stegopelta*.) From Albany County, Wyoming, this dinosaur is imperfectly known from limb bones, vertebrae, a left radius, ulna, sacrum, manus and armor scutes. Apparently the carapace was protected by numerous bony plates and a line of small lateral spikes and the tail was slender. *Nodosaurus* reached an approximate length of 5.2 meters (17.5 feet).

Notoceratops Tapia, 1918—*Orn., Hadro., U. Cret.* Originally thought to be ceratopsian, this small dinosaur is based on an incomplete left dentary from Chubut, Argentina.

Fragmentary mandible of *Notoceratops bonavelli*. (After Huene.)

Nuthetes Owen, 1854—*?Ther., ?Family, U. Cret.* (Possibly *Megalosaurus*.) Known from some small bones found in the Purbeck beds of England, this dinosaur has usually been classified as a junior synonym of *Megalosaurus*. Molnar believes it might be a juvenile theropod, possibly *Megalosaurus*; Long considers it distinct from *Megalosaurus* and possibly not even a dinosaur. Reportedly, the type specimen has been lost.

Nyasasaurus Charig, 1967—*Saur., ?Prosaur., ?Family, M. Trias.* (*Nyasaurus*.) If this is a dinosaur and not a thecodont, *Nyasasaurus* is one of the earliest known dinosaurs. It is known from Tanzania. No description of *Nyasasaurus* has yet been published.

Nyasaurus White, 1973—A misspelling of *Nyasasaurus*.

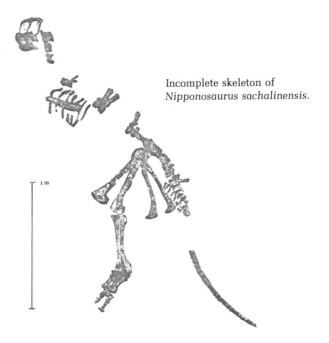

Incomplete skeleton of
Nipponosaurus sachalinensis.

Restoration of *Nodosaurus* prepared
for this book by William Stout.

Outlined skeleton of *Nodosaurus
tectilis* showing only some of the
armor. (After Lull.)

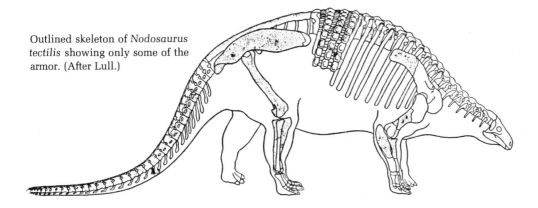

O

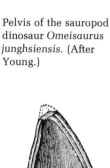

Pelvis of the sauropod dinosaur *Omeisaurus junghsiensis*. (After Young.)

Tooth of *Oplosaurus armatus*. (After Wright.)

Omeisaurus Young, 1939—*Saur., Sauro., Camar., Euhelo., U. Jur.* Related to *Euhelopus*, this sauropod is based on incomplete material, including a humerus, pubis, fibula, partial femur, two ilia and ischia and numerous vertebrae, from Sichuan, China.

Omosaurus Owen, 1875—(See *Dacentrurus.*)

Onychosaurus Nopcsa, 1902—*Ank., ?Nodo., U. Cret.* (Possibly *Struthiosaurus.*) Discovered in the Gosau Formation of Hungary, this dinosaur is known only from armor from the region of the tail. Nopcsa later considered *Onychosaurus* to be congeneric with *Struthiosaurus.*

Oölithes Young, 1954—This term has been given to dinosaur eggs found in Inner Mongolia, Gwangdon and Shandong, China, and southern Utah.

Opisthocoelicaudia Borsuk-Białynicka, 1977—*Saur., Sauro., Camar., U. Cret.* From Mongolia, this genus is a straight-backed sauropod of medium size, based on a skeleton lacking the neck and skull. The dorsal region is straight and the forelimbs relatively long. The dinosaur's most unusual feature is the structure of the tail, which was apparently carried off the ground in approximate alignment with the back.

Oplosaurus Gervais, 1852—*Saur., Sauro., Camar., Brachio., L. Cret.* (*Hoplosaurus;* probably *Brachiosaurus, Pelorosaurus.*) The genus is based on a single tooth, very similar to that of *Brachiosaurus*, found on the Isle of Wight, England.

Orinosaurus Lydekker, 1889—*Saur., Prosaur., Melan., U. Trias.* (*Orosaurus;* possibly *Euskelosaurus.*) From the Stormberg Series of South Africa, this dinosaur is known only from an indeterminate fragmentary and badly distorted left tibia.

Ornithoides Matthew, 1903—These fossil tracks were apparently left by a theropod dinosaur.

Ornitholestes Osborn, 1903—*Ther., ?Family, U. Jur.* This dinosaur, from the Morrison beds of Wyoming, retains many of the characteristics of its Triassic ancestors. The neck is moderately long, the body is lightweight and approximately 1.75 meters (6 feet) long. The strong hands,

Outlined incomplete skeleton of the sauropod *Opisthocoelicaudia skarzynskii*. (After Borsuk-Bialynicka.)

Restoration of *Opisthocoelicaudia* prepared for this book by George Olshevsky and Ken Steacy.

Opisthocoelicaudia skarzynskii

Dinosaurs that inhabited China during the Mesozoic Era. At the left are hadrosaurs of the genus *Tanius*, in the left foreground is *Sinocoelurus* and in the center is the armored *Heishanosaurus*, all from the Upper Cretaceous. In the water is the giant sauropod *Omeisaurus*; two stegosaurs of the genus *Chialingosaurus* are in the background, the theropod *Szechuanosaurus* stalks in the right background and the ornithopod *Sanpasaurus* stands in the right foreground, all probably from the Upper Jurassic. By Neave Parker. Courtesy of the *Illustrated London News*.

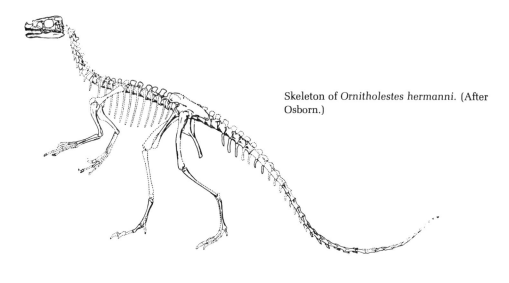

Skeleton of *Ornitholestes hermanni*. (After Osborn.)

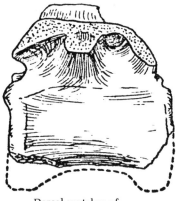

Dorsal vertebra of
*Ornithomimoides
mobilis*. (After Huene.)

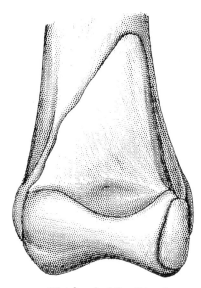

Distal end of the tibia of
Ornithomimus velox.
(After Marsh.)

each equipped with three fingers, were ideal for grasping its food, which probably consisted of small reptiles and other animals. The premaxillary teeth resemble those of the tyrannosaurs; the anterior teeth are not recurved but straight. *Ornitholestes* is often described as built for speed and running swiftly after its prey, but Colbert has suggested that the dinosaur was noncursorial.

Ornithomerus Seeley, 1881—(See *Rhabdodon*.)

Ornithomimipus Sternberg, 1926—*L. and U. Cret.* (Probably *Irenichnites*.) These dinosaur tracks are known from the Lower Cretaceous of British Columbia and the Upper Cretaceous of Alberta, Canada.

Ornithomimoides Huene and Matley, 1933—*Ther., ?Family. U. Cret.* This large theropod is known only from five dorsal vertebrae found in the Lameta Formation of Jabalpur, India.

Ornithomimus Marsh, 1890—*Ther., Ornith., U. Cret.* For a long time considered to be congeneric with *Struthiomimus*, this dinosaur, according to Russell, is a valid genus. Known from the Denver Formation of Colorado and the Oldman and Horseshoe Canyon formations of Alberta, Canada, this graceful-appearing dinosaur has long forelimbs, a long neck and small head terminating in a beak. The bones are hollow and the legs long, characteristics which made the animal a fast runner. *Ornithomimus* was more lightly built than *Struthiomimus* and was possibly an omnivore.

Illustration by Rod Ruth of *Ornithomimus*, from *Album of Dinosaurs* by Tom McGowen. Copyright 1972 by Rand McNally & Company.

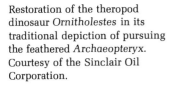

Restoration of the theropod dinosaur *Ornitholestes* in its traditional depiction of pursuing the feathered *Archaeopteryx*. Courtesy of the Sinclair Oil Corporation.

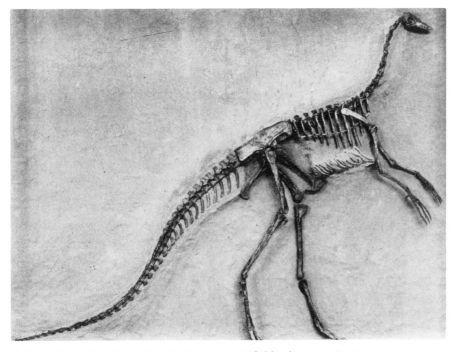

Skeleton of *Ornithomimus edmontonicus*, an ostrich-like dinosaur. Courtesy of the Royal Ontario Museum.

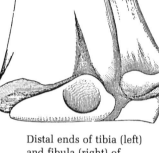

Distal ends of tibia (left) and fibula (right) of *Ornithotarsus immanis.* (After Cope.)

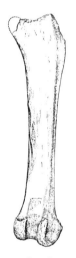

Femur of *Orthomerus dolloi.* (After Seeley.)

Ornithopsis Seeley, 1870—*Saur., Sauro., Camar., Brachio., U. Jur. and L. Cret.* (Probably *Brachiosaurus, Pelorosaurus;* possibly *Dinodocus.*) From the Isle of Wight, England, this sauropod is known from a dorsal vertebra approximately 23 centimeters (9 inches) long and a cervical vertebra about 36 centimeters (14 inches) long. The vertebrae, consisting of bony plates, are lightly constructed.

Ornithopus E. Hitchcock, 1848—*U. Trias.* (Probably *Steropoides.*) These ichnites from New England may have been made by a theropod dinosaur.

Ornithosaurus Riabinin, 1930—(Error; see *Ornithotarsus.*)

Ornithotarsus Cope, 1869—*Orn. Hadro., Hadrosaur., U. Cret.* From the Monmouth Formation of Monmouth County, New Jersey, this dinosaur is apparently quite large for a hadrosaur. According to Lull and Wright, it is probably similar to *Anatosaurus,* though the material is too poor to really tell. *Ornithotarsus* is known from a fragmentary tibia and fibula and other poor material. Recent studies indicate that this is a large individual of *Hadrosaurus.*

Orosaurus Lydekker, 1889—(See *Orinosaurus.*)

Orthogoniosaurus Das-Gupta, 1931—*Ther., ?Family, U. Cret.* This genus is based on a single indeterminate tooth from the Lameta Formation of Jabalpur, India.

Orthomerus Seeley, 1883—*Orn., Hadro., Hadrosaur., U. Cret.* Usually, *Orthomerus* is classified as a junior synonym of *Telmatosaurus;* but there is no real proof that the right femur ascribed to *Orthomerus,* found in Maastricht, Holland, is *Telmatosaurus.* Without good cause, hind limb material from the Crimea, U.S.S.R., has also been called *Orthomerus.*

Othnielia Galton, 1977—*Orn., Hypsil., U. Jur.* Formerly called *Nanosaurus rex, Laosaurus consors* and *L. gracilis,* this ornithopod is known from the Morrison Formation of Wyoming and Utah. The teeth of *Othnielia* are small and irregular. The animal reached a length of almost 3 meters (10 feet) and weighed approximately 80 kilograms (175 pounds).

Otozoum E. Hitchcock, 1847—*L. Jur.* Once believed to be a prosauropod, these ichnites are now usually considered to be thecodonts. Haubold (1971), however, still considers them to be the former. The tracks were discovered in the Connecticut Valley.

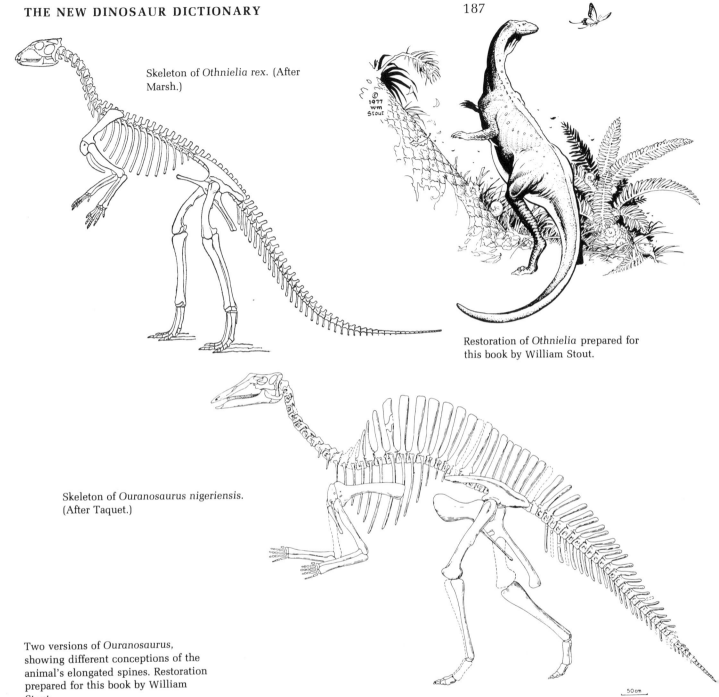

Skeleton of *Othnielia rex*. (After Marsh.)

Restoration of *Othnielia* prepared for this book by William Stout.

Skeleton of *Ouranosaurus nigeriensis*. (After Taquet.)

Two versions of *Ouranosaurus*, showing different conceptions of the animal's elongated spines. Restoration prepared for this book by William Stout.

50 cm

Ouranosaurus — Two Views

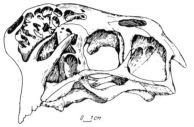

Skull of *Oviraptor philoceratops* showing the nasal
crest.

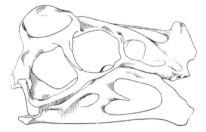

Skull of *Oviraptor
philoceratops*. (After Osborn.)

Skull of *Oviraptor* sp. (After
Osmólska.)

Ouranosaurus   Taquet, 1976—*Orn., Iguan., L. Cret.* Based on a skeleton from Niger, this ornithopod has an incipient crest similar to that of
Prosaurolophus and very long spines on the vertebrae. Some paleontologists propose that these spines formed the type of hump found in the
present-day bison. Other paleontologists think the spines created a sail-
back effect and that this fin may have served as a temperature regulator
to prevent the animal's overheating in a hot climate.

Oviraptor   Osborn, 1924—*Ther., Ovi., U. Cret. (Fenestrosaurus.)* Usually classified as an ornithomimid, recent studies indicate that *Oviraptor* belongs in its own family or in the North American Caenagnathidae.
The dinosaur is small, only about 2.8 meters (10 feet) long. The forelimbs are long and the hands quite large, with fingers not as curved as
those in most theropods. The head has a beak instead of teeth, intimating a possible omnivorous diet, and the snout is surmounted by a horn-
like protuberance. The animal was probably a rapacious killer of prey.
Its skeleton was discovered in Bayan Dzak, in Outer Mongolia, within
proximity of a nest of dinosaur eggs, the implication being that the
theropod had been trying to steal the eggs for consumption. Barsbold,
however, suggests that the animal's distinctive jaws were adapted for
crushing much harder food than eggs, such as mollusk shells.

Ovoraptor   Osborn, 1924—(See *Velociraptor*.)

P

Skull of *Pachycephalosaurus
grangeri*. Courtesy of the
American Museum of Natural
History.

Pachycephalosaurus   Brown and Schlaikjer, 1943—*Pach., Pachy., U.
Cret. (Tylosteus.)* This genus is the classic "bonehead" dinosaur, so
named because its brain was encased in a dome of solid bone some 23
centimeters (9 inches) thick. The snout and posterior region of the skull
is covered with a series of bumps and nodes. It has been postulated that
these nodes might have been used in digging up vegetation and that the
dome heads were used by the males in butting against each other during
the mating season as a test of strength. *Pachycephalosaurus* is the largest known member of its family, attaining an approximate length of 4.5
to 6 meters (15 to 20 feet). This dinosaur was discovered in the Hell
Creek Formation of Carter County, Montana, and is also known from
Wyoming and South Dakota.

Pachyrhinosaurus Sternberg, 1950—*Cer., Cerat., U. Cret.* From the St. Mary River and Horseshoe Canyon sediments of Alberta, Canada, this unusual appearing ceratopsian is closely related to *Styracosaurus.* Instead of horns, there is a rough boss of bone surmounting the upper part of the skull, covering the snout and extending behind the orbits. The frill may have had spikes, though smaller than those in *Styracosaurus.* In overall dimensions, *Pachyrhinosaurus* is much larger than *Styracosaurus.*

Domelike cranium of *Pachycephalosaurus wyomingensis.* (After Gilmore.)

Pachysauriscus Kuhn, 1959—*Saur., Prosaur., Plate., U. Trias.* (*Pachysaurops, Pachysaurus;* probably *Plateosaurus;* possibly *Gresslyosaurus.*) From Löwenstein, Germany, this dinosaur is based on incomplete material including vertebrae, cervicals, limb bones and various fragments. The dorsal column is longer than that in *Plateosaurus.*

Pachysaurops Huene, 1961—(See *Pachysauriscus.*)

Pachysaurus Huene, 1908—(See *Pachysauriscus.*)

Pachyspondylus Owen, 1853—(See *Massospondylus.*)

Domelike cranium of *Pachycephalosaurus reinheimeri.* (After Brown and Schlaikjer.)

Palaenornis Emmons, 1857—*?Theropod, Trias.* Originally described as an early avian, this small genus might actually be a theropod due to its Triassic age.

Palaeosauriscus Kuhn, 1959—*Saur., Prosaur., Anchi., U. Trias.* (*Palaeosaurus.*) This dinosaur is known only from a single tooth found in Bristol, England. The skeleton called *Palaeosaurus diagnosticus* in the paleontological literature is actually *Efraasia.*

Palaeosaurus Riley and Stutchbury, 1836—(See *Palaeosauriscus.*)

Palaeoscincus Leidy, 1856—*Ank., ?Nodo., U. Cret.* Although known only from a fossil tooth from the Judith River Formation of Fort Benton, Montana, this genus has traditionally been depicted with hard plates and sharp lateral spikes, based on specimens of *Panoplosaurus.*

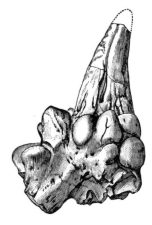

Spike of *Pachycephalosaurus* sp. (After Marsh.)

Panoplosaurus Lambe, 1919—*Ank., Nodo., U. Cret.* (*Edmontonia.*) From the Oldman and Horseshoe Canyon formations of Alberta, Canada, and also from Montana, Texas and possibly South Dakota, *Panoplosaurus* is a typical nodosaur. The carapace is covered with solid, bony plates, with lateral spikes running the length of the body and with especially large spikes in the shoulder region. The skull is pear-shaped when viewed from the top and long, measuring approximately 41 centimeters (16 inches) in length. The squat body is about 4.4 meters (15 feet) long.

Skull reconstruction of
Pachyrhinosaurus canadensis.
(After Langston.)

Restoration of the "bone-
headed" dinosaur
Pachycephalosaurus prepared
for this book by Jim Danforth.

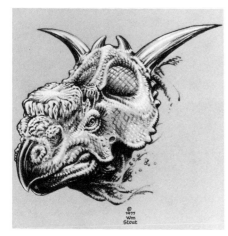

Restoration of *Pachyrhinosaurus* prepared for this book by William Stout.

Tooth of *Palaeoscincus
costatus.* (After Leidy.)

Tooth of *Palaeosauriscus
platyodon.*

Paracanthodon   Huene, 1956—A misspelling of *Paranthodon.*

Parachirotherium   Kuhn, 1958—*U. Trias. (Dinosaurichnium.)* These
German theropod ichnites have been placed in the footprint family
Parachirotheriidae.

Paragrallator   Ellenberger, 1970—*L. Jur.* These fossil footprints from
the uppermost Stormberg Series of Matsieng, in Lesotho, may have been
made by a small theropod.

Paranthodon   Nopcsa, 1929—*Steg., L. Cret. (Paracanthodon.)* This dinosaur is known only from a fragmentary jaw with teeth, found in the
Uitenhage beds of South Africa. Galton and Coombs have recently determined that it is a stegosaur.

Parasaurolophus   Parks, 1923—*Orn., Hadro., Lambeo., U. Cret.* From
the Oldman Formation of Alberta, Canada, the Fruitland and Ojo Alamo
formations of New Mexico, and from Utah, this giant dinosaur has a
crest resembling a great tube extending from the back of the skull. Some
artists have depicted the animal with a membrane attached from the
crest to the creature's back. In life this duck-billed dinosaur reached an
approximate length of 8.8 meters (30 feet) and weighed some 4.4 metric
tons (5 tons).

Traditional though hypothetical restoration of *Palaeoscincus* prepared for this book by Cathy Hill.

Parasauropodopus Ellenberger, 1970—*U. Trias.* These fossil tracks from the Keuper of d'Anduze, France, may have been left by an ornithischian dinosaur.

Paratetrasauropus Ellenberger, 1970—*U. Trias.* From the Lower Stormberg Series of Seaka, in Lesotho, these ichnites were made by a moderately large quadrupedal animal, presumably an ornithischian.

Paratrisauropus Ellenberger, 1970—*U. Trias.* These ornithopod tracks were discovered in the Lower Stormberg Series of Seaka and Maseru, in Lesotho.

Parksosaurus Sternberg, 1937—*Orn., Hypsil., U. Cret.* This genus is known from an incomplete skeleton from the Horseshoe Canyon Formation of Alberta, Canada. The incomplete skull shows that the eyes were large. The tibia is long, the femur short and the toes long and ending with sharp claws. The animal attained a length of about 2.4 meters (8 feet) and weighed approximately 68 kilograms (150 pounds).

Paronychodon Cope, 1876—*?Ther., ?Family, U. Cret. (Zapsalis.)* This dinosaur is known from Montana and Wyoming. It is based on teeth with a unique pattern of radiating ridges.

Parrosaurus Gilmore, 1945—*Saur., ?Sauro., ?Family, U. Cret. (Neosaurus.)* This dinosaur, discovered in the Ripley Formation of Bol-

Skull of *Panoplosaurus mirus.* Courtesy of R. A. Long, S. P. Welles and the National Museums of Canada.

Skull of *Panoplosaurus longiceps.* Courtesy of R. A. Long, S. P. Welles and the National Museums of Canada.

Model of the armored dinosaur *Panoplosaurus.* Courtesy of the Smithsonian Institution.

Skeleton (top view) of *Panoplosaurus rugosidens* showing the armored carapace. Courtesy of the American Museum of Natural History.

Fragmentary mandible of *Paranthodon oweni.* (After Owen.)

Skeleton of *Parasaurolophus walkeri*. Courtesy of
the Royal Ontario Museum.

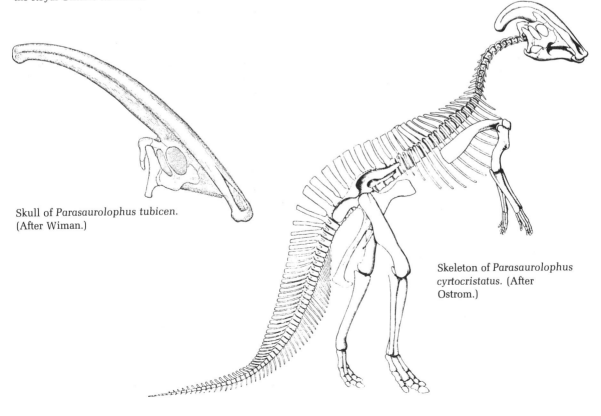

Skull of *Parasaurolophus tubicen*.
(After Wiman.)

Skeleton of *Parasaurolophus
cyrtocristatus*. (After
Ostrom.)

Dinosaurs of Upper Cretaceous Canada. To the far left is the horned dinosaur *Chasmosaurus*, while to its right is another ceratopsian *Pachyrhinosaurus* as it was formerly thought to have looked. In the center are two groups of hadrosaurs, *Corythosaurus* with the helmet-shaped crest and *Parasaurolophus* with the spikelike crest. To their right is the ostrich-like dinosaur *Struthiomimus* and the giant theropod *Albertosaurus*. The armored dinosaur *Ankylosaurus* dominates the right foreground. At the right, behind the tree, is another ankylosaurid *Euoplocephalus* (here depicted the way its junior synonym *Dyoplosaurus* was earlier thought to have looked) while on the hill at the upper right is another *Euoplocephalus* (depicted in an earlier conception of the junior synonym *Scolosaurus*). By Neave Parker. Courtesy of the *Illustrated London News*.

Tooth of *Paronychodon lacustris*.

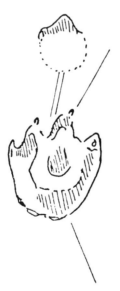

Footprints of *Paratetrasauropus seakensis*. (After Ellenberger.)

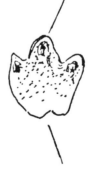

Footprint of *Paratrisauropus lifofanensis*. (After Ellenberger.)

Restoration of *Parksosaurus* by William Stout. The animal has just stepped from a rock and into a tree.

Skull of *Parksosaurus warreni*. Courtesy of R. A. Long, S. P. Welles and the Royal Ontario Museum.

linger County, Missouri, is known from a series of caudal vertebrae. Molnar believes *Parrosaurus* to be clearly not sauropod and possibly ornithischian, though most other paleontologists disagree.

Peishansaurus Bohlin, 1953—*?Ank., ?Family, U. Cret.* From Ehr-Chia-Wu-Tung, China, this armored dinosaur is known only from a partial left dentary of a juvenile individual.

Pelorosaurus Mantell, 1850—*Saur., Sauro., Camar., Brachio., U. Jur. and L. Cret. (Caulodon, Chondrosteosaurus, Eucamerotus;* probably *Brachiosaurus, Oplosaurus;* possibly *Dinodocus, Gigantosaurus* Seeley, *Ischyrosaurus, Morinosaurus, Ornithopsis.)* This genus is known from England, Portugal and France and is based on an incomplete right humerus. The vertebrae of the back and neck are enlarged and light.

Peltosaurus Glut, 1972—(Error; see *Sauropelta.*)

Caudal vertebrae of *Parrosaurus missouriensis.* (After Gilmore.)

Right humerus of
Pelorosaurus conybearii.
(After Owen.)

Footprint of
Pentasauropus erectus.
(After Ellenberger.)

Pentaceratops Osborn, 1923—*Cer., Cerat., U. Cret.* From the Fruitland Formation of San Juan County, New Mexico, this giant dinosaur is a descendant of *Chasmosaurus. Pentaceratops* was named for its five "horns." Actually, the genus is three-horned, one large horn over each orbit and a smaller horn above the snout. The two additional horns are really growths of bone extending from the cheek regions. The shield of *Pentaceratops* is exceptionally large. Sparse Mongolian material ascribed to this genus is probably not *Pentaceratops.*

Pentasauropus Ellenberger, 1970—*U. Trias.* From the Lower Stormberg Series of several locations in Lesotho, these tracks represent a new prosauropod family. The ichnites were left by a large, five-toed animal that may have walked on its toes.

Phaedrolosaurus Dong, 1973— *Ther., ?Dromae., L. Cret.* This dinosaur, represented largely by hind limb material from Wuerho, China, is believed to be ancestral or closely related to *Deinonychus.*

Phyllodon Thulborn, 1973—*Orn., Hypsil., U. Jur.* From Guimaroto Lignite, Portugal, this dinosaur is based on teeth from upper and lower jaws. The genus has been reconstructed as having six premaxillary teeth which oppose a predentary bone, thirteen maxillary teeth and fourteen dentary teeth.

Picrodon Seeley, 1898—*?Saur., ?Family, U. Trias.* (Possibly *Avalonianus, Gresslyosaurus.*) This genus from Somerset, England, is based on a tooth with referred vertebrae.

Pinacosaurus Gilmore, 1933—*Ank., Anky., U. Cret.* (*Syrmosaurus, Viminicaudus.*) From Mongolia and northern China, this primitive ankylosaurid has a body armed with symmetrical rows of pointed plates. These plates are separate from each other and protected the neck, back, limbs, tail and skull. The tail terminates in a bony club. The skull is slender, longer than it is wide, with a rounded beak lacking armor and with small teeth. A juvenile skull shows that the narial opening was accompanied by two accessory openings of unknown function. *Pinacosaurus* reached an approximate length of 4.4 meters (15 feet). Recent work by Maryańska shows that *Syrmosaurus* is a junior synonym of *Pinacosaurus.*

Pisanosaurus Casamiquela, 1967—*Orn., Heter., U. Cret.* This primitive ornithischian is known from fragmentary material including vertebrae, part of a left jaw, a right maxilla, a right tibia, a fibula and a pes.

Teeth of *Phyllodon
henkeli.* (After Thulborn.)

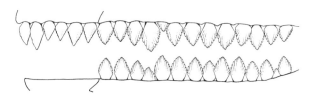

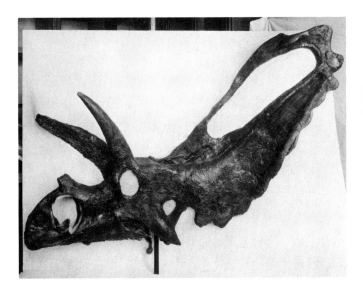

Skull of the horned dinosaur
Pentaceratops sternbergii. Courtesy of
the American Museum of Natural
History.

Restoration of the ceratopsian dinosaur *Pentaceratops* by
William Stout.

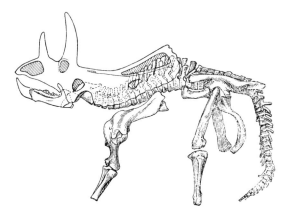

Incomplete skeleton of *Pentaceratops
fenestratus.* (After Lull.)

Tail of *Pinacosaurus
grangeri.* (After Maleev.)

The fragmentary pelvis is of primitive structure. *Pisanosaurus* is the earliest known ornithischian. Its remains were discovered in San Juan, Argentina.

Plastisauropus   Ellenberger, 1974—*U. Trias and L. Jur.* These ichnites may have been made by a moderately large theropod. They are from the Upper Stormberg Series of Moyeni and Mokanametsong.

Plateosauravus   Huene, 1932—*Saur., Prosaur, Melan., U. Trias.* (Possibly *Euskelosaurus, Melanorosaurus.*) This genus is known only from incomplete material discovered in the Red beds of Cape Province, South Africa. Van Heerden has proposed that *Melanorosaurus* be referred to *Euskelosaurus.*

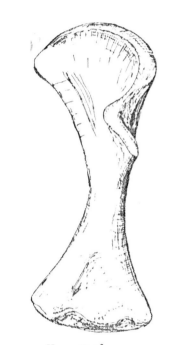

Humerus of *Plateosauravus cullingworthi.* (After Huene.)

Plateosaurus   Meyer, 1837—*Saur., Prosaur, Plate., U. Trias.* (Dimodosaurus, Platysaurus, Sellosaurus; probably *Pachysauriscus;* possibly *Gresslyosaurus.*) This prosauropod, known from Germany, France and Argentina, is one of the giants of the Triassic Period. *Plateosaurus* reached an approximate length of 6.2 meters (21 feet). The long neck and diminutive head suggest the later sauropods which descended from the prosauropods. *Plateosaurus* was a stocky creature, mostly bipedal, occasionally coming down on all fours.

Platypterna   E. Hitchcock, 1845—*U. Trias. and L. Jur. (Calopus.)* These fossil tracks from Massachusetts, Connecticut and Pennsylvania may have been made by a bipedal animal, possibly a small theropod or thecodont.

Platysauropus   Ellenberger, 1970—*U. Trias. or L. Jur.* From the Upper Stormberg Series of Phahamengo, in Lesotho, these ichnites may have been made by a saurischian.

Platysaurus   Agassiz, 1846—A misspelling of *Plateosaurus.*

Platytrisauropus   Ellenberger, 1970—*U. Trias. or L. Jur.* These saurischian ichnites are from the Upper Stormberg Series of Leribe, in Lesotho.

Plesiornis   E. Hitchcock, 1858—*L. Jur.* Though usually considered to be the tracks of a small theropod, these ichnites from New England are not distinct enough for a good classification.

Plesiothornidos   Harkness, 1850—*U. Trias.* These fossil tracks from England are presumably dinosaurian. The specimen is now lost.

Skull (top view) of a young individual of *Pinacosaurus grangeri*. Courtesy of the Institute of Paleobiology in Warsaw.

Incorrect restoration of *Pinacosaurus* based upon material once called *Syrmosaurus*. (After Maleev.)

Modern conception of *Pinacosaurus* as restored by George Olshevsky.

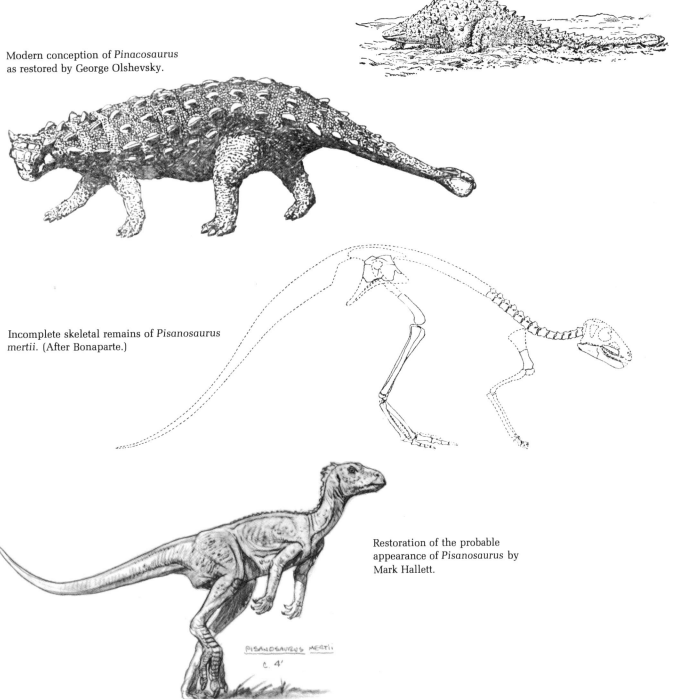

Incomplete skeletal remains of *Pisanosaurus mertii*. (After Bonaparte.)

Restoration of the probable appearance of *Pisanosaurus* by Mark Hallett.

Skeleton of *Plateosaurus engelhardti*. Courtesy of the Museum of Comparative Zoology, Harvard University.

Pleurocoelus Marsh, 1888—*Saur., Sauro., Camar., Brachio., L. Cret.* (Possibly *Astrodon, Brachiosaurus.*) Based on a vertebral centrum from a juvenile specimen, found in Prince Georges County, Maryland, *Pleurocoelus* is the smallest known American sauropod, approximately 8.8 meters (30 feet) long. The skull resembles that of *Camarasaurus*; the teeth are deep and narrow. The dinosaur has also been reported in Wyoming, Texas, Portugal, North Africa and Sussex, England.

Pleuropeltus Seeley, 1881—(See *Struthiosaurus.*)

Podokesaurus Talbot, 1911—*Ther., Podok., U. Trias.* (Possibly *Coelophysis.*) From Hampton County, Massachusetts, this small genus is only .88 meters (3 feet) long. The animal is quite primitive, lightly built, with the general form and characteristics of the pseudosuchians. *Podokesaurus* is closely related to or congeneric with *Coelophysis*. The original type specimen of *Podokesaurus*, a skeleton, was destroyed in a fire.

Poecilopleuron Fitzinger, 1843—A misspelling of *Poekilopleuron*.

Poecilopleurum Agassiz, 1846—A misspelling of *Poekilopleuron*.

Poekilopleuron Eudes-Delongchamp, 1838—*Ther., Megal., M. Jur.*

(*Poecilopleuron, Poecilopleurum, Poikilopleuron.*) Long considered to be a junior synonym of *Megalosaurus*, *Poekilopleuron* may perhaps be a valid genus. The dinosaur is based on incomplete skeletal remains from Caen, France, which were destroyed during World War II. The genus has a strong manus and a very short and stout arm with the primitive characteristic of five digits. Remains found in the U.S.S.R. have also been referred to *Poekilopleuron*.

Poikilopleuron   Owen, 1842—A misspelling of *Poekilopleuron*.

Polacanthoides   Nopcsa, 1929—*Ank., Nodo., L. Cret.* (Possibly *Hylaeosaurus*.) This genus is known from a tibia, humerus and scapula of unusual form, from the Isle of Wight, England.

Polacanthus   Hulke, 1881—*Ank., Nodo., L. Cret.* (See *Hylaeosaurus*.)

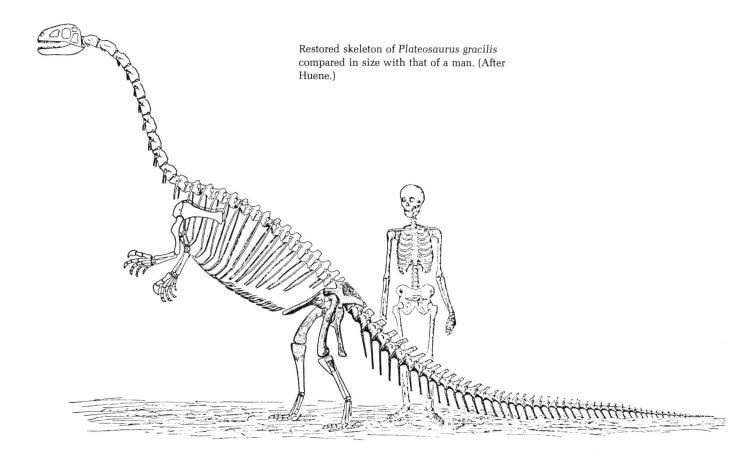

Restored skeleton of *Plateosaurus gracilis* compared in size with that of a man. (After Huene.)

A scene of the Upper Triassic dominated by
the large prosauropod *Plateosaurus,* which
lumbers on its hind legs while another of
that genus comes down on all fours in
search of food. The tiny dinosaur in the path
of *Plateosaurus* is *Podokesaurus.* In the
foreground is the mammal-like reptile
Cynognathus and to its right is the bipedal
thecodont *Saltoposuchus.* From a mural by
Rudolph F. Zallinger. Courtesy of the
Peabody Museum of Natural History, Yale
University.

Restoration of *Pleurocoelus*
prepared for this book by
Richard Hescox.

Skeleton of *Pleurocoelus* based on the
remains of *P. altus* and *P. nanus* and new
Texas material. (After Langston.)

Polemarchus E. Hitchcock, 1845—*U. Trias.* These ichnites from Massachusetts may have been made by a small theropod or thecodont.

Polyodontosaurus Gilmore, 1932—(See *Stenonychosaurus.*)

Polyonax Cope, 1874—*Cer., Cerat., U. Cret.* (Possibly *Triceratops.*) This genus is based on indeterminate remains, including fragmentary horn cores and three dorsal vertebrae, from the Laramie Formation of Colorado. It probably represents a young animal.

Prenocephale Maryańska and Osmólska, 1974—*Pach., Pachy., U. Cret.* This dinosaur is known from the Nemegt Formation of Mongolia. The cranial dome is quite high. The teeth in the back of the mouth are blunt while those in front are sharp and rather long. In life the animal attained an approximate length of .9 to 1.2 meters (3 to 4 feet).

Priconodon Marsh, 1888—*Ank., Nodo., L. Cret.* From the Arundel Formation of Prince Georges County, Maryland, this armored dinosaur is known only from teeth. At one time this genus was believed to be a stegosaur.

Priodontognathus Seeley, 1875—*?Ank., Nodo., U. Jur. or L. Cret.* (*Priodontosaurus.*) Known from a fragmentary maxilla from England, this genus was once considered to be a stegosaur, but is now known to be an ankylosaur.

Priodontosaurus Romer, 1966—A misspelling of *Priodontognathus.*

Probactrosaurus Rozhdestvensky, 1966—*Orn., Iguan., L. Cret.* From Ala Shan, China, this advanced iguanodont is very hadrosaur-like. The animal is known from material that includes a nearly complete skeleton and a good skull. The teeth are large.

Proceratops Lull, 1906—(See *Ceratops.*)

Proceratosaurus Huene, 1926—*Ther., ?Family, M. Jur.* From Gloucestershire, England, this dinosaur, long considered to be a species of *Megalosaurus*, is now a valid genus of its own. The animal is known from an incomplete low skull approximately .29 meters (1 foot) long. There are four premaxillary teeth and the indication of a small horn above the snout.

Procerosaurus Frič (Fritsch), 1905—*Orn., Iguan., U. Cret.* This genus is based on two poorly preserved and indeterminate limb bones from Bohemia.

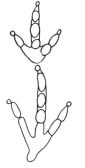

Footprints of *Plesiornis pilulatus.* (After Lull.)

Tooth of *Pleurocoelus valdensis.* (After Swinton.)

Part of a fibula of *Polyonax mortuaris*, a juvenile specimen.

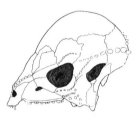

Skull of *Prenocephale prenes*. (After Maryańska and Osmólska.)

Procheneosaurus Matthew, 1920—*(Tetragonosaurus; see Corytho-saurus, Lambeosaurus.)*

Procompsognathus Fraas, 1913—*Ther., Podok., U. Trias.* (Possibly *Pterospondylus.*) This lightly built dinosaur has a relatively long neck. The hind legs are about three times as long as the forelegs. The skull measures approximately 7.8 centimeters (3 inches) in length and is filled with curved teeth. The animal is about 30 centimeters (12 inches) high at the hips. *Procompsognathus* is known from an incomplete skeleton found in Pfaffenhofen, Germany. Some of the material referred to this dinosaur is actually *Aetosaurus*, a thecodont.

Prodeinodon Osborn, 1924—*Ther., ?Tyran., L. Cret.* Based on two indeterminate teeth from Mongolia, this genus is significant in that it proves the existence of large theropods in that region's Lower Cretaceous. *Prodeinodon* may also be known from Fushi and Tebch, China. Large limb elements were found with the Tebch material but could not be collected due to the extreme cold climate at the time. But since the type specimen is indeterminate, any so-called geographical distribution of this genus is highly questionable.

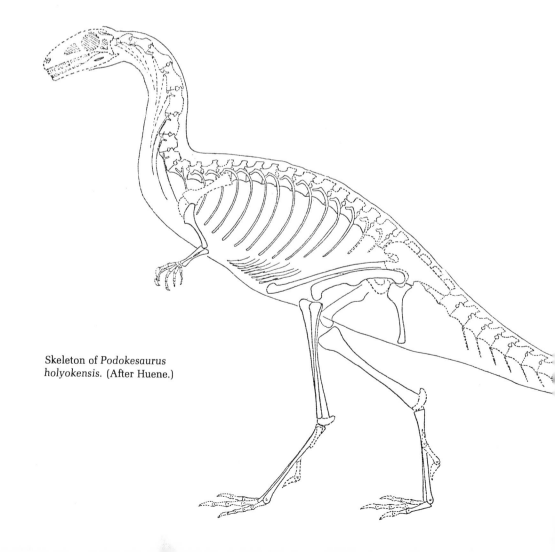

Skeleton of *Podokesaurus holyokensis*. (After Huene.)

Restoration of *Prenocephale* prepared
for this book by Richard Hescox.

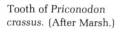

Tooth of *Priconodon
crassus.* (After Marsh.)

Restored skull of
Proceratosaurus bradleyi. (After
Huene.)

Model of the horned theropod
Proceratosaurus.

Limb bone of *Procerosaurus
exogyrarum.*

Restoration of the duck-billed *Prosaurolophus* prepared for this book by Linda L. Glut.

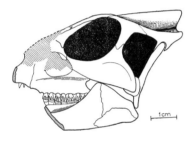

Incomplete skull of ?*Protoceratops kozlowskii.* (After Maryánska and Osmólska.)

Footprint of *Proto-trisauropodiscus minimus.* (After Ellenberger.)

Prosaurolophus Brown, 1916—*Orn., Hadro, Hadrosaur., U. Cret.* This large hadrosaur from the Oldman Formation of Alberta, Canada, has a skull similar to that of *Anatosaurus,* but with a low crest formed by an extension of the nasal bones, rising like knobs above the orbits. The crest is solid, leaving its function open to speculation. It has been suggested that *Prosaurolophus* is the female form of *Saurolophus,* though they occur in noncontemporaneous formations.

Protiguanodon Osborn, 1923—*Cer., Psittac., L. Cret.* (Probably *Psittacosaurus.*) From Mongolia, this primitive ceratopsian is most likely synonymous with *Psittacosaurus.* The large horned dinosaurs may have evolved from this genus. Gastroliths have been found within the rib cage of *Protiguanodon.*

Protoceratops Granger and Gregory, 1923—*Cer., Proto., U. Cret.* Though this ceratopsian is primitive, the true structure of its suborder is evident, revealing a definite transitional stage in the evolution of the horned dinosaurs. Though *Protoceratops* is usually hornless, old individuals did develop a nasal horn core. There is a well developed beak and shield, presaging the later horned giants of the suborder. Compared to these later horned dinosaurs, *Protoceratops* is small, reaching an approximate length of 2.35 meters (8 feet) to 2.7 meters (9 feet). The dinosaur exhibits marked sexual dimorphism in the frill and the structure of the skull roof. *Protoceratops* is known from Mongolia and Gansu. It is especially significant in that its fossil eggs were the first to be identified as those laid by a dinosaur. Now called *Elongatoolithus,* the eggs were discovered along with skeletons of *Protoceratops* in Mongolia's Gobi Desert by Roy Chapman Andrews in 1922. Brown and Schlaikjer report finding skeletons of fetal *Protoceratops,* also in Mongolia. Coombs has suggested that *Protoceratops* assumed a bipedal pose when running.

Protorosaurus Lambe, 1914—(See *Chasmosaurus.*)

Prototrisauropiscus Ellenberger, 1972—*U. Trias.* These ichnites, apparently those of a small theropod (described as "coelurosaur tracks"), are from South Africa.

Prototrisauropus Ellenberger, 1970—*U. Trias.* From the Lower Stormberg Series of several localities in Lesotho, and from France, these fossil footprints may have been made by a theropod.

Pseudotetrasauropus Ellenberger, 1970—*U. Trias.* These four-toed tracks were made by a large melanorosaur. They are from the Lower Stormberg Series of several localities in Lesotho, and from d'Anduze, France.

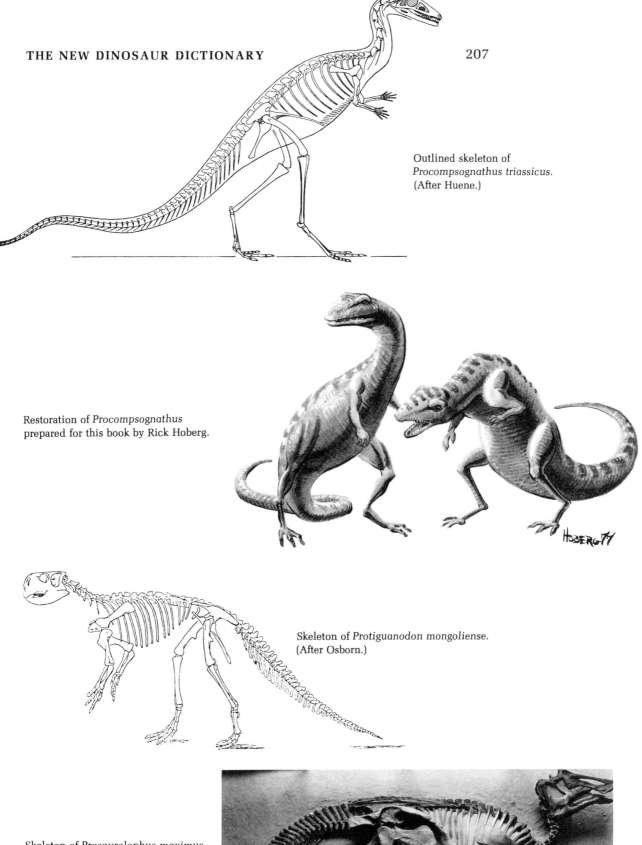

Outlined skeleton of
Procompsognathus triassicus.
(After Huene.)

Restoration of *Procompsognathus*
prepared for this book by Rick Hoberg.

Skeleton of *Protiguanodon mongoliense.*
(After Osborn.)

Skeleton of *Prosaurolophus maximus.*
Courtesy of the Royal Ontario
Museum.

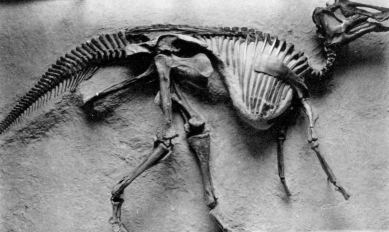

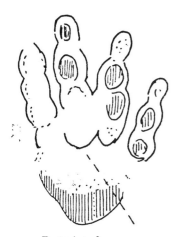

Footprint of *Pseudotetrasauropus mekulingensis.* (After Ellenberger.)

Footprint of *Pseudotrisauropus humilis.* (After Ellenberger.)

Footprint of *Psilotrisauropus subengensis.* (After Ellenberger.)

Pseudotrisauropus   Ellenberger, 1970—*U. Trias.* From the Lower Stormberg Series of several localities in Lesotho, these fossil footprints may have been made by a theropod.

Psilotrisauropus   Ellenberger, 1970—*U. Trias.* The term has been given to footprints, possibly dinosaurian, from the Lower Stormberg Series of Subeng, in Lesotho. Ellenberger believes they belong to an ornithischian.

Psittacosaurus   Osborn, 1923—*Cer., Psittac., L. Cret.* (Probably *Protiguanodon.*) From Mongolia, Siberia, the U.S.S.R. and Shandong, China, this dinosaur may have been a direct ancestor of the later ceratopsians. *Psittacosaurus* is bipedal, its hind legs being about twice the length of the forelimbs. The skull has a parrot-like beak and is of the design expected of an ancestral ceratopsian. At least one species had an incipient nasal horn and well developed jugal "horns." The animal grew to an approximate length of 1.5 meters (5 feet) and weighed some 22.5 kilograms (50 pounds). Some paleontologists believe the psittacosaurids to be ornithopods instead of ceratopsians.

Pteropelyx   Cope, 1889—*Orn., Hadro., Lambeo., U. Cret.* (Probably *Corythosaurus.*) The genus is known from an incomplete skeleton lacking the skull, discovered in the Judith River Formation of Cow Island, Montana. On the basis of the known material, it is presumed to be a crested hadrosaur.

Pteroplax   Huene, 1956—A misspelling of *Pteropelyx.*

Pterospondylus   Jaekel, 1913—*Ther., ?Podok., U. Trias.* (Possibly *Procompsognathus.*) This genus is based on a single dorsal vertebra found in Halberstadt, Germany.

Q

Qemetrisauropus   Ellenberger, 1970—*U. Trias.* From the Lower Stormberg Series of Qeme and Maphutseng, in Lesotho, these fossil footprints may have been left by a moderately large theropod.

Qomoqomosauropus   Ellenberger, 1970—*L. Jur.* These ichnites from the uppermost Stormberg Series of Qomoqomong, in Lesotho, may have been made by a large theropod.

Skeleton of *Protoceratops andrewsi* and its eggs, now called *Elongatoolithus*. Courtesy of the Field Museum of Natural History.

Restoration of the primitive ceratopsian *Protoceratops* and its eggs *Elongatoolithus*. From a mural by Charles R. Knight. Courtesy of the Field Museum of Natural History.

Skull of *Psittacosaurus youngi*.
(After Steel.)

Restoration of the primitive ceratopsian *Psittacosaurus* prepared for this book by Cathy Hill.

Footprints of *Ralikhompus aviator* with feather-like imprints. (After Ellenberger.)

Fragmentary mandible of *Psittacosaurus osborni*. (After Steel.)

Metacarpal of *Rapator ornitholestoides*. (After Huene.)

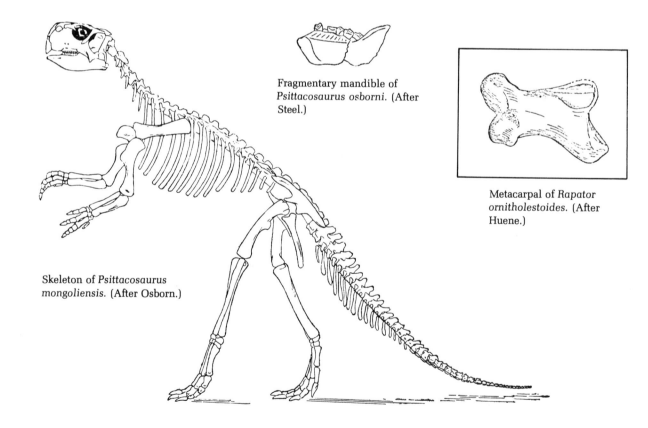

Skeleton of *Psittacosaurus mongoliensis*. (After Osborn.)

Scapula of *Rebbachisaurus garasbae*. (After Lavocat.)

R

Skull of *Psittacosaurus sinensis*. (After Young.)

Rabdodon Matheron, 1869—(See *Rhabdodon*.)

Ralikhompus Ellenberger, ?1972—*U. Trias. or L. Jur.* This term has been given to birdlike dinosaur footprints, with feather-like imprints, found in South Africa.

Rapator Huene, 1932—*Ther., ?Family, L. Cret.* This large genus is based on a metacarpal found in New South Wales. A dorsal vertebra perhaps belonging to *Rapator* suggests a large *Allosaurus*-like form about 10 meters (34 feet) long. The metacarpal is also like that of *Allosaurus* in shape and size.

Rebbachisaurus Lavocat, 1954—*Saur., Sauro., Diplod., Titano., L. Cret.* Known from Morocco and Tunisia, this genus is based on a sacrum, humerus, eleven vertebrae and right scapula. The dorsal vertebrae are high and graceful, the last one being nearly 1.45 meters (5 feet) tall. The scapular blade is broad, unlike that of most other sauropods.

Regnosaurus Mantell, 1848—*?Saur., ?Sauro., ?Diplod., ?Titano., L. Cret.* (Possibly *Hylaeosaurus*.) This genus is known from an incomplete right lower jaw with teeth crowns. For a long time considered to be an ankylosaur, *Regnosaurus* might actually be, according to Ostrom, a sauropod.

Footprint of *Qemetrisauropus princeps*. (After Ellenberger.)

Rhabdodon Matheron, 1869—*Orn., Iguan., U. Cret. (Mochlodon, Rabdodon.)* This genus is an unspecialized ornithopod, not unlike *Camptosaurus*. This animal is primarily known from an incomplete skeleton of an individual slightly more than 4.7 meters (16 feet) long. It is known from Provence, France, and also from Austria, Hungary, Transylvania and perhaps Spain.

Rhadinosaurus Seeley, 1881—(See *Struthiosaurus*.)

Rhaetosaurus Lapparent and Lavocat, 1955—A misspelling of *Rhoetosaurus*.

Rhodanosaurus Nopcsa, 1929—*Ank., Acanth., U. Cret.* (Probably *Struthiosaurus*.) This genus is based on a vertebra and seven dermal plates found in Provence, France. Recent histological work shows similarities between *Rhodanosaurus* and pachycephalosaurs.

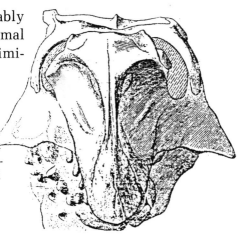

Anterior view of the skull of *Psittacosaurus mongoliensis* showing dermal armor below the right quadratojugal horn. (After Osborn.)

Rhoetosaurus Longman, 1925—*Saur., Sauro., Camar., Cetio., L. Jur.* (*Rhaetosaurus.*) From Queensland, this sauropod is known from incomplete skeletal material including a femur, pelvic fragments, a sacrum and cervical, dorsal and caudal vertebrae. The vertebra centrum measures approximately 18 centimeters (7 inches) long and 25 centimeters (9½ inches) wide. The anterior vertebrae have long, slender centra. *Rhoetosaurus* is one of the more ancient sauropods.

Riojasaurus Bonaparte, 1969—*Saur., Prosaur., Melan., U. Trias.* (*Strenusaurus.*) Based on a nearly complete skeleton and skull fragments found in La Rioja Province, Argentina, this quadrupedal prosauropod superficially resembles a slender sauropod. The neck is serpentine and the tail was probably carried off the ground when the animal walked. *Riojasaurus* is a large prosauropod, approximately 5.9 meters (20 feet) long.

S

Saichania Maryańska, 1977—*Ank., Anky., U. Cret.* This armored dinosaur is known from a skeleton found in the Barun Goyot Formation, Khulsan, Nemegt Basin, in the Gobi Desert. The carapace is covered with numerous pointed armor projections. The skull is armed with bony protuberances. The animal attained a length of approximately 7 meters (24 feet). *Saichania* has a more advanced development of the accessory cranial sinuses than in *Pinacosaurus* and the palatal region has a stronger ossification. The dinosaur differs from *Euoplocephalus* mainly in the structure and shape of the nostrils.

Saltasaurus Bonaparte and Powell, 1980—*Saur., Sauro., Atlan., Titano., U. Cret.* From the Lecho formation in El Brete, in the southern Salta province of Northwestern Argentina, this sauropod, related to *Titanosaurus,* is based on a complete sacrum fused to both ilia, with referred vertebrae, scapulae, coracoids, sternal plates, ischia, pubes, metacarpals, metatarsals, a phalanx, dermal scutes and small dermal ossicles. *Saltasaurus* is the only genus of this family with good evidence of osteoderms and plates, though Depéret suggested in 1896 that *Titanosaurus madagascariensis* had such armor, based upon a single fragmentary plate.

Restoration of *Rebbachisaurus* by George Olshevsky and the author.

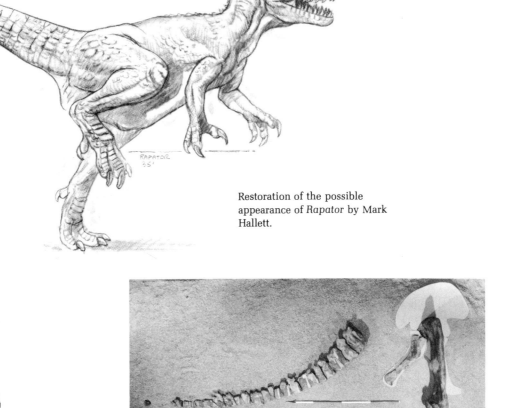

Restoration of the possible appearance of *Rapator* by Mark Hallett.

Humerus (left) and femur (right) of *Rhabdodon priscum*. (After Lapparent.)

Vertebrae, femur and incomplete pelvis of *Rhoetosaurus brownei*, the knee joint having been restored at Langman's direction. Courtesy of the Queensland Museum.

Old painting of *Rhoetosaurus* with body contours inaccurately based on those of *Camarasaurus*. Courtesy of the Queensland Museum.

First scientific restoration of
Rhoetosaurus and its habitat.
From Geology leaflet No. 2,
Queensland Museum, 1980
(2nd Ed.) Courtesy Ralph
Molnar.

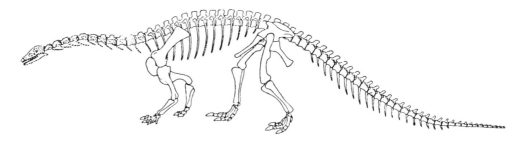

Skeleton of the prosauropod
Riojasaurus incertus. (After
Bonaparte.)

Restoration of *Riojasaurus*
prepared for this book by
William Stout.

Excavation of the skull and anterior part of the trunk of the armored dinosaur *Saichania chulsanensis* during the 1971 Polish-Mongolian Paleontological Expedition to the Nemegt Basin in the Gobi Desert.

Full-scale restoration of *Saichania* at the Valley of Dinosaurs in the Silesian Park of Culture and Recreation, Chorzów, Poland.

Saltopoides de Lapparent and Montenant, 1967—*L. Jur.* These dinosaur ichnites were discovered in France. They resemble *Grallator* and have been placed in the footprint family Anchisauripodidae.

Sanpasaurus Young, 1946—*Orn., ?Iguan., U. Jur.* From Sichuan, China, this dinosaur is based on an incomplete skeleton which shows the femur and fibula to be relatively small and the forelimbs to be quite long. Most of the material appears to be iguanodont, though some of the elements referred to *Sanpasaurus* might be sauropod.

Sarcolestes Lydekker, 1893—*Ank., Nodo., U. Jur.* From the Oxford Clay of Petersborough, England, this dinosaur is known only from an incomplete lower jaw with teeth, which Nopcsa claimed lacked a predentary. Some paleontologists believe that *Sarcolestes* is synonymous with *Scelidosaurus;* the latter, however, occurs in the Lower Jurassic. Recent work by Galton indicates that *Sarcolestes* is a nodosaurid.

Chevron of *Sanpasaurus yaoi.*

Dentary of *Sarcolestes leedsi.* (After Lydekker.)

Sarcosaurus Andrews, 1921—*Ther., ?Family, L. Jur.* This genus is based on a hind leg, vertebrae and a small pelvis found in Leicestershire, England. The bones of the pelvis have fused together.

Sarmientichnus Casamiquela, 1964—*M. Jur.* From Argentina, these ichnites possibly show two toes very closely appressed, giving the appearance of a single toe. They may have been left by a theropod.

Satapliasaurus Gabuniia, 1951—*L. Cret.* From Georgia (U.S.S.R.) and England, these tracks were made by a large theropod. The ichnites are tridactyl, with an occasional showing of a first digit. Along with these tracks were prints almost 50 centimeters (19 inches) long, apparently made underwater by a sauropod or ornithopod.

Sauraechinodon Owen, 1861—(See *Echinodon.*)

Saurichnium Gürich, 1926—*?Age.* The term has been given to so-called dinosaur tracks found in southwest Africa. They are probably too old to have been made by dinosaurs.

Saurischichnus Huene, 1941—*U. Trias.* These ichnites from Italy may have been made by a prosauropod.

Saurolophus Brown, 1912—*Orn., Hadro., Hadrosaur., U. Cret.* This duck-billed dinosaur from the Horseshoe Canyon Formation of Alberta, Canada, from Mongolia and from the Moreno Formation of California, has a solid spikelike crest, formed by an extension of the nasal bones, rising high above the posterior end of the skull. The crest's function is unknown and suggests a "horn." *Saurolophus* is a large hadrosaur, reaching an average length of 8.8 meters (30 feet); but a large Mongolian specimen measures 12 meters (40 feet), and there are reports of even larger specimens from that region. According to Brown, *Saurolophus* is a very abundant form.

Sauropelta Ostrom, 1970—*Ank., Nodo., L. Cret. (Peltosaurus.)* Based on an incomplete skeleton lacking the skull from the Cloverly Formation of Bighorn County, Montana, this ankylosaur has a carapace covered with flat and keeled dorsal plates, with long triangular spines projecting laterally. Apparently the skull was deep, long and narrower than in most ankylosaurs. *Sauropelta* is of medium size, reaching a length of about 5.3 meters (18 feet) and weighing some 3.1 metric tons (3.5 tons).

Saurophagus Ray, 1941—(See *Allosaurus.*)

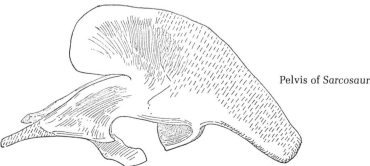

Pelvis of *Sarcosaurus woodi.*

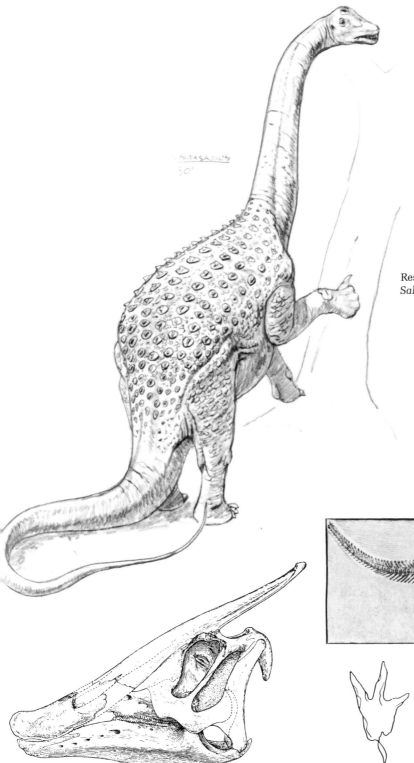

Restoration of the armored sauropod *Saltasaurus* by Mark Hallett.

Skeleton of the hadrosaur *Saurolophus osborni*. Courtesy of the American Museum of Natural History.

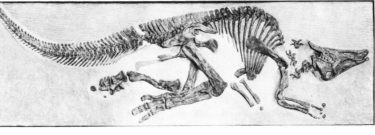

Skull of *Saurolophus angustirostris*. (After Rozhdestvensky.)

Footprints of *Satapliasaurus*. From left to right, *S. tchaboukanii, S. dzotsenidzei, S. kandelakii* and a print possibly made by an ornithopod. (After Gabouniia.)

Dinosaurs of Upper Cretaceous Mongolia. *Tarbosaurus*, a huge theropod, enters the scene at the far left. In its path are two dinosaurs of the genus *Protiguanodon*, in front of which are two closely related (or synonymous) parrot-beaked dinosaurs *Psittacosaurus*. The large duck-billed dinosaur *Saurolophus* turns its head as the great flesh-eater approaches. To the right is a giant hypothetical ceratopsian based only on a fragment of probable ankylosaur bone. And to the lower right are two *Protoceratops*. By Neave Parker. Courtesy of the *Illustrated London News*.

Skeleton of the nodosaurid *Sauropelta edwardsi*. Courtesy of the American Museum of Natural History.

Hypothetical restoration of *Sauroplites* by George Olshevsky.

Sauroplites Bohlin, 1953—*Ank., Ankylo., L. Cret.* From Gansu, China, this genus is known from incomplete material, including several dermal plates and an incomplete ischium. *Sauroplites* might be similar to either *Nodosaurus* or *Euoplocephalus.*

Sauropodopus Ellenberger, 1970—*U. Trias.* These fossil tracks were perhaps made by one of the most ancient sauropods. They were found in the Lower Stormberg Series of Falatsa, in Lesotho.

Sauropus E. Hitchcock, 1845—*L. Jur. (Aethyopus, Amblonyx, Chimera, Chimerichnus, Fulicopus.)* From New England, *Sauropus* has usually referred to the front feet impressions, with the junior synonym *Fulicopus* referring to the hind feet of the same animal. Some scientists believe that these ichnites were made by an ornithischian similar to *Hypsilophodon* with hands like *Camptosaurus.* Haubold (1969), however, places *Sauropus* in its own footprint family Sauropodidae and considers the sauropodids to be theropods.

Trackway of *Sauropodopus antiquus.* (After Ellenberger.)

Restoration of the armored dinosaur *Sauropelta* prepared for this book by Rick Hoberg. *The dinosaur is known to have lateral spikes.*

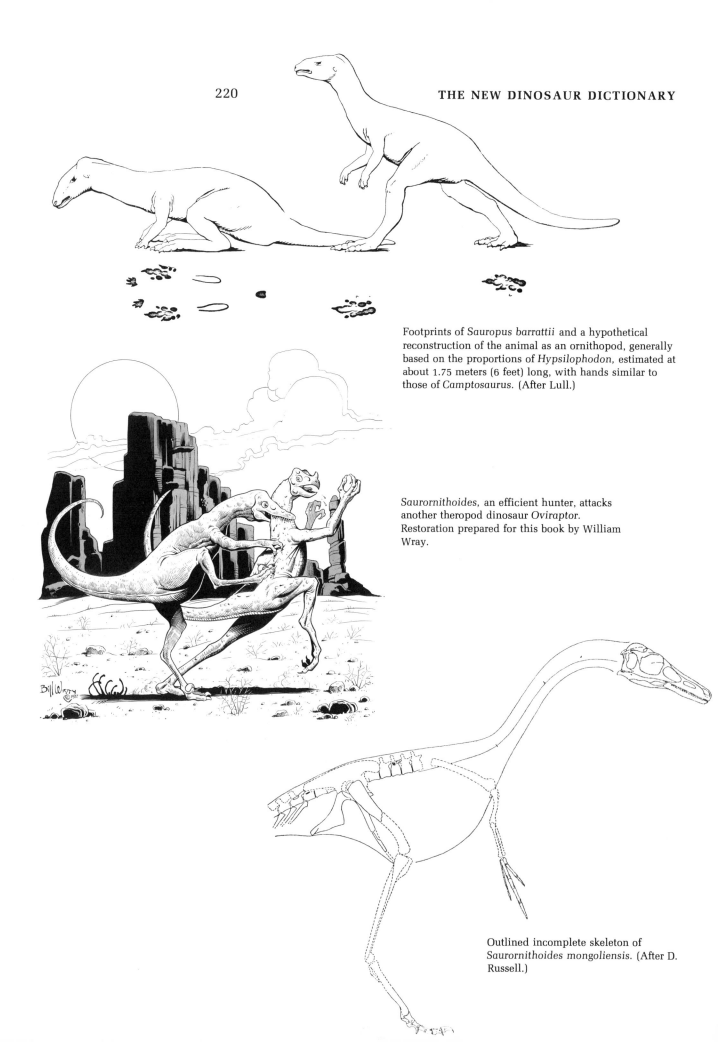

Footprints of *Sauropus barrattii* and a hypothetical reconstruction of the animal as an ornithopod, generally based on the proportions of *Hypsilophodon*, estimated at about 1.75 meters (6 feet) long, with hands similar to those of *Camptosaurus*. (After Lull.)

Saurornithoides, an efficient hunter, attacks another theropod dinosaur *Oviraptor*. Restoration prepared for this book by William Wray.

Outlined incomplete skeleton of *Saurornithoides mongoliensis*. (After D. Russell.)

Skeleton of *Scelidosaurus harrisonii*. Courtesy of the British Museum (Natural History).

Ilium and pubis of the hadrosaur *Secernosaurus koerneri*. Courtesy of M. Brett-Surman and the Field Museum of Natural History.

Restoration of *Scelidosaurus* as a primitive stegosaur or ankylosaur by Neave Parker. Recent studies indicate that the animal was probably a bipedal ornithopod with a relatively long neck. Courtesy of the British Museum (Natural History).

Reconstructed left manus of *Saurornitholestes langstoni*, with proportions based upon *Velociraptor* and *Deinonychus*. (After Sues.)

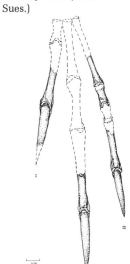

Footprint of *Seakatrisauropus divergens*. (After Ellenberger.)

Saurornitholestes langstoni

Restoration of *Saurornitholestes* prepared for this book by George Olshevsky and Ken Steacy.

Footprints of *Senqutrisauropus priscus*. (After Ellenberger.)

Saurornithoides Osborn, 1924—*Ther., Saurorn., U. Cret.*, (*Ornithoides*; possibly *Stenonychosaurus*.) This birdlike dinosaur, with a relatively long neck and large head, is known from Bain Dzak in Outer Mongolia. The hands are equipped with manipulative fingers and the hind feet have an enlarged claw, utilized in slashing the flesh of its victims. The brain was large, possibly making *Saurornithoides* one of the most intelligent of the dinosaurs. The large eyes permitted stereo vision. Russell proposes that *Saurornithoides* and similar dinosaurs might have hunted and caught small mammals, even at twilight. The dinosaur grew to an approximate length of 1.8 to 2.1 meters (6 to 7 feet).

Saurornitholestes Sues, 1978—*Ther., Dromae., U. Cret.* Based on a frontal, some phalanges and unguals from the manus, two teeth and a few miscellaneous bones, the material apparently indicates a dinosaur smaller than *Stenonychosaurus*. The specimens were discovered in the Oldman Formation of Alberta, Canada.

Scalosaurus Mehl, 1936—A misspelling of *Scolosaurus*.

Scelidosaurus Owen, 1859—*Orn., Scelid., L. Jur.* The oldest known ornithischian, *Scelidosaurus* had long been classified as a primitive stegosaur and, in more recent years, as an ankylosaur. Charig proposed that the dinosaur be assigned its own suborder Scelidosauria; Thulborn suggested that it is a hypsilophodont. Based on these studies, *Scelidosaurus* is now classified as an ornithopod and is considered to be bipedal, with a relatively long and slender neck. The hind legs of the animal are longer than the forelimbs and the feet are broad. The body is heavily built and covered with small armor plates which run in rows along the neck, back and tail. There are small vertical plates along the neck and tail. The skull is small and has weak jaws. The animal attained a length of about 3.5 meters (12 feet) and weighed some 125 kilograms (275 pounds). The original type specimen referred to *S. harrisoni* is now known to be the knee joint of a megalosaurid theropod. The dinosaur is known from England.

Scolosaurus Nopcsa, 1928—(See *Euoplocephalus*, W. P. Coombs, personal communication.)

Seakatrisauropus Ellenberger, 1970—*U. Trias.* From the Lower Stormberg Series of Seaka, in Lesotho, these ichnites may have been made by a theropod.

Secernosaurus Brett-Surman, 1975—*Orn., Hadro., Hadrosaur., U. Cret.* Based upon a prepubis, scapula, fibula, caudals, two ilia and a

Footprints of *Selenichnus falcatus* and a hypothetical restoration of the animal, based on the proportions of the thecodont *Saltopus*. (After Lull.)

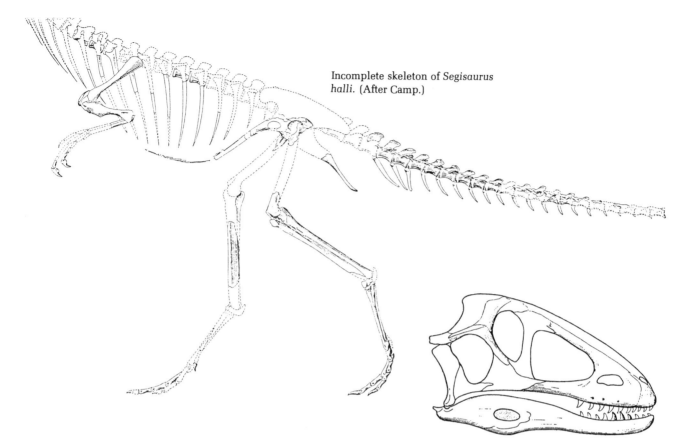

Incomplete skeleton of *Segisaurus halli.* (After Camp.)

Skull of *Shanshanosaurus huoyanshanensis.* (After Dong.)

Restoration of *Shanshanosaurus* prepared for this book by William Stout. The animal is depicted as about to consume some ants.

Restoration of *Segisaurus* by the author.

Tooth of *Sinocoelurus fragilis*. (After Young.)

partial braincase from the San Jorgé Formation, Rio Chico, Patagonia, Argentina, this hadrosaurine is relatively small and occurs in the latest Cretaceous. Unlike any other hadrosaur or iguanodont, the postacetabular process of the ilium is elongate and deflected dorsomedially and the antitrochanter is relatively smaller than that in any other known duck-billed dinosaur of equal size. *Secernosaurus* is the second most primitive of all known hadrosaurs and only the second to be found in Gondwanaland.

Segisaurus   Camp, 1936—*Ther., Segi., L. Jur.* This lightweight genus from Keet Seel, Arizona, is known from an incomplete skeleton. The bones are thick-walled and the clavicles are present, unusual characteristics for a theropod. Elements of this genus resemble those in *Compsognathus*. Camp has suggested that *Segisaurus* was adapted for quick turning, digging, or both.

Selenichnus   E. Hitchcock, 1858—*L. Jur.* From the Connecticut Valley, these didactyl footprints are not distinct enough for reliable classification. The animal that made them was apparently bipedal and perhaps a theropod. Some workers place *Selenichnus* in its own footprint family Selenichnidae.

Sellosaurus   Huene, 1908—(See *Plateosaurus*.)

Incomplete maxilla of *Sinosaurus triassicus*. (After Young.)

Senqutrisauropus   Ellenberger, 1970—These ichnites from the Lower Stormberg Series of Morobong, in Lesotho, may have been made by a theropod.

Shanshanosaurus   Dong, 1977—*Ther., Shanshan., U. Cret.* From Xinjiang, in central Asia, this is a small theropod with a small skull, caniniform teeth, relatively long neck and short forelimbs. The bones are thin-walled. The tibia is longer than the femur and the humerus is about one third as long as the femur. Part of the animal's diet may have consisted of insects. *Shanshanosaurus* was a cursorial animal. It now belongs to its own family Shanshanosauridae.

Shantungosaurus   Hu, 1973—*Orn., Hadro., Hadrosaur., U. Cret.* From Shandong, China, this flat-headed hadrosaur is one of the largest known duck-billed dinosaurs, measuring approximately 15 meters (51 feet) in length. The neural spines are long. The tail has long chevrons, intimating that the animal might have been amphibious.

Shensipus   Young, 1966—*M. Jur.* From Shensi and Tungchuan, China, these ichnites may have been made by a small theropod or a large bird.

Hypothetical restoration of *Sinosaurus* by the author.

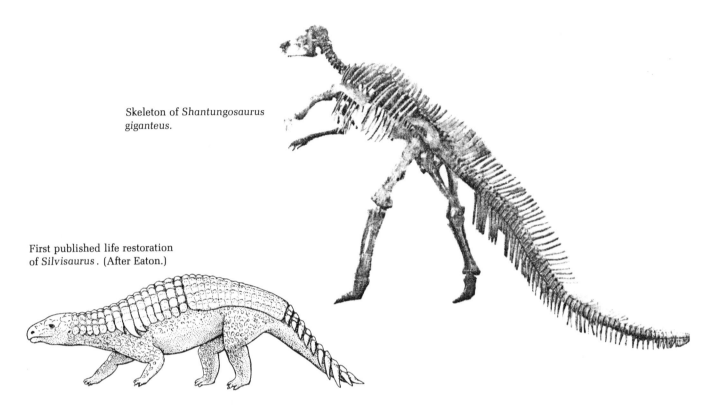

Skeleton of *Shantungosaurus*
giganteus.

First published life restoration
of *Silvisaurus*. (After Eaton.)

Restoration of the flat-headed
hadrosaur *Shantungosaurus*.

More correct restoration of
Silvisaurus by George
Olshevsky.

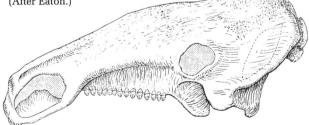

Skull of *Silvisaurus condrayi*.
(After Eaton.)

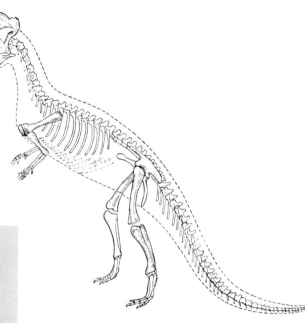

Outlined skeleton of *Stegoceras validus*. (After Gilmore.)

Restoration of the unusual theropod *Spinosaurus* prepared for this book by William Stout.

Elongated vertebral spines of *Spinosuchus caseanus*.

Domelike cranium of *Stegoceras lambei*. Recent studies indicate that *S. lambei* may be a junior synonym of *S. validus*. (After Sternberg.)

Domelike cranium of *Stegoceras edmontonensis*. (After Brown and Schlaikjer.)

Outlined incomplete skeleton of *Staurikosaurus pricei*. (After Galton.)

Sillimanius   E. Hitchcock, 1845—*U. Trias.* From New England, these fossil tracks may have been made by a small theropod.

Silvisaurus   Eaton, 1960—*Ank., Nodo., U. Cret.* This primitive armored dinosaur is known from a skull and incomplete skeleton, including many dermal elements, found in the Dakota Formation of Ottawa County, Kansas. The neck is relatively long. In life the animal probably had armor plates covering the dorsal area of the neck and shoulders, the prepelvic area of the back, and the tail, with lateral spikes particularly long above the shoulders and toward the end of the tail. The hips were protected by an armor sheath. The under part of the body was protected by numerous small scutes. *Silvisaurus* attained a length of about 3.25 meters (11 feet). The skull is one fourth longer than it is wide and Eaton noted it has a number of sinus chambers, as did other ankylosaurs. Eaton believed these sinus chambers were used for resonance and calculated that the animal could reach a high C.

Sinocoelurus   Young, 1942—*Ther., ?Family, U. Jur.* This genus is based on four small indeterminate teeth found in Sichuan, China.

Sinoichnites   Kuhn, 1958—*U. Jur.* These ichnites from north Shensi, China, may have been made by a large iguanodont.

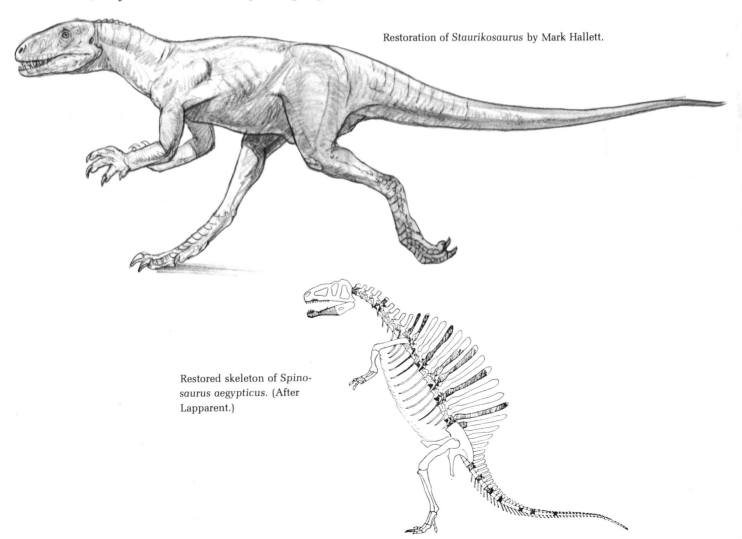

Restoration of *Staurikosaurus* by Mark Hallett.

Restored skeleton of *Spinosaurus aegypticus.* (After Lapparent.)

Domelike cranium of
Stegoceras sternbergi.
Recent studies indicate that
S. lambei may be a junior
synonym of *S. validus.*
(After Brown and
Schlaikjer.)

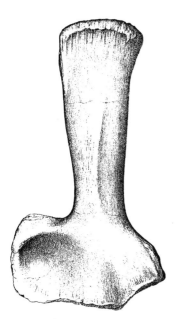

Scapula coracoid of
Stegosaurus sulcatus. (After
Marsh.)

Sinosaurus Young, 1948—*Ther., ?Family, U. Trias.* This genus is based on a left maxilla and jaw fragments found in Yunnan Lufeng, China. The maxillary teeth resemble those in *Teratosaurus.* The remains indicate a large carnivorous animal.

Skolosaurus Huene, 1954—A misspelling of *Scolosaurus.*

Smilodon Plieninger, 1846—(See *Zanclodon.*)

Sphenospondylus Seeley, 1883—(See *Iguanodon.*)

Sphingopus Demathieu, 1966—*M. Trias.* From France, these fossil footprints may have been made by an early theropod. Haubold (1971) has placed *Spingopus* in the footprint family Parachirotheriidae.

Spinosaurus Stromer, 1915—*Ther., Spino., U. Cret.* This genus from Baharije, Egypt, is probably one of the largest of the theropod dinosaurs. In life the animal reached a length of about 15 meters (50 feet) and probably weighed over 6.2 metric tons (7 tons). The truly remarkable aspect of *Spinosaurus* is the series of huge neural spines, some of which attained lengths of 1.75 meters (6 feet). A membrane was probably attached to these spines, creating a sail-back effect that puzzles paleontologists. The teeth in *Spinosaurus* are straight, not curved. All the specimens referred to this genus—including vertebrae, a dentary and partial maxilla—were destroyed during World War II. A recent suggestion by some paleontologists is that *Spinosaurus* may have been quadrupedal.

Spinosuchus Huene, 1932—*?Ther., ?Family, U. Trias.* This long-spined genus is based on seven cervical and fifteen dorsal vertebrae from Crosby County, West Texas. Possibly the form is not a dinosaur but a thecodont.

Spondylosoma Huene, 1938—*?Saurischia, ?Suborder, M. Trias.* This genus is based on an almost complete vertebral column, a humerus, a scapula and a fragmentary femur; it is known from Rio Grande de Sul, Brazil. Colbert suggests that the animal had a long neck and small head. *Spondylosoma* is probably not a dinosaur but a thecodont.

Staurikosaurus Colbert, 1970—*Ther., Staurik., M. Trias.* From the Santa Maria Formation of Rio Grande do Sul, this dinosaur is based on incomplete skeletal material including vertebrae, both hind legs, a pelvis and lower jaws. From the size of the jaws, Colbert and Galton have suggested that the creature had a large head. *Staurikosaurus* now belongs to its own family Staurikosauridae.

Restoration of *Stegosaurus ungulatus*, with longer legs, shortened tail and eight tail spikes, based on the mounted skeleton at Yale University. (Modified after Lull.)

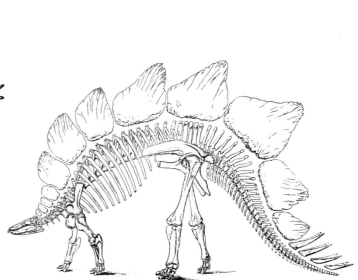

Skeleton of *Stegosaurus ungulatus*. (After Marsh.)

Skeleton of *Stegosaurus stenops*. Courtesy of the Smithsonian Institution.

Incomplete remains of *Stegosaurus laticeps*. (After Marsh.)

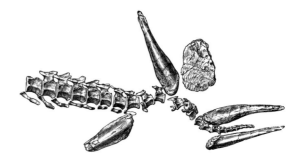

Distal end of left tibia of
Stenonychosaurus inequalis.

Footprint of *Stenonyx
lateralis.* (After E.
Hitchcock.)

Stegoceras Lambe, 1902—*Pach., Pachy., U. Cret.* (In part, "*Troödon*" of Gilmore, 1924.) This is a moderate-sized pachycephalosaur, less than 2.35 meters (8 feet) long and weighing less than 55 kilograms (120 pounds). The animal has a fairly large cranial dome. *Stegoceras* is known from the Belly River Series of Alberta, Canada, and possibly from Gansu.

Stegopelta Williston, 1905—(See *Nodosaurus.*)

Stegosaurides Bohlin, 1953—*?Ank., ?Family, L. Cret.* (*Stegosauroides.*) From Hui-Hui-Pu, west Gansu, China, this genus is known only from fragments, including the base of a dermal spine and two vertebral centra. *Stegosaurides* bears a slight resemblance to *Acanthopholis.*

Stegosauroides Colbert, 1961—A misspelling of *Stegosaurides.*

Stegosaurus Marsh, 1877—*Steg., Stego., U. Jur.* (*Diracodon*; in part, *Hypsirhophus.*) This odd-looking dinosaur was discovered in the Morrison Formation of Jefferson County, Colorado. Two series of alternating, erect, leaf-shaped bony plates surmount the neck, back and tail. Once thought to serve as armor, these plates are now known to contain blood vessels and were probably used in heat regulation. The animal's real protection came from the four spikes at the end of the tail, which could smash into its theropod attackers with deadly impact. (*S. ungulatus*, a species with longer legs and a shorter tail, might have had eight tail spikes.) This dinosaur is perhaps best known for its supposed "three brains," two of which were actually enlargements of the spinal cord in the shoulder and pelvic regions. These enlargements, much larger than the actual brain, controlled the movements of the head and tail. This arrangement was not uncommon among dinosaurs and is even found in mammals. *Stegosaurus* grew to a length of about 7.4 meters (25 feet) and weighed approximately 3.5 metric tons (4 tons). Some paleontologists have proposed that the animal might have been able to rear up on its hind legs or that the plates lay flat against the body. *Stegosaurus* is also known from Wyoming, Oklahoma, Montana, Utah and Gloucestershire, England.

Stenonychosaurus Sternberg, 1932—*Ther., Saurorn., U. Cret.* (*Polyodontosaurus*; possibly *Saurornithoides.*) This genus is based on fragmentary material, including vertebrae, a partial left tibia, the first metacarpal, pes and astragalus, found in the Oldman and Horseshoe Canyon formations of Alberta, Canada. The dinosaur is quite similar to

Restoration of *Stegoceras* prepared for
this book by William Stout.

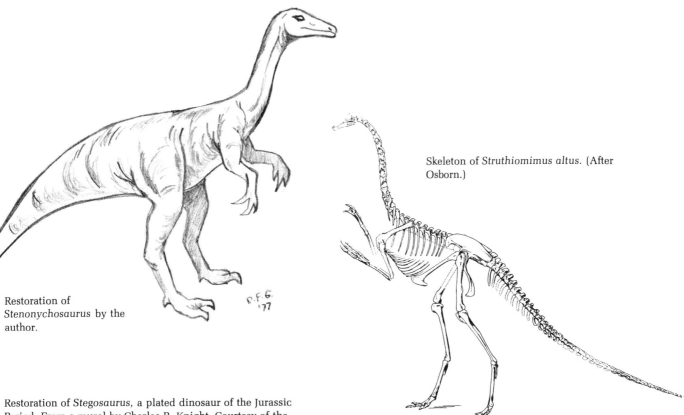

Restoration of *Stenonychosaurus* by the author.

Skeleton of *Struthiomimus altus*. (After Osborn.)

Restoration of *Stegosaurus*, a plated dinosaur of the Jurassic Period. From a mural by Charles R. Knight. Courtesy of the Field Museum of Natural History.

Ilium of *Stokesosaurus
clevelandi.* Courtesy of J. H.
Madsen, Jr.

One of Baron Nopcsa's fanciful
restorations of the armored dinosaur
Struthiosaurus.

Previously unpublished restoration of
Struthiomimus by Charles R. Knight.

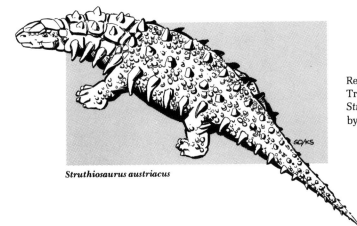

Struthiosaurus austriacus

Restoration of the small armored
Transylvanian dinosaur
Struthiosaurus prepared for this book
by George Olshevsky and Ken Steacy.

Saurornithoides and Russell believes them to be congeneric. Russell also proposes that *Stenonychosaurus* was a crepuscular hunter of small mammals. The dinosaur reached a length of about 1.75 meters (6 feet) and weighed some 27 kilograms (60 pounds).

Stenonyx   Lull, 1904—*L. Jur. (Leptonyx.)* These fossil footprints from the Connecticut Valley were made by a podokesaurid. They have been placed in the footprint family Anchisauripodidae.

Stenopelix   von Meyer, 1857—*?Pach., ?Pachy., L. Cret.* Though once considered to be a psittacosaurid, this genus is now classified as a primitive pachycephalosaur. It is known from hind legs, vertebrae and a pelvis from Bückeburg, Germany. Galton and Sues are currently restudying the genus.

Stenopelyx   Nopcsa, 1917—A misspelling of *Stenopelix.*

Stephanosaurus   Lambe, 1902—(See *Lambeosaurus, Kritosaurus.*)

Stereocephalus   Lambe, 1902—(See *Euoplocephalus.*)

Stereosaurus   Seeley, 1876—This series of apparently dinosaurian vertebrae was never formally described. The bones were placed in the Sedgwick Museum and cited in Seeley's Woodward Museum index. No other information is available.

Steropezoum   E. Hitchcock—(See *Steropoides.*)

Steropoides   E. Hitchcock, 1845—*U. Trias. (Steropezoum, Tridentipes.)* From Massachusetts and Connecticut, these fossil footprints may have been made by a theropod dinosaur.

Sterrholophus   Marsh, 1891—(See *Triceratops.*)

Stokesosaurus   Madsen, 1974—*Ther., ?Tyrann., U. Jur.* Based on a premaxilla and two ilia from the Morrison Formation of east central Utah, this genus is a small theropod approximately 4 meters (13 feet 6 inches) long. The ilium roughly resembles that of *Allosaurus* and also that of the later tyrannosaurids, yet the animal seems closest to *Deinonychus* in its general shape.

Strenusaurus   Bonaparte, 1969—(See *Riojasaurus.*)

"Streptospondylus"   von Meyer, 1830—(See *Eustreptospondylus.*)

Struthiomimus   Osborn, 1917—*Ther., Ornith., U. Cret.* This genus from the Oldman and Horseshoe Canyon formations of Alberta, Canada,

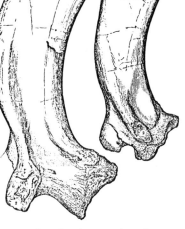

Left and right scapulae of *Struthiosaurus austriacus.* (After Seeley.)

is a hollow-boned theropod descriptively referred to as the "ostrich dinosaur." Its shape suggesting an ostrich, *Struthiomimus* has a long neck and exceptionally long forelimbs. The mouth forms a hard, flat beak which may have been used in consuming small reptiles, insects, fruits and various forms of vegetation. *Struthiomimus* reached a length of approximately 4.1 meters (14 feet) and a height of 2.35 meters (8 feet).

Struthiosaurus   Bunzel, 1871—*Ank., Acanth., U. Cret. (Danubiosaurus, Pleuropeltus, Rhadinosaurus; possibly Crataeomus.)* From Wiener-Neustadt, Austria, and Hungary and Transylvania, this dinosaur is known from two incomplete skulls, various pieces of armor, plates and large dermal spines. Nopcsa made fanciful restorations of *Struthiosaurus* with a birdlike head and somewhat resembling *Hylaeosaurus*. *Struthiosaurus* reached an approximate length of 2 meters (6.8 feet).

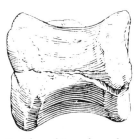

Vertebra of *Symphyrophus musculosus*. (After Osborn and Marsh.)

Struthopus   Ballerstedt, 1921—*L. Cret.* The term has been given to didactyl ornithopod footprints found in Germany. Some paleontologists consider them to be of *Iguanodon* origin.

Styracosaurus   Lambe, 1913—*Cer., Cerat., U. Cret.* This dinosaur is a short-frilled ceratopsian, the shield being endowed with a number of long spikes. There is one very long horn surmounting the snout and two extremely short horns above the orbits. The animal grew to a length of about 5.25 meters (18 feet) and weighed approximately 3.5 metric tons (4 tons). *Styracosaurus* was discovered in the Oldman Formation of Alberta, Canada, and is also known from Montana. Sternberg suggested that *Styracosaurus* occasionally congregated in swampy areas; but the rarity of *Styracosaurus* in sediments deposited near Oldman swamps suggests that such congregating was infrequent, if it occurred at all.

Succinodon   Huene, 1941—*Saur., Sauro., ?Diplod., ?Titano., U. Cret.* This dinosaur is known only from an incomplete jaw with teeth found in Poland.

Swinnertonichnus   Sargeant, 1967—*M. Trias.* These possible English theropod tracks are based on tridactyl ichnites from Nottingham. They have been placed in the footprint family Anchisauripodidae.

Sacral vertebrae of *Syngonosaurus macrocercus*. (After Seeley.)

Sygmosaurus   Sauvage, 1882—A misspelling of *Syngonosaurus*.

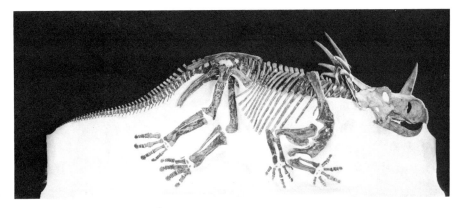

Skeleton of *Styracosaurus parksi*.
Courtesy of the American Museum of
Natural History.

Skull of *Styracosaurus albertensis*.
Courtesy of the National Museums of
Canada.

The spike-frilled *Styracosaurus* and the
crested *Corythosaurus*. Restoration by
Robert T. Bakker. Courtesy of the
National Museums of Canada.

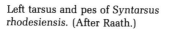

Symphyrophus Cope, 1878—*Orn., ?Iguan., U. Jur. (Symphyrosaurus; probably Camptosaurus.)* This genus is based on a vertebral centrum and the distal end of a femur from the Morrison Formation of Fremont County, Colorado. Originally the material was thought to be sauropod and later crocodilian.

Symphyrosaurus Huene, 1908—A misspelling of *Symphyrophus.*

Syngonosaurus Seeley, 1879—*Orn., Iguan., L. Cret. (Sygmosaurus.)* From Cambridge, England, this dinosaur is known from nineteen incomplete vertebrae and other material possibly applicable.

Syntarsus Raath, 1969—*Ther., Podok., U. Trias.* This genus is based on most of the postcranium with the exception of the cervical column, from the Nyamandhlovu district of Rhodesia; and there is much new undescribed material applicable to *Syntarsus.* The genus is small and has a crest at the back of the skull. The tibia and some tarsal bones are similar to those in birds. The animal may have been insulated by feathers and probably weighed approximately 30 kilograms (63 pounds). Raath believes that *Syntarsus* was a desert dweller.

Syrmosaurus Maleev, 1952—(See *Pinacosaurus.*)

Szechuanosaurus Young, 1942—*Ther., ?Family, U. Jur. to L. Cret.* Based on a lower jaw and teeth, this dinosaur was discovered in north Sichuan, China. The teeth are probably not all from the same animal. A jaw fragment referred to *Szechuanosaurus*, found in Sinkiang, resembles that of *Labocania.*

Left tarsus and pes of *Syntarsus rhodesiensis.* (After Raath.)

Broken tooth of *Szechuanosaurus campi.* (After Young.)

T

Talarurus Maleev, 1952—*Ank., Anky., U. Cret.* From Bayan Shireh, Mongolia, this armored dinosaur is known from an incomplete skeleton with a fragmentary skull. There are keeled plates about 5 centimeters (almost 2 inches) thick on the back, hips and tail. The sides of the body and tail are armed with sharp spines. The skull, when complete, was probably narrow. In life the animal grew to an approximate length of 5 meters (17 feet). *Talarurus* is probably closely related to *Euoplocephalus.*

Talmontopus de Lapparent and Montenat, 1967—*L. Jur.* The term has

Restoration of the feathered theropod *Syntarsus* by William Stout. The feathers at the crest are speculation.

Modern and more correct restoration of *Talarurus* by George Olshevsky.

First published life restoration of *Talarurus*. (After Maleev.)

been given to theropod footprints found in France. The tracks have been placed in the footprint family Anchisauripodidae.

Tanius Wiman, 1929—*Orn., Hadro., Hadrosaur., U. Cret.* This duck-billed dinosaur is known from a nearly complete skeleton from Shandong, China. The skull lacks the anterior part but intimates that *Tanius* had a low, flat head. The genus is closely allied with, though more primitive than, *Telmatosaurus.*

Tarbosaurus Maleev, 1955—*Ther., Tyrann., U. Cret.* This genus from the Nemegt Formation is the Mongolian equivalent of the American *Tyrannosaurus.* The dinosaur is of the general tyrannosaurid form, with each manus equipped with two sharp claws and rugged bony protuberances above the snout. One specimen of *Tarbosaurus* is about 6.8 meters (23 feet) long, some 2.8 meters (almost 10 feet) high at the hips, with a skull 1.15 meters (almost 4 feet) long and a manus over 14 centimeters

Hind foot bones of *Talarurus plicatospineus.* (After Maleev.)

Distal caudal vertebra of *Caudocoelus sauvagei.* (After Huene.)

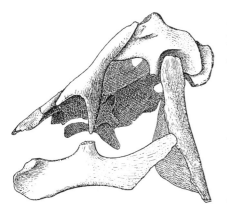

Fragmentary skull of *Tanius sinensis*. (After Wiman.)

Sacrum of *Tanius laiyangensis*.

Mandible of *Tatisaurus oehleri*. (After Simmons.)

(5½ inches) long; but the animal probably grew to a length of 11.75 meters (40 feet). *Tarbosaurus* is one of the few dinosaurs for which several growth stages are known.

Tarchia Maryańska, 1978—*Ank., Anky., U. Cret.* This armored dinosaur was discovered during the 1971 Polish-Mongolian Paleontological Expedition to Mongolia. The dinosaur once called *Dyoplosaurus giganteus* is referable to this genus as well. The skull of *Tarchia* is approximately the same size as that of *Saichania*, though the brain case is larger.

Tarsodactylus E. Hitchcock, 1858—*U. Trias.* These ichnites from Massachusetts may have been made by a theropod, a thecodont or a crocodilian.

Tatisaurus Simmons, 1965—*Orn., ?Family, U. Trias.* Based on a fragmentary left mandible with teeth found in Yünnan, China, this dinosaur might be an ornithopod or a prosauropod, probably the former.

Taupezia Delair, 1962—*U. Jur.* These fossil footprints from England are presumably dinosaurian.

Teinurosaurus Nopcsa, 1928—*Ther., ?Family, U. Jur. (Caudocoelus.)* Based on a single caudal vertebra from Boulogne, France, originally referred to *Iguanodon prestiwichi* by Sauvage (1897–98). Nopsca Recognized it as theropod and gave it its own generic name, *Teinurosaurus*. Two footnote errors (corrected by Nopcsa in 1929) made it look as if he were naming it *Saurornithoides* and giving the name *Teinurosaurus* to Leidy's *Deinodon*. This correction was not noticed by Huene, who named the specimen *Caudocoelus* in 1932. *Teinurosaurus* has clear priority over *Caudocoelus* and should be the preferred name for the specimen. (G. Olshevsky, personal communication.)

Telmatosaurus Nopcsa, 1903—*Orn., Hadro., Hadrosaur., U. Cret. (Hecatasaurus, Limnosaurus;* in part, *Orthomerus.)* This primitive hadrosaur is known from Transylvania and has recently been reported in France. The femur is almost 52 centimeters (20 inches) long and a tibia measures more than 30 centimeters (11½ inches). There are twelve cervical vertebrae lacking neural spines and being wider than they are deep. The teeth, unlike those of most hadrosaurs, are compressed from back to front. The jugal bone is narrow.

Tenontosaurus Ostrom, 1970—*Orn., Iguan., L. Cret.* An iguanodont discovered in the Cloverly Formation of Wheatland County, Montana,

Hypothetical restoration of
Tatisaurus by the author.

Restoration of the armored
dinosaur *Tarchia* by George
Olshevsky.

Skeleton of the giant Asian
theropod *Tarbosaurus bataar*.
Courtesy of the Institute of
Paleobiology in Warsaw.

Even a dangerous predator like
Gallimimus flees from the
monstrous *Tarbosaurus*.
Restoration by William Stout.

Skull of the armored dinosaur
Tarchia gigantea. (After
Tumanova.)

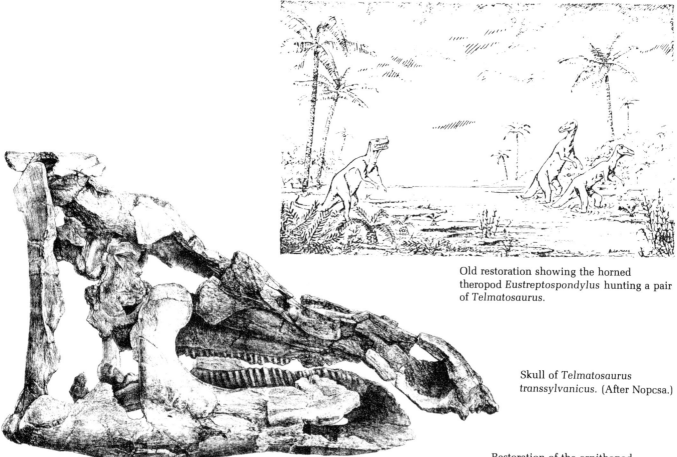

Old restoration showing the horned
theropod *Eustreptospondylus* hunting a pair
of *Telmatosaurus*.

Skull of *Telmatosaurus
transsylvanicus*. (After Nopcsa.)

Restoration of the ornithopod
Tenontosaurus prepared for this book
by William Stout.

Skeleton of *Tenontosaurus tilletti*. Courtesy
of R. A. Long, S. P. Welles and the
American Museum of Natural History.

Tenontosaurus has a skull similar to that of *Iguanodon* and an extremely long tail. The tail is strengthened by ossified tendons and chevrons. The hind feet are equipped with powerful claws that were probably used in defending itself against predators. *Tenontosaurus* reached a length of approximately 7.3 meters (25 feet) and weighed about .88 metric tons (1 ton). Molnar suggests this dinosaur is related to hypsilophodonts rather than to iguanodonts. *Tenontosaurus* is also known from the Trinity Group of Texas and Oklahoma.

Teratosaurus   von Meyer, 1861—*?Ther., Terat., U. Trias.* This genus is based on a right maxilla discovered in Stuttgart, Germany. Colbert has hypothetically described the animal as a giant dinosaur almost 6 meters (20 feet) long and weighing over 450 kilograms (1,000 pounds), with a short, muscular neck, a large head with a mouth filled with formidable teeth, the forelimbs about one third shorter than the hind legs and each manus equipped with three large claws. In private correspondence, Long has proposed that *Teratosaurus* might actually be a giant thecodont.

Tetragonosaurus   Parks, 1931—(See *Procheneosaurus.*)

Tetrapodosaurus   Sternberg, 1932—*L. Cret.* Originally believed to be ceratopsian, these fossil tracks from the Peace River area of British Columbia were probably made by an ankylosaur. The tracks are both three-toed and four-toed, indicating a quadrupedal animal. Sternberg has put *Tetrapodosaurus* in its own footprint family Tetrapodosauridae.

Tetrasauropus   Ellenberger, 1970—*U. Trias.* From the Lower Stormberg Series of Falatsa and Seaka, in Lesotho, and from France, these very large, five-digit footprints were made by a prosauropod of an unknown family.

Thecocoelurus   Huene, 1926—*Ther., ?Family, L. Cret.* (Possibly *Aristosuchus, Calamosaurus.*) This genus is based on half an indeterminate cervical vertebra, found on the Isle of Wight, England, representing a moderate-sized form.

Thecodontichnus   Huene, 1941—*U. Trias.* These theropod ichnites were found in Toscana. Haubold (1971) placed them in the footprint family Parachirotheriidae.

Thecodontosaurus   Riley and Stutchbury, 1836—*Saur., Prosaur., Anchi., U. Trias.* (Possibly *Hortalotarsus.*) This dinosaur is more primitive than *Plateosaurus.* The genus has serrated and leaf-shaped teeth. It has

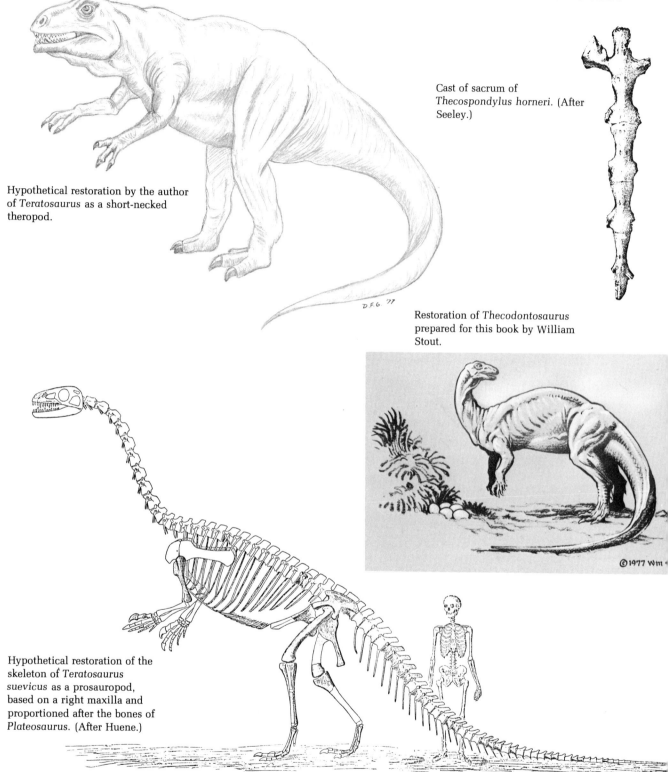

Hypothetical restoration by the author of *Teratosaurus* as a short-necked theropod.

Cast of sacrum of *Thecospondylus horneri*. (After Seeley.)

Restoration of *Thecodontosaurus* prepared for this book by William Stout.

Hypothetical restoration of the skeleton of *Teratosaurus suevicus* as a prosauropod, based on a right maxilla and proportioned after the bones of *Plateosaurus*. (After Huene.)

been reported from North and South America, Asia, Africa, Australia and Europe, but probably only the records from Bristol, England, can be correctly referred to this genus. Two small dinosaurs from Poland's fissure fills might also be *Thecodontosaurus*. The type specimens, based on several individuals, have been destroyed, but other specimens have been preserved at Yale.

Thecospondylus Seeley, 1882—*Ther., ?Family, L. Cret.* Known only from a sacrum found in Kent, England, this genus may be closely related to *Elaphrosaurus*. Its true affinities are not yet really understood.

Therizinosaurus Maleev, 1954—*Ther., Theriz., U. Cret.* Originally thought to be a turtle, this theropod from the Nemegt Basin of the Gobi Desert in Mongolia, and possibly from Kazakhstan, is known only from several phalanges and a front limb. The claws are enormous, the largest theropod talons known, measuring almost 80 centimeters (30 inches). Rozhdestvensky has suggested that it fed on ants, using the claws to tear open ant hills.

Therosaurus Fitzinger, 1843—(See *Iguanodon*.)

Thescelosaurus Gilmore, 1913—*Orn., ?Hypsil., U. Cret.* Related to *Hypsilophodon*, this dinosaur is known from the Lance Formation of Converse County, Wyoming, and also from Montana and western Canada. In life this slender, swiftly moving ornithopod reached a length of about 3.5 meters (12 feet) and weighed some 250 kilograms (550 pounds). Some paleontologists believe that possibly this genus belongs to its own family Thescelosauridae.

Thespesius Leidy, 1856—*Orn., Hadro., Hadrosaur., U. Cret.* (Possibly *Anatosaurus*.) This genus is known from two caudal centra and a phalanx, discovered in the Lance Formation of Grand River, South Dakota.

Thotobolosaurus Ellenberger, 1970—*Saur., ?Prosaur., ?Melan., U. Trias.* From the Lower Stormberg Series of Lesotho and South Africa, this dinosaur is reportedly a large, possibly quadrupedal melanorosaurid very much like a true sauropod. The form corresponds to the ichnite *Pseudotetrasauropus*. A description of the genus has not yet been published.

Tichosteus Cope, 1877—*U. Jur.* Based on a vertebral centrum of a juvenile individual, discovered in the Morrison Formation of Fremont County, Colorado, this genus has usually been attributed to the Theropoda. *Tichosteus* might be a hypsilophodont similar to *Laosaurus*, or

Footprints of *Tetrasauropus gigas*. (After Ellenberger.)

Manus of *Thecodontosaurus antiquus*. (After Steel.)

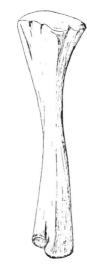

Left tibia of *?Thecodontosaurus minor*.

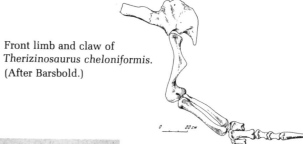

Front limb and claw of
Therizinosaurus cheloniformis.
(After Barsbold.)

Skeleton of *Thescelosaurus neglectus.*
Courtesy of the Smithsonian
Institution.

Caudal vertebra and phalanx of
Thespesius occidentalis. (After
Lull-Wright.)

Immature vertebral centrum of
Tichosteus lucasanus. (After
Osborn and Mook.)

Model of the ornithopod *Thescelosaurus* by
Charles Whitney Gilmore. Courtesy of the
Smithsonian Institution.

Restoration of the duck-billed dinosaur *Thespesius* by Charles R. Knight.

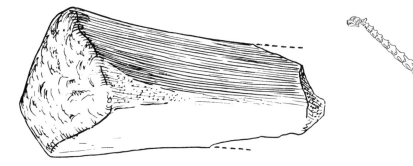

Incomplete left radius of *Titanosaurus indicus*. (After Huene.)

Reconstructed skeleton of *Tienshanosaurus chitaiensis* based on a general outline from the reconstruction of *Camarasaurus*. (After Young.)

Restoration of the sauropod *Titanosaurus* by G. Biese under the direction of Huene.

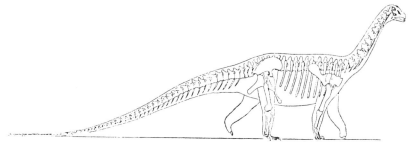

Outlined skeleton of *Titanosaurus australis.*
(After Huene.)

Femur of *Titanosaurus falloti.*
(After Hoffet.)

not a dinosaur at all. Another specimen of *Tichosteus* was discovered by Long in 1963.

Tiejiangosaurus   Dong, Li, Zhou and Chang, 1978—A misspelling of *Tuojiangosaurus.*

Tienshanosaurus   Young, 1937—*Saur., Sauro., Camar., Euhelo., L. Cret.* This dinosaur is known from an incomplete skeleton without the skull, found in Sinkiang, China. It is a relatively small sauropod.

Titanosaurus   Lydekker, 1877—*Saur., Sauro., Diplod., Titano., U. Cret.* Despite its name, *Titanosaurus* is actually a slender and relatively small sauropod. It is based on two vertebrae from the Lameta Formation of Jabalpur, India. *Titanosaurus* has also been reported from Argentina, Brazil, Uruguay, England, France, Spain, Laos and Niger, though there is no definite proof that any of the non-Indian material actually belongs to this genus. Armor plates originally described as *Loricosaurus* and *Lametasaurus* might actually belong to *Titanosaurus.*

Titanosaurus   Marsh, 1877—(See *Atlantosaurus.*)

Tomodon   Leidy, 1865—(See *Diplotomodon.*)

Tornieria   Sternfeld, 1911—*Saur., Sauro., Diplod., Titano., U. Jur.* (*Gigantosaurus* Fraas.) From the Tendaguru Formation of Tanzania and also Malawi, this genus is based on incomplete material, including a right tibia .74 meters (2 feet 6 inches) long, a right fibula, a partial right femur and a right pes. Some of the material referred to *Tornieria* might belong to some other genus and is reportedly quite large.

Anterior dorsal vertebra of
Tornieria robusta.

Torosaurus   Marsh, 1891—*Cer., Cerat., U. Cret.* The termination of one line of ceratopsian development is illustrated in *Torosaurus.* The genus has the longest skull of any terrestrial animal, measuring 2.6 me-

Fanciful early restoration of *Tornieria* compared in size with the "smaller" *Diplodocus* and a man.

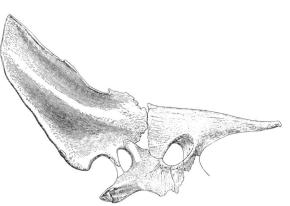

Incomplete skull of *Torosaurus utahensis.* (After Gilmore.)

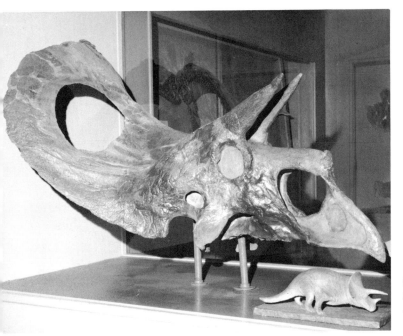

Skull and model of the giant ceratopsian dinosaur *Torosaurus latus.* Courtesy of the Academy of Natural Sciences.

Traditional depiction of *Trachodon* based on the general appearance of *Anatosaurus.* Copyright © 1964 by Sinclair Oil Corporation.

Some of the last dinosaurs to become extinct. The armored
Euoplocephalus stands at the left while in front of it is the
theropod *Albertosaurus*. In the background are the horned
dinosaur *Triceratops*, the duck-billed *Anatosaurus* and a
larger theropod *Tyrannosaurus*. Dominating the scene at the
right is the huge ceratopsian *Torosaurus* and in the far
upper right is spike-frilled *Styracosaurus*. Also in the scene
are various pterosaurs and small mammals. By Neave Parker.
Courtesy of the *Illustrated London News*.

Models of *Apatosaurus*, then
possibly a new sauropod,
Torvosaurus and
Allosaurus, sculpted by
J.A. Jensen. Courtesy of J.A. Jensen and the
Earth Sciences Museum, Brigham Young Uni-
versity.

James A. Jensen compares the
humerus of *Torvosaurus
tanneri* with the smaller
humerus of *Allosaurus*.
Courtesy of J. A. Jensen and the
Earth Sciences Museum,
Brigham Young University.

ters (nearly 9 feet) long including the enormous shield. Like *Triceratops*, *Torosaurus* has three horns, two long horns above the orbits and one small horn over the snout. But, unlike *Triceratops*, the frill of *Torosaurus* has fontanelles. *Torosaurus* is known from the Lance Formation of Wyoming, the Hell Creek Formation of South Dakota, the Tornillo Formation of Texas and the North Horn Formation of Utah.

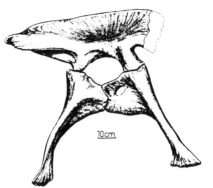

Right pelvic girdle of *Torosaurus tanneri*. (After Galton and Jensen.)

Torvosaurus Galton and Jensen, 1979—*Ther., Megal., U. Jur.* Based on the left and right long bones of the forelimb found in the Upper or Brushy Basin Member of the Morrison Formation of western Colorado, *Torvosaurus* is the largest theropod known from the Morrison. The referred skull is short with jaws resembling those of *Poekilopleuron*. The forelimbs are short with the referred phalanges relatively massive. Both forelimb and the referred pelvic girdle of this genus make *Torvosaurus* more similar to the European megalosaurids than to the American allosaurids.

Trachodon Leidy, 1865—*Orn., Hadro., ?Lambeo., U. Cret.* This genus is based on a single mandibular tooth discovered in the Judith River Formation of Montana. A popular misconception is that *Trachodon* is synonymous with *Anatosaurus*. Actually the Judith River specimen is too early to be *Anatosaurus* and seems likely to be from a crested hadrosaur.

Triaenopus E. Hitchcock, 1845—*U. Trias.* From Connecticut, these fossil tracks may have been made by a small theropod.

Triceratops Marsh, 1889—*Cer., Cerat., U. Cret.* (*Diceratops, Sterrholophus*; possibly *Agathaumas, Claorhynchus, Polyonax*.) *Triceratops* is the largest of the ceratopsians. The largest known individual may have measured 9 meters (30 feet) in length and weighed approximately 10.5 metric tons (12 tons). The skull alone measures over 2 meters (7 feet) long, with a short, solid frill and three horns. One short horn surmounts the snout while two long horns appear above the orbits. The edge of the frill was probably armed with a series of bony nodes. *Triceratops* is a fierce-looking animal, well fortified in defending itself against the giant Cretaceous predators and against other *Triceratops*. Skulls often show puncture wounds and one specimen reveals that a brow horn had broken and later healed. *Triceratops*, along with *Torosaurus*, culminates the evolution of the Ceratopsia and was one of the last dinosaurs to suffer extinction. The dinosaur was discovered in the Lance Formation of Converse County, Wyoming. It is also known in the Dakotas, Montana, Saskatchewan and Alberta. In 1887 a pair of horn cores, now

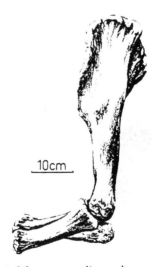

Left humerus, radius and ulna of *Torvosaurus tanneri*. (After Galton and Jensen.)

Skull of *Triceratops hatcheri.*
(After Marsh.)

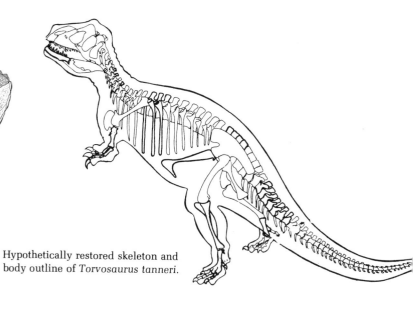

Hypothetically restored skeleton and
body outline of *Torvosaurus tanneri.*

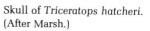

Tooth of *Trachodon
mirabilis.* (After Lull-
Wright.)

Skeleton of *Triceratops prorsus.* Courtesy of
the Smithsonian Institution.

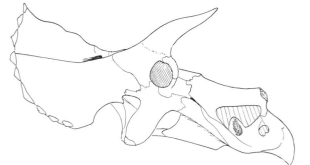

Skull of *Triceratops serratus.*
(After Huene.)

Skull of *Triceratops calicornis.* Courtesy of the Field Museum of Natural History.

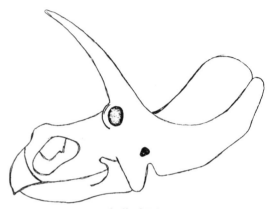

Skull of *Triceratops eurycephalus.* (After Steel.)

Nasal horn core of *Triceratops galeus.* (After Steel.)

Skull of *Triceratops flabellatus.* (After Marsh.)

known to be *Triceratops,* was found at Green Mountain Creek and described by Marsh as belonging to an artiodactyl *Bison alticornis.* Brown had reportedly seen over five hundred *Triceratops* skulls, most of them incomplete, during seven years in the field, making this animal one of the most commonly known of dinosaurs.

Trichristolophus Ellenberger, 1972—*U. Trias.* These ichnites from Lesotho are said to be those of an anchisaurid.

Tridentipes E. Hitchcock, 1858—(See *Steropoides.*)

Trihamus E. Hitchcock, 1865—*L. Jur.* These fossil tracks from Massachusetts and Connecticut may have been made by a small theropod.

Trimucrodon Thulborn, 1973—*Orn., Fabro., U. Jur.* This dinosaur is known only from three teeth from Porto Pinheiro, Portugal. The animal appears to be closely related to *Echinodon.*

Trisaurodactylus Ellenberger, 1974—*U. Trias. or L. Jur.* The term has been given to very birdlike dinosaur tracks found only in the Upper Stormberg sediments of Matsepe, in Lesotho.

Trisauropodiscus Ellenberger, 1970—From the Lower Stormberg Series of Thejane and Maphutseng, in Lesotho, these ichnites may have been made by a small theropod.

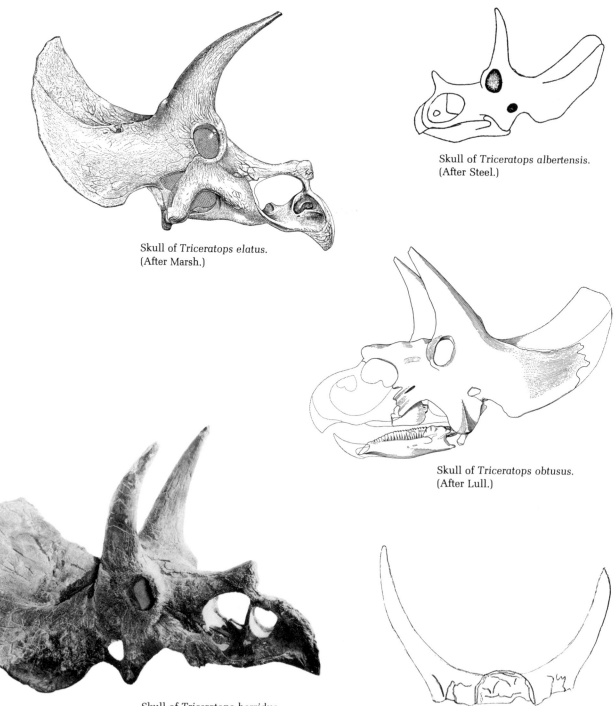

Skull of *Triceratops elatus*.
(After Marsh.)

Skull of *Triceratops albertensis*.
(After Steel.)

Skull of *Triceratops obtusus*.
(After Lull.)

Skull of *Triceratops horridus*.
Courtesy of the Museum of Geology,
South Dakota School of Mines and
Technology.

Orbital horn cores of *Triceratops
alticornis* originally believed to have
been those of a bison. (After Steel.)

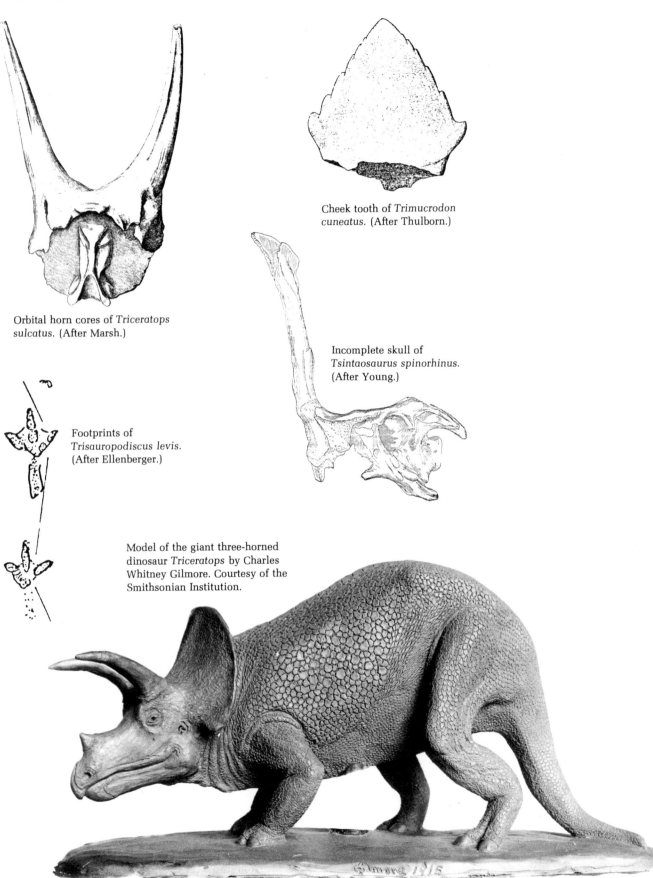

Orbital horn cores of *Triceratops
sulcatus*. (After Marsh.)

Cheek tooth of *Trimucrodon
cuneatus*. (After Thulborn.)

Incomplete skull of
Tsintaosaurus spinorhinus.
(After Young.)

Footprints of
Trisauropodiscus levis.
(After Ellenberger.)

Model of the giant three-horned
dinosaur *Triceratops* by Charles
Whitney Gilmore. Courtesy of the
Smithsonian Institution.

Footprints of
Tritotrisauropus medius.
(After Ellenberger.)

Tritotrisauropus   Ellenberger, 1970—*U. Trias.* These fossil footprints from the Lower Stormberg Series of Maphutseng, in Lesotho, may have been made by a saurischian dinosaur.

Troödon   Leidy, 1856—*Ther., Troödon., U. Cret.* This genus is based on fossil teeth from the Judith River Formation of Alberta, Canada. Generally the teeth resemble those of *Saurornithoides.* The jaw from Montana, referred to this genus by Russell, is probably *Stenonychosaurus.* Discoveries of eggs, nests and juvenile skeletons of Troödon by John R. Horner, however, indicate that this genus might actually be the first known carnivorous ornithischian.

"Troödon"   Gilmore, 1924—(See *Stegoceras.*)

Tsintaosaurus   Young, 1958—*Orn., Hadro., Lambeo., U. Cret.* From Shandong, China, this large duck-billed dinosaur has a solid crest in the shape of a vertical blade above the orbits. The crest is formed by an extension of the nasal bones. Some Russian scientists believe *Tsintaosaurus* to be congeneric with *Tanius.*

Tueojiangosaurus   Dong, Li, Zhou and Chang, 1977—A misspelling of *Tuojiangosaurus.*

Tugulusaurus   Dong, 1973—*Ther., Ornith., L. Cret.* This dinosaur may be an ancestral ornithomimid. It is known from a femur and other limb bones discovered in Sinkiang, China.

Tuojiangosaurus   Dong, Li, Zhou and Chang, 1977—*Steg., Stego., U. Jur.* Discovered in 1974 near the Fushi River, on the outskirts of Tzekung in southeast Sichuan, China, *Tuojiangosaurus* is the first plated dinosaur known in Asia from a complete skeleton. In general appearance, the animal resembles *Stegosaurus,* but with smaller plates, fifteen pairs of them, running in two rows along the back and tail, and with two pairs of sharp spikes on the tail. The skull is small, narrow, pointed in front and with small teeth having low crowns. The animal measures 7 meters (23.5 feet) in length and is 2.5 meters (8.4 feet) high. *Tuojiangosaurus* is said to have fed on tender branches and leaves and lived among lush vegetation near a lake on the high land.

Tuojiongosaurus   Dong, Li, Zhou and Chang, 1977—A misspelling of *Tuojiangosaurus.*

Tylocephale   Maryánska and Osmólska, 1974—*Pach., Pachy., U. Cret. Tylocephale* is based on an incomplete, high-domed skull from the Barun Goyot Formation of Mongolia. The dinosaur rather resembles

Restoration of the hadrosaur *Tsintaosaurus* by C. C. Flerow.

Skeleton of the Chinese stegosaur *Tuojiangosaurus multispinus*.

Skeleton of the giant theropod *Tyrannosaurus rex*. Courtesy of the American Museum of Natural History.

Restoration of the plated dinosaur *Tuojiangosaurus* prepared for this book by Richard Hescox.

Stegoceras. In life *Tylocephale* was probably not much over .9 meters (1 yard) in length.

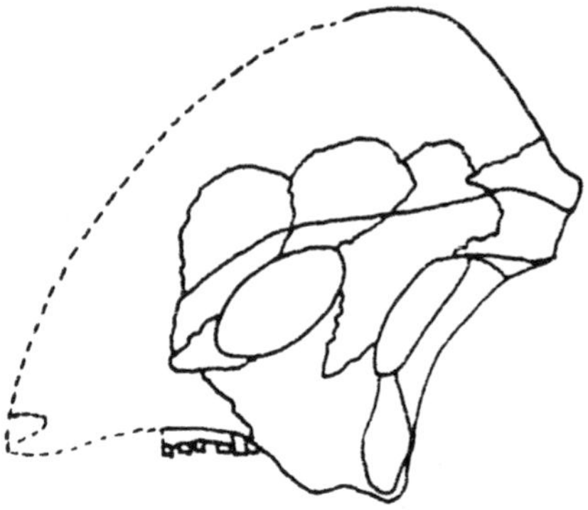

Partial skull of *Tylocephale gilmorei*. (After Maryańska and Osmólska.)

Tylosteus Leidy, 1872—(See *Pachycephalosaurus*.)

Tyrannosauropus Haubold, 1971—*U. Cret.* From the Mesaverde Group of Utah and Colorado, these giant ichnites were made by a very large theropod. The tracks are almost 80 centimeters (30 inches) long.

Tyrannosaurus Osborn, 1905—*Ther., Tyrann., U. Cret. (Dynamosaurus, Manospondylus.)* One of the most highly evolved of all known theropods, this "tyrant lizard" was one of the most powerful carnivores ever to walk this planet. Also one of the largest theropods, this dinosaur stands some 5.3 meters (18 feet) tall and is approximately 11.75 meters (40 feet) long, with a newly discovered specimen even larger. The head is gigantic, with daggerlike teeth measuring 7.8 to over 15.5 centimeters (3 to over 6 inches) in length. The forelimbs are small, almost useless appendages, each equipped with two claws. (Although a manus of *Tyrannosaurus* has never been found, all other tyrannosaurids found with well-preserved hand bones have indicated only two claws.) New-

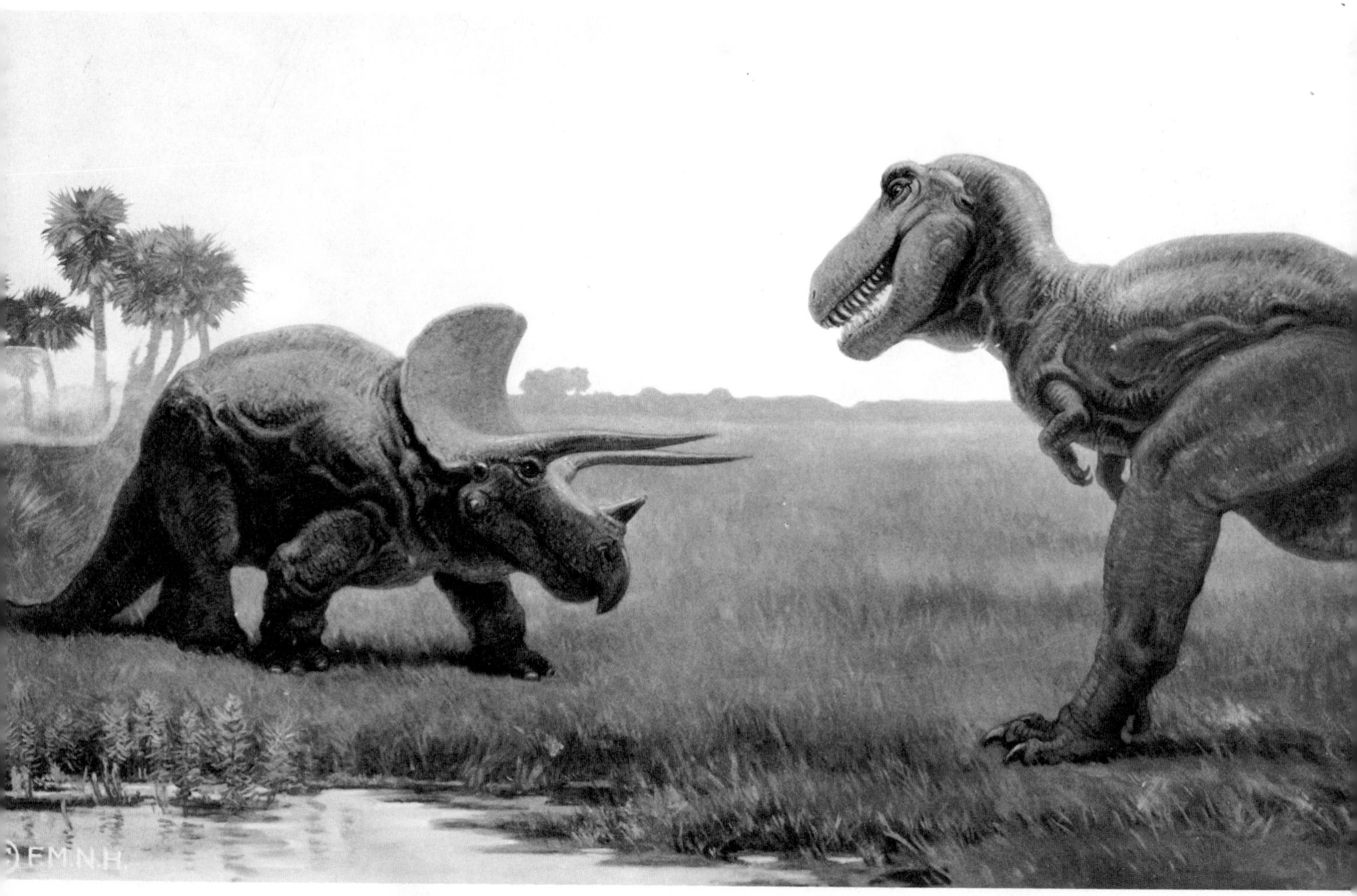

The classic dinosaur confrontation of the Cretaceous period, the carnivorous *Tyrannosaurus* versus the three-horned herbivore *Triceratops*. From a mural by Charles R. Knight. Courtesy of the Field Museum of Natural History.

man has suggested that these tiny forelimbs were utilized in helping the animal rise off the ground to stand up after its repose and that such animals walked with their bodies horizontal to the ground, their head and tail counterbalancing one another. Some paleontologists have proposed that giant predators like *Tyrannosaurus* were slow-moving scavengers; but the creature was probably an active and sometimes swift hunter, using its massive jaws and deadly taloned hind feet to kill the larger, stockier herbivores. *Tyrannosaurus* was discovered in the Hell Creek beds of Dawson County, Montana, and is also known from Wyoming, Texas, possibly North and South Dakota, and Alberta and Saskatchewan, Canada. It has also been reported from poor, probably indeterminate material, from Shandong, China.

U

Uintasaurus Holland, 1924—(See *Camarasaurus*.)

Incomplete fibula of *Velocipes* gürichi. (After Huene.)

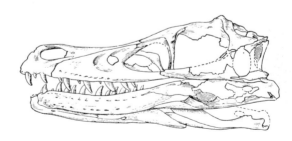

Skull of *Velociraptor mongoliensis*. (After Osborn.)

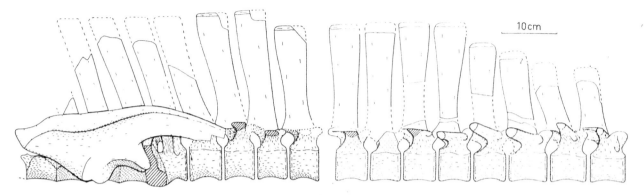

Vertebrae, sacrum and right ilium of
Vectisaurus valdensis. (After Galton.)

V

Valdosaurus   Galton, 1977—*Orn., Hypsil., L. Cret.* Formerly called
Dryosaurus canaliculatus, this hypsilophodont, from the Wealdon of
southern England, is based on a femur.

Vectisaurus   Hulke, 1879—*Orn., Iguan., L. Cret.* From the Isle of
Wight, England, this dinosaur is known from incomplete material including six large vertebrae with moderately long spines, a partial right
ilium, plus other specimens. A skull fragment not unlike *Stegoceras*
might apply to *Vectisaurus.*

Velocipes   Huene, 1932—*?Ther., ?Family, U. Trias.* Based on an indeterminate fibula, this genus is known from Slasks, Germany.

Velociraptor   Osborn, 1924—*Ther., Coel., U. Cret. (Ovoraptor.)* Discovered in the Djatochta Formation of Bain Dzak in Outer Mongolia,
this dinosaur was apparently a hunter of small herbivores. *Velociraptor*
was small, agile and swift. The limbs are slender and the fingers long.
The head is long, measuring 15.5 centimeters (6 inches), with teeth running to the back of the mouth. The eyes are large. The presence of a
collarbone is a quite avian characteristic of this animal. *Velociraptor* is
also known from Toogreeg; it has also been reported from Kazakhstan
and Shanxi, based on indeterminate specimens. A specimen of *Velociraptor,* clutching a *Protoceratops* skull, was found during the 1971
Polish-Mongolian Paleontological Expedition.

Restoration of *Vectisaurus* prepared for this book by George Olshevsky and Ken Steacy.

Restoration of the probable appearance of *Volkeimerie* by Mark Hallett.

Skeleton of *Velociraptor mongoliensis* (right) found in association with that of *Protoceratops andrewsi* (left) during the 1971 Polish-Mongolian Paleontological Expedition. Courtesy of the Institute of Paleobiology in Warsaw.

Restoration of *Velociraptor* prepared for this book by George Olshevsky and Ken Steacy.

Velociraptor mongoliensis

Viminicaudus   Huene, 1958—(Error; see *Pinacosaurus*.)

Vulcanodon   Raath, 1972—*Saur., ?Prosaur., ?Melan., U. Trias.* or *L. Jur.* Based on incomplete material, including limb bones, pelvic elements and caudal vertebrae from Rhodesia, this large quadrupedal genus may be a prosauropod with a length of more than 7 meters (25 feet). *Vulcanodon* might also be a sauropod. According to Raath, associated teeth suggest that the dinosaur was carnivorous, though some paleontologists believe that these teeth belong to a different animal.

Caudal vertebra of
Walgettosuchus woodwardi.
(After Huene.)

W

Frontal regions of the skull
of *Yaverlandia bitholus.*
(After Galton.)

Walgettosuchus   Huene, 1932—*Ther., ?Family, L. Cret.* This dinosaur is known only from a caudal vertebra found in New South Wales. The specimen is unlike that of other theropods, the centrum being flattened dorsoventrally and with a very long and probably high neural spine.

Walteria   Mehl, 1931—*U. Cret.* These fossil footprints from the early Upper Cretaceous of Colorado were made by a quadrupedal dinosaur, possibly an ankylosaur.

Wannanosaurus   Hou, Chao and Chu, 1977—*Pach., Pachy., U. Cret.* From China, this very small pachycephalosaur is known from a skull with jaws, a femur, a tibia, a rib head and other elements. The femur is approximately 8 centimeters (3.1 inches) long and the tibia is about 8.8 centimeters (3.75 inches). The entire length of the animal may have been less than 1 meter (39.37 inches).

Wealdenichnites   Kuhn, 1958—*L. Cret.* These ichnites, found in Germany, were almost certainly made by *Iguanodon*.

Wildeichnus   Casamiquela, 1964—*M. Jur.* The term has been given to dinosaur tracks, probably made by a theropod, found in Santa Cruz, Argentina. *Wildeichnus* has been placed in the footprint family Anchisauripodidae.

Wuerhosaurus   Dong, 1973—*Steg., Stego., L. Cret.* The only definite Cretaceous stegosaur, *Wuerhosaurus* was discovered in the Tugulo Series of Sinkiang, China. It is known from various parts of the skeleton, but with no skull material. The plates are apparently low. The spines of the vertebrae are longer than in any other stegosaur. The anterior processes of the ilium are long and spread wide laterally.

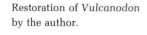

Restoration of *Vulcanodon*
by the author.

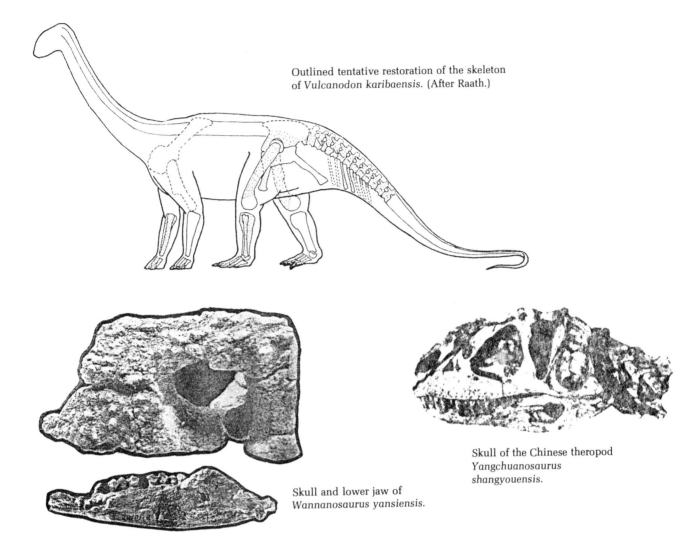

Outlined tentative restoration of the skeleton of *Vulcanodon karibaensis*. (After Raath.)

Skull and lower jaw of *Wannanosaurus yansiensis*.

Skull of the Chinese theropod *Yangchuanosaurus shangyouensis*.

Restoration of *Wuerhosaurus* prepared for this book by George Olshevsky and Ken Steacy.

Hypothetical restoration of *Zanclodon* from *The Book of Prehistoric Animals* (1935), by Raymond L. Ditmars. Courtesy of Charles Scribner's Sons.

Restoration of *Yangchuanosaurus* by the author.

Restoration of *Yaverlandia* by the author.

Y

Yaleosaurus Huene, 1932—(See *Anchisaurus*.)

Yangchuanosaurus Dong, Li, Zhou and Chang, 1978—*Ther., Megal., U. Jur.* This dinosaur is based on a nearly complete and articulated skeleton found in the Szechuan Province of China. The skeleton seems to be of the general proportions of *Allosaurus*. The skull is similar to that of *Allosaurus*, but with more premaxillary teeth but fewer dentary and maxillary teeth. In *Yangchuanosaurus* there are 4 premaxillary teeth, 14 to 15 dentary teeth and 14 to 15 maxillary teeth. There are 10 cervical vertebrae, 13 dorsals and 5 sacrals.

Yangtzepus Young, 1960—*U. Jur.* These dinosaurian ichnites were discovered in Sichuan, China. They might be ornithischian in origin.

Yaverlandia Galton, 1971—*Pach., Pachy., L. Cret.* (Possibly *Stenopelix*.) The earliest known pachycephalosaur, *Yaverlandia* is based on the frontal part of a skull from the Isle of Wight, England. In this form the dome is hardly developed at all, the frontals being merely slightly thickened.

Yaxartosaurus Young, 1958—A misspelling of *Jaxartosaurus*.

Yünnanosaurus Young, 1942—*Saur., Prosaur., Anchi., U. Trias.* (Probably *Lufengosaurus*.) Known from an almost complete skeleton from the Lower Lufeng Series of Yünnan Province, China, this dinosaur is similar to *Lufengosaurus* and is probably a juvenile of that genus.

Z

Zanclodon Plieninger, 1846—*?Ther., ?Terat., M. Trias.* (*Smilodon*.) Based on a jaw fragment with teeth, which are smooth with the edges serrated or whole, *Zanclodon* is known from Gaildorf, Germany. The type specimen may very well be a thecodont, and most other material referred to this genus is nondinosaurian. For a long time thought to be referable to the lizard-like *Tanystrophaeus*, recent work has shown that *Zanclodon* is in fact an archosaur.

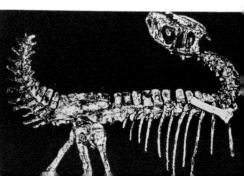

Skeleton of *Yangchuanosaurus shangyouensis*.

Zapsalis Cope, 1876—(See *Paronychodon*.)

Zatomus Cope, 1871—?*Ther., ?Family, U. Trias.* From the Dan River—Deep Rover Coal of Chatham County, North Carolina, this genus is known only from a sharp, serrated tooth. Though possibly a theropod, it has also been referred to the prosauropods and might actually be a thecodont.

Zigongosaurus Hou, Chao and Chu, 1976—*Saur., Sauro., Camar., Brachio., U. Jur.* This large brachiosaur is known from limb bones, vertebrae, teeth and other elements, found near the Fushi River, on the outskirts of Tzekung in southeast Sichuan, China.

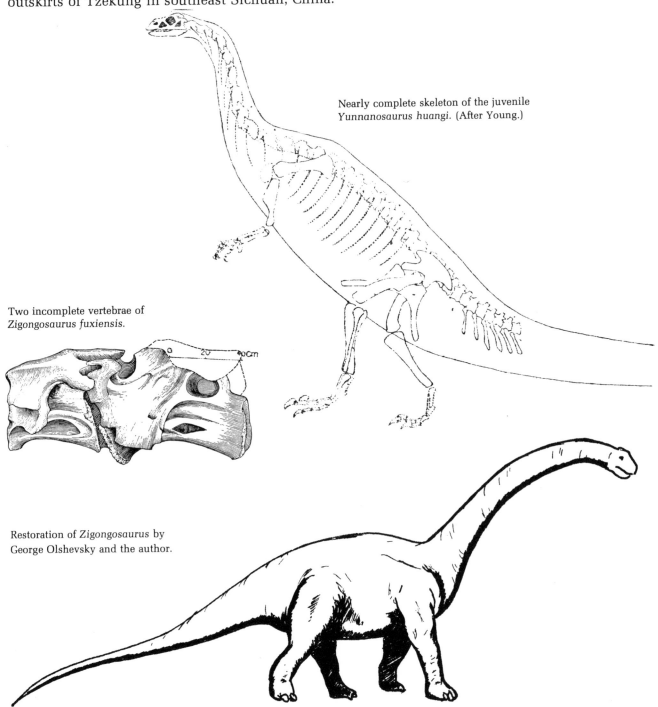

Nearly complete skeleton of the juvenile *Yunnanosaurus huangi*. (After Young.)

Two incomplete vertebrae of *Zigongosaurus fuxiensis*.

Restoration of *Zigongosaurus* by George Olshevsky and the author.

Brachiosaurus (left) compared with the larger
"Ultrasaurus" (right). Restoration by Harry Pincus. Copyright © 1979 by Harry Pincus.

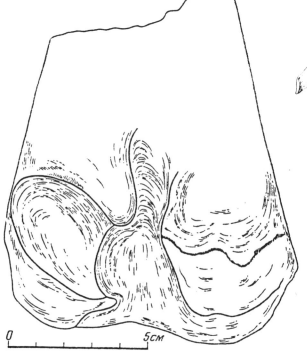

Distal end of a femur found
in association with the type
specimen of *Arstanosaurus
akkurganensis.* (After Suslov.)

Skull of *Garudimimus
brevipes.* (After Barsbold.)
(See Addendum III.)

Erlikosaurus as restored by George Olshevsky and the author.

ADDENDA

ADDENDUM I

The following is a compilation of dinosaur genera which arrived too late for inclusion in the main list of this book:

Abalonia   Romer, 1966—A misspelling of *Avalonia*.

Aeposaurus   Romer, 1966—A misspelling of *Aepisaurus*.

Aepysaurus   Gervais, 1859—A misspelling of Aepisaurus.

Breviparopus   Dutuit and Ouazzou, 1980—*L. Cret.* These sauropod footprints were discovered in Taghbalout, Morocco. They indicate an enormous and exceedingly long animal.

Callovosaurus   Galton, 1980—*Orn., Iguan., M. Jur.* The genus is based on a femur from the Lower Oxford Clay of England, originally the type specimen of *Camptosaurus leedsi*. The femur is more slender than that of *Camptosaurus*. Based on the femur's shape, Galton places *Callovosaurus* as intermediate between *Dryosaurus* and *Camptosaurus* and advocates that *Callovosaurus* and *Camptosaurus* be given their own family Camptosauridae.

265

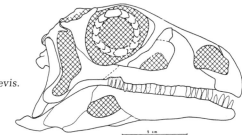

Skull of *Coloradia brevis.* (After Bonaparte.)

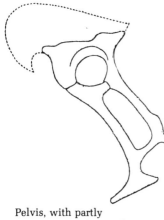

Pelvis, with partly reconstructed ilium, of "segnosaurian indet." (After Barsbold and Perle.)

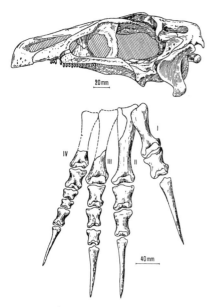

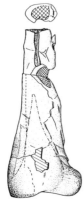

Slightly reconstructed skull and right pes of *Erlikosaurus andrewsi*. (After Barsbold and Perle.)

Distal portion of the tibia of *Kakuru kujani*. (After Molnar.)

Chinshakiangosaurus Yeh, 1975—*Saur., Sauro.* Not yet described, but mentioned in *Mesozoic Redbirds of Yunnan* (1975).

Coloradia Bonaparte, 1978—*Saur., Prosaur., Plate., U. Trias.* This plateosaurid, known from a skull and jaws found in the Los Colorados Formation of La Rioja, Argentina, is related to *Plateosaurus* and *Lufengosaurus* but has a shorter snout. The preorbital opening of the skull is partially below the orbit. The nasals are short and the frontals are elongated. Since the name *Coloradia* is preoccupied, the genus will be renamed after the date of this writing.

Dracopelta Galton, 1980—*Ank., Nodo., U. Jur.* This genus is the first Upper Jurassic ankylosaur to be described from articulated bones. It is based on a partial rib cage, with thirteen dorsal vertebrae and five different types of dorsal armor, from Ribomar, Portugal. Two kinds of dorsal armor show a partial overlapping of adjacent plates.

Dravidosaurus Yadagiri and Ayyasami, 1979—*Steg., Stego., U. Cret.* What appears to be the first known Upper Cretaceous stegosaur, *Dravidosaurus* is based on plates, limb bones and vertebrae from the Kallamedu Formation, near Kallamedu, in the Tiruchirapalli district of India.

Erlikosaurus Perle, 1980—*Ther., ?Segno., U. Cret.* A medium-sized possible segnosaurid, this dinosaur is based on a skull with mandible, left humerus, right pes and disarticulate cervical vertebrae from the Baysheen Tsav suite of southeastern Mongolia. The skull has a moderately elongated snout with long nostrils. The premaxilla and anterior portion of the maxilla are toothless and were, in life, covered by a horny sheet. The pes is short with massive metatarsals. The pedal unguals are strongly laterally compressed and recurved. In the form of the mandible and the character of dentition, *Erlikosaurus* resembles the larger *Segnosaurus*, but the former has a greater number of mandibular teeth and also differs in the longer length of the mandible's edentulous portion and in the pedal unguals' lateral compression. The genus is only tentatively assigned to the Segnosauridae because the pelvis is not known.

Gravitholus Wall and Galton, 1979—*Pach., Pachy., U. Cret.* From the Oldman Formation, near Jenner Ferry, of Alberta, this genus is based on an enlarged and extremely wide dome with a relatively small endocranial cavity.

Hadrosaurichnus Alonso, 1980—Dinosaur footprints. No other information is presently available.

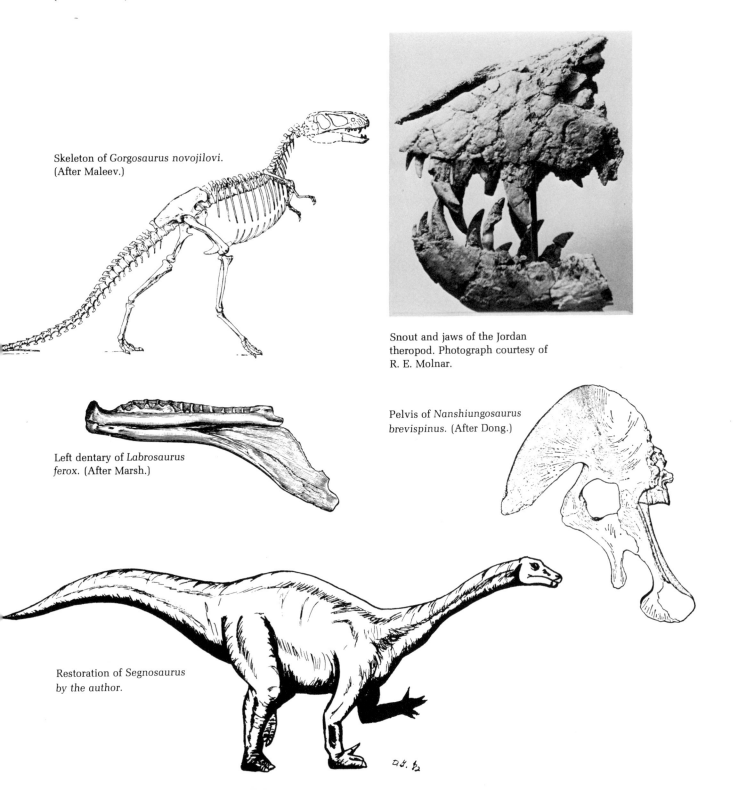

Dentary referred to *Chirostenotes pergracilis*.
(After Gilmore.)

Skeleton of *Gorgosaurus novojilovi*.
(After Maleev.)

Snout and jaws of the Jordan
theropod. Photograph courtesy of
R. E. Molnar.

Left dentary of *Labrosaurus
ferox*. (After Marsh.)

Pelvis of *Nanshiungosaurus
brevispinus*. (After Dong.)

Restoration of *Segnosaurus*
by the author.

Restoration of Micropachycephalosaurus by the author.

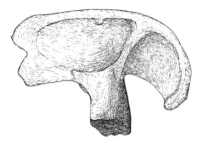

Ilium of ?Apatosaurus
alenquerensis. (After
Lapparent and Zbyszewski.)

Ventral armor of Minmi
paravertebra. Courtesy of Ralph
Molnar.

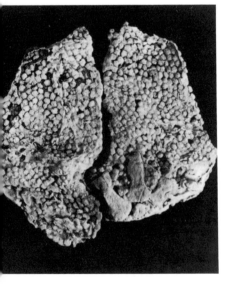

Kakuru   Molnar and Pledge, 1980—*Ther., Coel., U. Cret.* This genus is based on a tibia found in southern Australia. Except for *Acrocantho-saurus*, the medial malleolus of *Kakuru* is more strongly developed than in any other known theropod. Distally the tibia differs from that of other known theropods but resembles in form that of *Calamosaurus* and *Coelurus*, and in proportion that of *Ornitholestes* and *Microvenator*. The knee joint is medially expanded. Referred to *Kakuru* is a pedal phalanx. *Kakuru* is a relatively small theropod, probably attaining a length of some 3 meters (over 10 feet).

Maiasaura   Horner and Makela, 1979—*Orn., Hadro., Hadrosaur., U. Cret.* Discovered in the Two Medicine Formation of Teton County, Montana, this genus is based on an adult skull more than .8 meters (2 feet 9 inches) long, with a long bony knob over the snout, of a large hadrosaur. Referred to the same genus are the skeletons of fifteen infants, each one meter (almost 3 feet 4 inches) long, found in an oval, concave nest with eggshell. The infants seem to be approximately twice the size of a hatchling and one-tenth that of an adult. What is especially remarkable about the find is the implication that at least some kinds of dinosaurs were maternal.

Majungatholus   Sues and Taquet, 1979—*Pach., Pachy., U. Cret.* From the Majunga District of northwestern Madagascar, this dinosaur is known from a partial skull discovered in the early twentieth century, but only recently recognized as a pachycephalosaur. The specimen has a frontal dome and quite large upper temporal fenestrae which differentiate the genus from other dome-headed dinosaurs. Since pachycephalosaurs have previously been known only from the Northern Hemisphere, the presence of *Majungatholus* in Madagascar supports the theory of a land connection existing during the Cretaceous between Gonwanaland and Laurasia.

Microhadrosaurus   Dong, 1979—*Orn., Hadro., Hadrosaur., U. Cret.* Based upon an incomplete dentary lacking teeth, from Nanshiung on the south China coast, *Microhadrosaurus* is a small hadrosaur, but probably no smaller than *Secernosaurus*, and may be a juvenile.

Micropachycephale   Dong, 1979—A misspelling of *Micropachy-cephalosaurus*.

Micropachycephalosaurus   Dong, 1978—*Pach., Pachy., U. Cret.* A small pachycephalosaur, this genus is based on a sacrum and ilium found in the Wang Formation, Laiyany, Shantung, China. To date, *Micropachycephalosaurus* has the longest generic name of any dinosaur.

Restoration of *Maiasaura* by
the author.

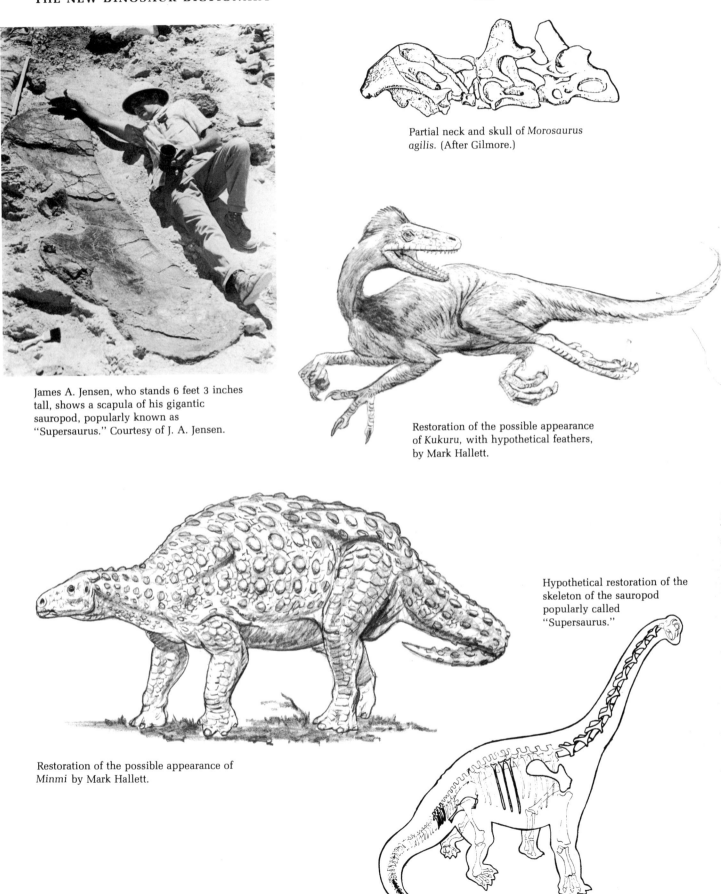

James A. Jensen, who stands 6 feet 3 inches tall, shows a scapula of his gigantic sauropod, popularly known as "Supersaurus." Courtesy of J. A. Jensen.

Partial neck and skull of *Morosaurus agilis.* (After Gilmore.)

Restoration of the possible appearance of *Kukuru*, with hypothetical feathers, by Mark Hallett.

Restoration of the possible appearance of *Minmi* by Mark Hallett.

Hypothetical restoration of the skeleton of the sauropod popularly called "Supersaurus."

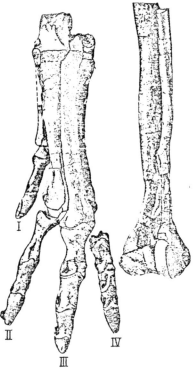

Outline of tooth and jaw fragment of the ornithopod described by Rao and Seschar in 1927.

Minmi Molnar, 1980—*Ank., ?Family, L. Cret.* From the Minmi Member of the Bungil Formation, north of Roma, southern Queensland, this armored genus is based on eleven dorsal vertebrae with bases of ribs, five incomplete ribs, three paravertebrae, one incomplete pes and ventral armor. Posterior processes are elongate and imply muscle attachment. The first two paravertebrae extend distally to the tips of the transverse processes, with the third extending well beyond the tip, possibly allowing for movement of armor and skin. The neural spines are low and more or less square. Metacarpals or metatarsals are short and robust. Ventral armor consists of small round ossicles though dorsal armor, if present, has not been preserved. In life this small ankylosaur probably measured 3 meters (approximately 10 feet) long or less. To date, *Minmi* has the shortest generic name of any dinosaur.

Mussaurus Bonaparte and Vince, 1979—*Saur., Prosaur., Mussauridae, U. Trias.* This genus, establishing the new family Mussauridae, is based upon the nearly complete, articulated skeleton with skull of a hatchling prosauropod, found in the upper section of the El Tranquillo Formation of northern Santa Cruz province, Argentina. The short and high skull has a very short snout and elongated frontals and parietals, with a short and high preorbital opening near the large orbit. The teeth are elongated and almost rounded. The cervical vertebrae are short and high as in the thecodont *Lagosuchus.*

Muttaburrasaurus Bartholomai and Molnar, 1981—*Orn., Iguan., L. Cret.* Based on a complete skeleton from the Mackunda Formation at the top of the Albian, this dinosaur has a bump-like rise between the snout and the orbits, and, like *Iguanodon,* spiked thumbs. A scapula discovered near Hughenden, in northern Queensland, may also be referred to *Muttaburrasaurus.* The dinosaur attained an approximate length of 7.4 meters (25 feet).

Nannosaurus Nopcsa, 1928—A misspelling of *Nanosaurus.*

Nanshiungosaurus Dong, 1979—*Saur., Sauro., ?Diplod., ?Titano., U. Cret.* This peculiar sauropod is based on a presacral column and pelvis found in Nanshiung, a province on the south China coast. The dinosaur is rather small for a sauropod. The entire vertebral column, if complete, probably measured approximately 10 meters (34 feet) or less. The pelvis is coossified with a parallel ischium and pubis, the former having a "pubic boot." The ilium has a very long preacetabular process and almost no postacetabular process.

Left forefoot and distal portion of left tibia and fibula of *Laosaurus minimus.*

I

II   IV

III

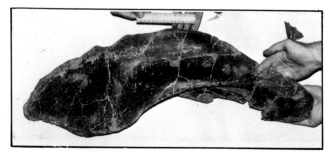

Ilium of a new stegosaur first mentioned as the "questionable ankylosaurid" from the Cleveland-Lloyd Dinosaur Quarry. Courtesy of R. A. Long.

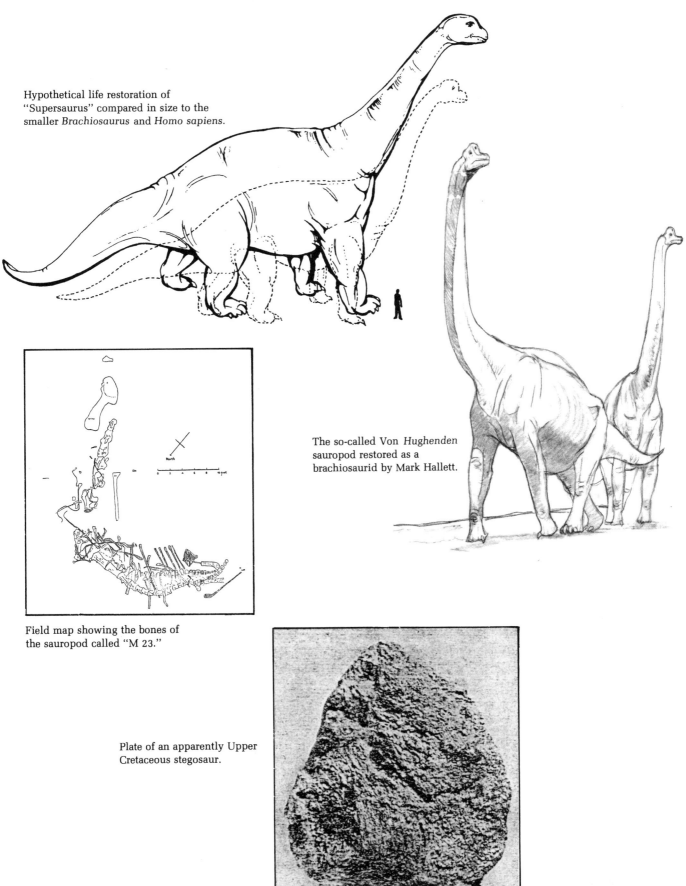

Hypothetical life restoration of
"Supersaurus" compared in size to the
smaller *Brachiosaurus* and *Homo sapiens*.

The so-called Von *Hughenden*
sauropod restored as a
brachiosaurid by Mark Hallett.

Field map showing the bones of
the sauropod called "M 23."

Plate of an apparently Upper
Cretaceous stegosaur.

Femur of the unnamed "Lightning Ridge hypsilophodont." Courtesy of Ralph Molnar.

Navahopus   Baird, 1980—*U. Jur.* The name has been given to a dinosaur trackway from the Upper Navajo Sandstone, Glen Canyon Group, two miles north of the Copper Mine Trading Post, on the Kaibito Plateau, Navajo Indian Reservation, Coconino County, Arizona. The footprints indicate a quadrupedal prosauropod similar to *Ammosaurus*. Impressions of the manus show a laterally pointing claw.

Ohmdenosaurus   Wild, 1978—*Saur., Sauro., ?Family, L. Jur.* This genus is based on a right tibia, calcaneum and astragalus found in Germany. The tibia was long believed to be the humerus of a plesiosaur.

Ornithoides   Osborn, 1924—(See *Saurornithoides.*)

Ovaloolithus   Zhao, 1979—Dinosaur eggs. No other information is presently available.

Paraspheroolithus   Zhao, 1979—Dinosaur eggs. No other information is presently available.

Patagosaurus   Bonaparte, 1979—*Saur., Sauro., Camar., Cetio., M. Jur.* Based on a nearly complete postcranial skeleton found in the Callovian-Oxford beds of Patagonia, this dinosaur is similar to and approximately the same size as *Cetiosauriscus leedsi. Patagosaurus* displays generic differences from *Cetiosaurus* in the shape of the neural spines of the caudal vertebrae and in the distal part of the ischium. The shape of the vertebrae indicate that the dinosaur is more advanced than *Amygdalodon* and more primitive than *Haplocanthosaurus*.

Phaceloolithus   Zeng and Zhang, 1979—Dinosaur eggs. No other information is presently available.

Piatnitzkysaurus   Bonaparte, 1979—*Ther., Megal., M. Jur.* From the Callovian-Oxford beds of Patagonia, this genus is based on an incomplete skeleton lacking evidence of the hand and foot. The animal is similar to *Allosaurus*, but with a more primitive pelvis, with a supposedly longer humerus, and with differences in the dorsal vertebrae.

Placoolithus   Zhao, 1979—Dinosaur eggs. No other information is presently available.

Poicilopleuron   Leidy, 1870—A misspelling of Poekilopleuron.

Scutellosaurus   Colbert, 1981—*Orn., Fabro., U. Trias.* This genus is based on incomplete postcranial material, plus a jaw, from the Kayenta Formation of northern Arizona. The tail is extremely long, about two and one-half times the length of the body. The entire animal is about

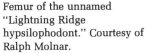

Horn cores referred to *Monoclonius recurvicornis.* (After Steel.)

Pelvis and right metatarsus of *Segnosaurus galbinensis.* (After Barsbold and Perle.)

200 mm

50 mm

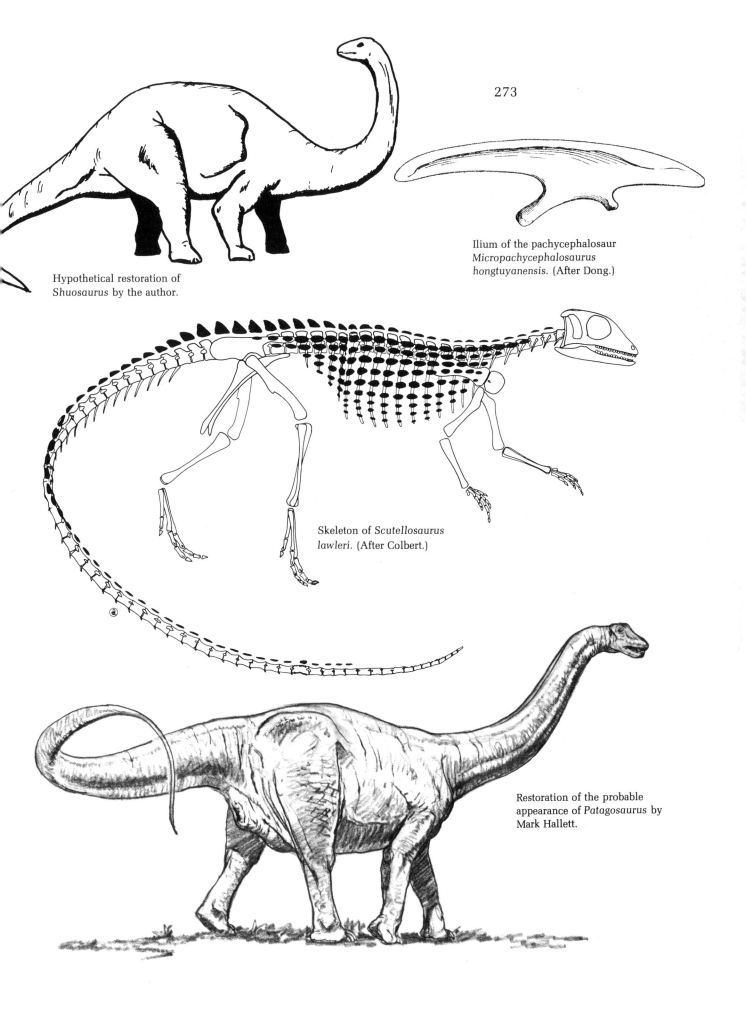

273

Hypothetical restoration of *Shuosaurus* by the author.

Ilium of the pachycephalosaur *Micropachycephalosaurus hongtuyanensis*. (After Dong.)

Skeleton of *Scutellosaurus lawleri*. (After Colbert.)

Restoration of the probable appearance of *Patagosaurus* by Mark Hallett.

1.175 meters (4 feet) long. Present is extensive bony armor plating. The animal is related to the African *Lesothosaurus* and provides the first good information on the evolution of North American ornithischians.

Segnosaurus Perle, 1979—*Ther., Segno., U. Cret.* This large and unusual theropod, based on an incomplete skeleton from the Baysheen-Tsav suite in Mongolia, establishes the new family Segnosauridae. The animal is approximately 1.8 meters (6 feet) high at the pelvis. The tibia and femur are each approximately 86 centimeters (33 inches) long. The feet are tetradactyl and the large forelimbs are more than half the length of the hindlimbs. The teeth of the lower jaw resemble those of a prosauropod like *Plateosaurus*. The pelvis is approximately 1.3 meters (nearly 4 and one half feet) wide at the front. The ilia are extremely deep and well separated from each other, and with very large, outward deflecting anterior wings. The pubis is oriented parallel to the ischium. This type of opisthopubic pelvis is similar to that in primitive ornithischians, somewhat relating to each other the two orders of dinosaurs.

Shuosaurus —*Saur., Sauro., L. Jur.* Not yet described, this primitive sauropod is similar to *Barapasaurus*. The name is mentioned in Chou's "Vertebrate Paleontology in China, 1949–1979," published in *Vertebrata PalAsiatica*, volume 17, number 4.

Sousaichnium Leonardi, 1976—*L. Cret.* These fossil footprints from Paraiba, Brazil were made by an ornithischian, possibly an iguanodont. The tracks are especially interesting in that ornithischian bones in the Cretaceous of South America are rare.

Spheroolithus Zhao, 1979—Dinosaur eggs. No other information is presently available.

Tanystrosuchus Kuhn, 1963—*?Ther., ?Podok., U. Trias.* This genus is based on a distal caudal vertebra from the Stubensandstein of Heslach, Germany. The specimen is 3.9 centimeters long, 2.1 centimeters wide and 1.2 centimeters high. Huene (1908) described the specimen as a lepidosaur, *Tanystropheus posthumus*. Peyer (1931) referred it to the dinosaur *Coelophysis*, Kuhn (1965) to the proterosaurids, and Steele (1970) to the dinosaur *Halticosaurus*. *Tanystrosuchus* may actually be a valid genus of dinosaur.

Unquillosaurus Powell, 1979—*Ther., U. Cret.* This "carnosaur" is known from the Los Blanquitos Formation of El Ceibal, Argentina.

Volkheimeria Bonaparte, 1979—*Saur., Sauro., Camar., Cetio., M. Jur.* This genus is based on an incomplete postcranial skeleton found in the

Unprepared skull, still in its plaster jacket, of the adult *Maiasaura peeblesorum*. The scale is 12 inches. Courtesy of J. R. Horner.

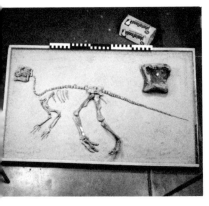

Composite skeleton of the juvenile *Maiasaura peeblesorum* compared with a third phalange of the adult. The scale is in centimeters. Courtesy of J. R. Horner.

Incomplete skull of *Yezosaurus mikasaensis.* (After Obata and Muramoto.)

Callovian-Oxford beds of Patagonia. The primitive sauropod has a *Cetiosaurus* type ischium, but with a distal thickening. The neural spines of the dorsal vertebrae are laterally compressed and the neural arches are quite low.

Yezosaurus   Obata and Muramoto, ?1977—*Ther., ?Tyrann., U. Cret.* From Japan, this genus is based on tooth-bearing portions of the upper and lower jaws. It may actually be a Cretaceous marine reptile.

Zephyrosaurus   Sues, 1980—*Orn., Hypsil., L. Cret.* This small hypsilophodont is known from parts of the skull and other bones from the Cloverly Formation of Montana. The skull structure differs enough from the superficially similar *Hypsilophodon* and *Dryosaurus* to indicate that *Zephyrosaurus* might represent its own line of hypsilophodont evolution. The small number of preserved bones provide information on this dinosaur's tooth replacement, the cranial nerve structure and the lymphatic system.

Partial right femur of *Astrodon pusillus.*

Jacques van Heerden has proposed that the name Palaeopoda be used in place of Prosauropoda, and that there are only three valid genera of the family Plateosauridae known in South Africa—*Aristosaurus, Euskelosaurus* and *Massospondylus,* with *E. africanus* and *Plateosauravus cullingworthi* referred to *E. browni,* and *Eucnemesaurus fortis, Gigantoscelus molengraaffi, Melanorosaurus readi, Orosaurus capensis* and *Plateosauravus stormbergensis* referred to the genus *Euskelosaurus,* and the teeth genera *Avalonianus sanfordi, Basutodon ferox* and *Picrodon herveyi* considered to be *nomina dubia.*

In addition, van Heerden will define a new family of possibly carnivorous forms similar to remains referred to *Sinosaurus* and *Riojasaurus.* A new dinosaur genus based on good postcranial material will be the type of the new family. The dinosaur has short, high cervical vertebrae, four sacrals, and shortened forelimbs.

ADDENDUM II

The following is a list of forms which have appeared in the paleontological literature and which, at the time of writing, are mostly in the very preliminary stages of research. Some of the following material is not supported by much in the way of substantial evidence. But it is possible that some of these forms may emerge as new dinosaur genera in the future:

Attempted reconstruction of the skull of *Zephyrosaurus schaffi.* (After Sues.)

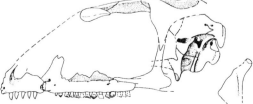

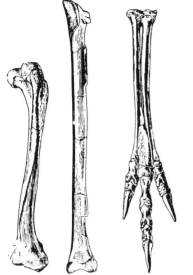

Hind limb and foot of
Avimimus portentosus. (After Kurzanov.)
(See Addendum III.)

Theropods:

From Australia, the so-called Cape Patterson allosaur.

The jaws referred by Gilmore to *Chirostenotes pergracilis.*

From the Fruita Paleontological Area, a tiny coelurosaur represented by at least four individuals known mostly by hind limb fragments. One individual has most of a humerus measuring about two-thirds the length of the femur; the humerus is 38 mm long and the femur approximately 56 mm. The very well-developed fourth trochanter of the femur might indicate that these individuals are neither hatchlings nor very young juveniles (G. Callison, personal communication).

The so-called Jordan theropod, described by Molnar in 1978, known from a fragmentary skull collected by Harley Garbani in 1966 from a dark gray clay of the Hell Creek Formation in Garfield County, Montana. The Upper Cretaceous form, still known too incompletely for naming, was originally thought to be a juvenile *Tyrannosaurus,* yet it is smaller than any known tyrannosaurid and the preserved part of the snout is longer relative to its height than in any other family tyrannosaurid. This moderate-size theropod may, in fact, be an exceptionally large dromaeosaur. The partial endocranial mold is similar to those of the tyrannosaurids and to *Ceratosaurus* and suggests well developed optic lobes and a relatively wide olfactory passage. It has been suggested that the Jordan theropod fed upon relatively small prey.

A possible dromaeosaurid, mentioned by Osmólska (1978), from the Nemegt Formation of Mongolia.

Lagosuchus and *Lagerpeton* (both Romer, 1971), which are classified as thecodonts and assigned to the family Lagosuchidae (Bonaparte, 1975) but which might actually be the most primitive known saurischian dinosaurs.

The Cretaceous "bird genera" of Harrison and Walker, including *Wyleyia* (1973), *Bradycneme* (1975) and *Heptasteornis* (1975). In a paper delivered at the 1978 meeting of the Society of Vertebrate Paleontology, Michael Brett-Surman reported that these genera are actually small dinosaurs, an opinion supported by Dr. Storrs Olson and Dr. R. T. Bakker, leading world authorities respectively on fossil birds and dinosaurs. Brett-Surman also reported a new theropod family from the Upper Cretaceous of Montana and Argentina making this the first theropod family from both Laurasia and Gondwanaland in the Cretaceous. The picture is complicated, however, by Harrison and Walker's plan to name an identical form as another bird order.

Teeth of *Pectinodon bakkeri.* (After Carpenter.) (See Addendum III.)

A completely preserved pelvic girdle and limb bones of a theropod from the Kallamedu Formation of the Upper Cretaceous sequence near Kallamedu, in the Tiruchirapalli district of India. Previously theropod dinosaurs from these beds were only represented by a single tooth and some bone fragments.

Two "carnosaurs," one of which includes a preserved brain cavity, from the Lower Jurassic Kota Formation near Yamanpalli, Andra Pradesh, India, excavated by Yadagiri in 1979.

What used to be called *Gorgosaurus novojilovi* (which some paleontologists believe to be a juvenile *Tarbosaurus bataar*), but which Maryańska (1979) believes to be a new genus.

The left dentary called *Labrosaurus ferox* Marsh, 1884, which some paleontologists believe to be a new genus, since it is quite early into the Jurassic to be *Allosaurus*, and because a notch in the specimen seems to indicate a possibly sabre-toothed theropod.

Tracks, originally called avian, which may all be dinosaurian: *Kouphichnium lithographicum* Oppel, 1862 (*Hypornithes jurassica* Jaekel, 1929, *Ornithichnites caudatus* Jaekel, 1929, *Ptorornis bavarica* Jaekel, 1929), from the Upper Jurassic, Solnhofen limestone, Bavaria, apparently left by a compsognathid (Baird believes these tracks may have been made by arthropods); *Ornithichnites palmatus* E. Hitchcock, 1836 (*Sauroidichnites palmatus* E. Hitchcock, 1836, *Palamopus anomalus* E. Hitchcock, 1848), Triassic, from Horse Race in Gill, Massachusetts.

The following Triassic ichnites, classified as avian, though they might be dinosaurian: *Deanea* Reichenbach, 1852, originally called *Ornithichnites fulicoides*, from Massachusetts; *Bellona* Reichenbach, 1852, originally called *Ornithichnites giganteus*, from Northampton, Massachusetts; and *Cybele* Reichenbach, 1852, originally called *Ornithichnites tuberosus*, from Northampton, Massachusetts.

From the Upper Cretaceous Bayan Shireh suite at Khara Khutul in southeastern Mongolia, a pelvic girdle lacking the upper portion of the ilia. The unnamed form has been referred to as "segnosaurian indet" and "dinosaur from Khara Khutul." Apparently the ilia were broadly separated from one another, their anterior wings deflecting outwards. The pelvis is segnosaurian but is smaller than that of *Segnosaurus* and has a narrower ischium and pubis.

A birdlike theropod from the Nemegt Formation, about to be described by Kurzanov.

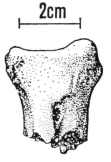

2cm

Indeterminate partial tarsometatarsus which may be a new genus of elmisaurid. (After Osmolska.) (See Addendum III.)

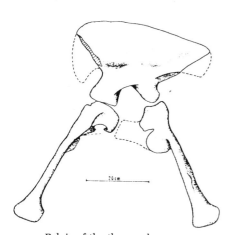

Pelvis of the theropod
Piatnitzkysaurus floresi. (After
Bonaparte.)

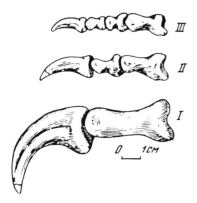

Manus bones of *Ingenia
yanshini.* (After Barsbold.)
(See Addendum III.)

Sauropodomorphs:

PROSAUROPODS:

The "Blikana dinosaur," mentioned by Charig, Attridge and Crompton in 1965.

SAUROPODS:

The popularly named "Supersaurus" from Colorado, discovered by
Jensen in 1972, with a single cervical vertebra 1.5 meters (5 feet) long
and a neck that could measure 14.5 meters (50 feet) in length.

Larger than "Supersaurus," the popularly called "Ultrasaurus," represented by a 9-foot long scapula discovered in southwestern Colorado
by Jensen.

A brachiosaur formerly called *Apatosaurus alenquerensis.*

A camarasaur from Colorado, mentioned by Jensen in 1972.

A brachiosaur formerly called *Morosaurus agilis.*

From the Cloverly Formation of Wyoming, an exceptionally long cervical centrum, which might refer to Pleurocoelus.

From Kweichow, China, an unusual dorsal vertebra with an antero-
posteriorly flattened neural spine, as opposed to the side-to-side flatten-
ing in other sauropods.

What Rozhdestvensky called a "sauropod from Fergan" in 1968.

Two sauropod skulls, generically different because of the position of
the frontals, parietals, supratemporal fossae and paraoccipitals, discovered by Yadagiri in 1979 in the Lower Jurassic Kota Formation near
Yamanpalli, Andra Pradesh, India.

From Australia, the so-called Winton sauropod, Hughenden sauropod
and Lightning Ridge sauropod.

The first sauropod known from the Kallamedu Formation of the Upper Cretaceous near Kallamedu, in the Tiruchirappalli district of India.

A sauropod about to be described by Kurzanov and Bannikov from the
Nemegt Formation of Mongolia.

The so-called "M 23" sauropod informally described in the British
Natural History (vol. 3, no. 19, 1931), discovered in Tendaguru, near
Kindope, and presumably Jurassic age. This East African dinosaur is
apparently like *Brachiosaurus* but with well-developed lateral "wings"
projecting off the dorsal neural spines. The ilium is described (though
not sketched) as like that of *Apatosaurus.* The anterior dorsal neural
spines are deeply forked like those of *Dicraeosaurus,* but different from
those of that genus. The dorsals are short, the cervicals long, the cervical
neural spines moderately well-developed and, unlike those of *Brachiosaurus,* moderately high. The femur is shorter than the scapula.

Hypothetical restoration of
Chaoyoungosaurus by the
author. (See Addendum III.)

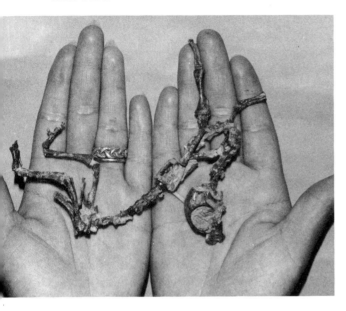

Skeleton of *Mussasaurus
patagonicus.* Courtesy of
J. F. Bonaparte.

"Family tree" of Mesozoic eggs
showing the families Megaloolithidae,
Faveoloolithidae, Spheroolithidae
(and the genera *Spheroolithus,
Ovaloolithus* and *Paraspheroolithus*)
and Elongaloolithidae. (After Zhao.)

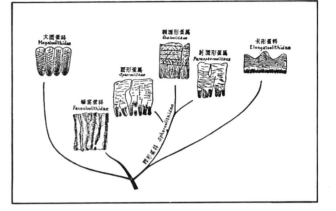

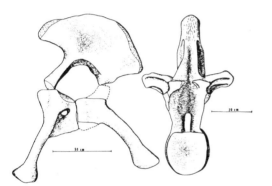

Pelvis and posterior dorsal
vertebra of the sauropod
Patagosaurus fariasi. (After
Bonaparte.)

Reconstruction of the
skull of
*Muttaburrasaurus
langdoni.* (After
Bartholomai and Molnar.)

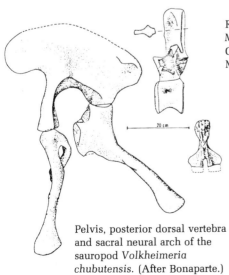

Pelvis, posterior dorsal vertebra
and sacral neural arch of the
sauropod *Volkheimeria
chubutensis.* (After Bonaparte.)

Restoration of
Muttaburrasaurus.
Courtesy of Ralph
Molnar.

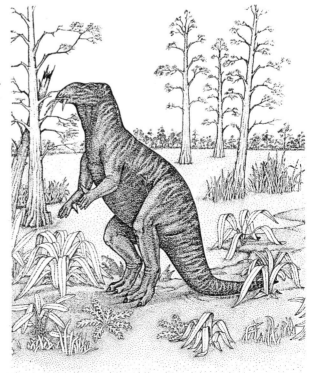

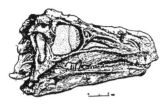

Skull of *Huayangosaurus taibaii.* (After Dong, Tang and Zhou.) (See Addendum III.)

ORNITHOPODS:

From Australia, the so-called Coober Pedy Ornithopod and Lightning Ridge hypsilophodont.

A fabrosaur from Nova Scotia being studied by Baird, mentioned in *Guidebook A59, 24th Int. Geol. Cong.* (1972) as "a turkey-sized herbivorous dinosaur similar to the South African *Fabrosaurus,* represented by a scrap of jaw. This is the only Triassic ornithischian found to date in North America."

A flat-headed hadrosaur from Baishin-Tsav, mentioned by Kurzanov in 1976.

A new genus of iguanodontid from the Lower Cretaceous of Mongolia, based on several nearly complete skeletons including a skull with an exceptionally large snout, and teeth that were originally described by Rozhdestzensky (1952) as *Iguanodon orientalis.*

An incomplete and poorly preserved hadrosaur from Chubut, Argentina, incorrectly described by Casamiquela as a Paleocene genus.

Numerous hypsilophodont-type dinosaurs from Uruguay, Switzerland and New South Wales.

An Upper Cretaceous, southern Indian ornithopod, possibly an iguanodont and apparently from Mysore State, described in 1927 by Rao and Seschar.

A new fabrosaurid from the Fruita Paleontological Area, known from a left maxilla fragment with a complete tooth, a mandible fragment, vertebrae and various limb fragments. The morphology of the tooth suggests that this dinosaur more closely resembles *Echinodon* than *Nanosaurus* (G. Callison, personal communication).

Thecodontosaurus gibbidens will be redescribed as probably ornithischian by Galton.

A lambeosaurine hadrosaur, known from a partial pelvis and hind limbs, from the Upper Cretaceous, Nemegt Formation, of Mongolia, to be described by Osmólska.

The mounted skeleton of a juvenile iguanodont or hadrosaur, exhibited in Japan during the late 1970s by the USSR, and labeled with the unofficial name "Gadolosaurus." The undescribed skeleton, which measures over one meter in height, was discovered in Mongolia. The skull has no crest and the ischium is slender and lacks a "foot." Possibly this is a new genus or a juvenile of an already-known hadrosaur such as *Tanius* or *Shantungosaurus.*

Stegosaurs:

Four dermal scutes resembling those of *Hylaeosaurus,* from the Kimmeridge Clay of Rodbourne, England.

Hypothetical restoration of *Honghesaurus* by the author based on an old restoration of *Iguanodon.* (See Addendum III.)

From the Portland beds at Swindon, England, a caudal spine bearing affinities to *Kentrosaurus*.

The so-called "questionable ankylosaurid" from the Cleveland-Lloyd Dinosaur Quarry, mentioned by Madsen in his August, 1976 paper on *Allosaurus fragilis*. The specimen is now believed to refer to a peculiar stegosaur with an ankylosaurlike ilium.

A stegosaur, discovered by Yadagiri in 1979, from the Lower Jurassic Kota Formation near Yamanpalli, Andra Pradesh, India.

The first stegosaur from the Kallamedu Formation of India, based on a humerus, phalange, three plates and later referred material including a sacrum, ilium, more plates, skull and isolated teeth, recorded in 1979 by Yadagiri and Ayyasami.

Hypothetical restoration of *Huayangosaurus* by the author. (See Addendum III.)

Ankylosaurs:

An incomplete skull, which Riabinin suggested was ceratopsian, resembling the skull of *Euoplocephalus*, discovered at the Sary Agach station of Kazakhstan, U.S.S.R.

Teeth, called *Stegosaurus madagascariensis* by Piveteau, discovered in Malagasy, Madagascar, which are too late into the Cretaceous to be *Stegosaurus*.

Ceratopsians:

From Coahuila, Mexico, fragments reported by Janensch, which could be *Monoclonius*, *Chasmosaurus* or a new genus.

Horn cores referred to *Monoclonius recurvicornis*, which are not *Monoclonius* and could be a new genus of dinosaur.

EXCLUSIONS

Hypothetical restoration of *Tenchisaurus* by the author. (See Addendum III.)

The following, all of which have appeared in the paleontological literature, are no longer classified as dinosaurs:

AACHENOSAURUS Smets, 1888—Petrified wood.

ANKISTRODON Huxley, 1865—(See *Epicampodon*.)

BATHYGNATHUS Leidy, 1854—A pelycosaur.

BRASILEOSAURUS Huene, 1931—A crocodilian.

CHIROTHERIUM Lull, ?date—Pseudosuchian footprints.

CLARENCEA Brink, 1959—A thecodont of the family Ornithosuchidae.

CLEPSYSAURUS Lea, 1853—(*Palaeoctonus, Suchoprion*.) A thecodont of the suborder Phytosauria.

COLONOSAURUS Marsh, 1872—of the type specimen of ichthyornis, a toothed bird.

Hypothetical restoration by the author of *Gongbusaurus*. (See Addendum III.)

DAHUTHÉRIUM   Montenat, ?date—Footprints, possibly crocodilian.

DASYGNATHOIDES   Kuhn, 1961—(See *Ornithosuchus*.)

DASYGNATHUS   Huxley, 1877—(See *Ornithosuchus*.)

DORATODON   Bunzel, 1871—A crocodilian.

EPICAMPODON   Huxley, 1865—*(Ankistrodon.)* A thecodont of the suborder Proterosuchia.

EUPODOSAURUS   Boulenger, 1891—Possibly a nothosaurid.

GRACILISUCHUS   Romer, 1972—A thecodont of the family Ornithosuchidae.

GWYNEDDOSAURUS   Bock, 1945—A protorosaurid.

HALLOPUS   Marsh, 1881—A crocodilian of the family Hallopodidae.

HERBSTOSAURUS   Casamiquela, 1974—A pterodactyl.

HYPSELORHACHIS   Charig, 1967—A thecodont of the family Lotosauridae.

KROKODILOPUS   Nopcsa, 1923—Possibly crocodilian footprints.

MACELOGNATHUS   Marsh, 1884—A crocodilian.

MARCELLOGNATHUS   Romer, 1966—A misspelling of *Macelognathus*.

OLIGOSAURUS   Seeley, 1881—A macelognathid.

ORNITHICHNITES   E. Hitchcock, 1836—Obsolete term once used to label any tridactyl ichnite.

ORNITHOIDES   Matthew, 1903—Carboniferous or Permian ichnite.

ORNITHOSUCHUS   Newton, 1894—*(Dasygnathoides, Dasygnathus.)* A thecodont of the family Ornithosuchidae.

OTOUPHEPUS   Cushman, 1904—Invalid name for footprints.

PALAEOCTONUS   Cope, 1877—(See *Clepsysaurus*.)

PNEUMATARTHRUS   Cope, 1871—(See *Pneumatoarthrus*.)

PNEUMATOARTHRUS   Cope, 1871—*(Pneumatarthrus.)*—A gigantic protostegid sea turtle, either *Archelon* or a close relative.

POPOSAURUS   Mehl, 1915—A thecodont of the family Poposauridae (R. A. Long, personal communication).

RIGALITES   Huene, 1931—Pseudosuchian footprints.

RIOJASUCHUS   Bonaparte, 1969—A thecodont of the family Ornithosuchidae.

SALTOPUS   Huene, 1910—A thecodont.

SCLEROMOCHLUS   Woodward, 1907—An advanced thecodont of the family Scleromochlidae.

SUCHOPRION   Cope, 1878—(See *Clepsysaurus*.)

TANYSTROPHAEUS   Huene, 1908—(See *Tanystropheus*.)

TANYSTROPHEUS   Meyer, 1852—*(Tanystrophaeus.)* A lepidosaur.

TAPINOSAURUS   Rabeck, 1925—A plesiosaur.

TRIASSOLESTES   Reig, 1963—A thecodont of the family Triassolestidae.

VENATICOSUCHUS   Bonaparte, 1972—A thecodont of the family Ornithosuchidae.

Femur (specimen F3390) tentatively identified as *Austrosaurus* sp. (After Coombs and Molnar.) (See Addendum III.)

Head of a femur (specimen F7880) tentatively identified as *Austrosaurus* sp. (After Coombs and Molnar.) (See Addendum III.)

Distal caudal vertebrae (specimen F637) tentatively identified as *Austrosaurus* sp. (After Coombs and Molnar.) (See Addendum III.)

ADDENDUM III

In an effort to keep this book as current and inclusive as possible, the following new material is being added as the final document goes to press:

Arstanosaurus Suslov, 1982—is a hadrosaur of uncertain subfamily, from the Upper Cretaceous of Kazakhstan, U.S.S.R., known from a left maxilla and possibly an associated distal end of a femur.

Avimimus Kurzanov, 1981—is an Upper Cretaceous theropod establishing the new family Avimimidae and was discovered in the Gobi Desert during the Soviet-Mongolian Expedition.

Elmisaurus Osmolska, 1981—is an Upper Cretaceous theropod establishing the new family Elmisauridae. The genus is based on a complete left tarsometatarsus, plus a referred incomplete manus, incomplete pes and various indeterminable fragmentary and long limb bones, all from three individuals, from the Nemegt Formation of Mongolia. The dinosaur is a medium-sized, lightly built theropod having limb bones with very thin walls. The manus is slender with three long digits, the pes is long and slender with three functional toes and a shortened first digit. The partial fusion within the metatarsus is an avian character common to *Elmisaurus* and some other theropods and provides more evidence concerning the dinosaurian ancestry of birds. A proximal portion of tarsometatarus found in the same formation shows a stronger fusion of elements than in *Elmisaurus* and, if it were more complete, might represent a new genus. Osmolska also refers the genera *Chirostenotes* Gilmore and *Macrophalangia* Sternberg to the family Elmisauridae.

Garudimimus Barsbold, 1981—is an Upper Cretaceous theropod establishing the new family Garudimimidae. Its remains from the Gobi Desert were discovered during the Soviet-Mongolian Expedition.

Huayangosaurus Dong, Tang and Zhou, 1982—is a primitive and median stegosaur establishing its own subfamily Huayangosaurinae. The animal is 4 meters (13½ feet) long. It has dorsal plates and spines varying in shape and apparently has tail spikes. Teeth are present in the front of the mouth. The genus is known from the Middle Jurassic of Dashanpe, in Zigong, Szechuan, from an assembly of sauropods, carnosaurs and stegosaurs yet to be described.

Hulsanpes Osmolska, 1982—is a deinocheirid from the Upper Cretaceous, Barung Goyot Formation of Mongolia, known from a foot.

Ingenia Barsbold, 1981—is an Upper Cretaceous theropod establishing the new sub family Ingeniinae. It was discovered during the Soviet-Mongolian Expedition in the Gobi Desert.

Pectinodon Carpenter, 1982—is a saurornithoidid from the Lance Formation, Upper Cretaceous, of eastern Wyoming, based on a relatively large adult tooth, about 6 millimeters (.23 inches) long, with large poste-

Left humerus (specimen F7292) tentatively identified as *Austrosaurus* sp. (After Coombs and Molnar.) (See Addendum III.)

Distal end of femur (specimen F7291) tentatively identified as *Austrosaurus* sp. (After Coombs and Molnar.) (See Addendum III.)

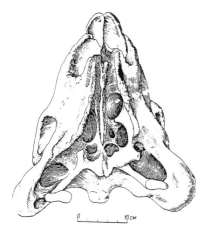

Skull of *Shamosaurus*. (After Tumanova.) (See Addendum III.)

rior serrations. Referred to this genus are some small teeth probably from infants.

These dinosaur names have appeared in the paleontological literature though formal descriptions of the genera have not, as of this writing, yet been published: *Chaoyoungosaurus*, an Upper Jurassic Chinese pachycephalosaurian probably establishing a new family Chaoyoungosauridae: *Gongbusaurus*, an Upper Jurassic Chinese hypsilophodont; *Honghesaurus*, presumably a camptosaurid of slender iguanodontid from the Upper Jurassic of China; *Questiosaurus* Kurzanov and Bannikov, an Upper Cretaceous sauropod known from at least an incomplete skull from the Djadokhta Formation of Mongolia; *Roccosaurus* van Heerden, possibly a carnivorous prosauropod which will establish a new prosauropod family; *Shamosaurus*, an Upper Cretaceous Mongolian ankylosaur based at least upon a skull; *Tenchisaurus*, a Jurassic ankylosaurid; and *Tianchungosaurus*, an Upper Jurassic Chinese pachycephalosaurian probably establishing a new family Tianchungosauridae.

Michael Brett-Surman will describe a birdlike theropod based on a complete metatarsus. The dinosaur is known from Montana and Argentina and is the first Upper Cretaceous theropod species known from both Eurasia and Gondwanaland. (M. Brett-Surman, personal communication.)

Walter P. Coombs, Jr., and Ralph E. Molnar have described (1981) five new sauropod specimens (F3390, F6737, F7291, F7292 and F7880) from the Winton Formation, Upper Cretaceous, in Queensland, Australia. The specimens include pectoral and pelvic girdles, metacarpals, fore- and hindlimb bones and caudal vertebrae. Though fragmentary, the specimens indicate a relatively primitive sauropod with few similarities to *Rhoetosaurus*. The material is indistinguishable from *Austrosaurus* and is tentatively named *Austrosaurus* sp.

Dale A. Russell and Robert A. Long will describe some new Upper Cretaceous dinosaurs based upon elements from the Hell Creek beds of Montana, including a new species of large ornithomimid, a new genus or new genera of dromaeosaurid, a new type of ceratopsian and a new saurischian larger than *Tyrannosaurus*.

Michael Cooper has made the following junior synonyms of *Massospondylus carinatus*: *Leptospondylus capensis* Owen, *Pachyspondylus orpenii* Owen, *Hortalotarsus skirtopodus* Seeley, *Massospondylus browni* Seely, *M. harriesi* Broom, *M. schwarzi* Haughton, *Aetonyx palustris* Broom, possibly *Gryponyx africanus* Broom, *G transvaalensis* Broom, *G. taylori* Haughton, *Thecodontosaurus dubius* Haughton, *Aristosaurus erectus* Van Hoepen and *Dromicosaurus gracilis* Van Hoepen, and the genera *Gyposaurus* and *Lufengosaurus*.

And Peter Galton has identified the incomplete right femur, once identified as *Astroden pusillus*, as a stegosaur.

Restoration of "Gadolosaurus" by the author.

BIBLIOGRAPHY

The amount of reference works pertaining to dinosaurs is virtually limitless. Some of these works, from which I obtained a wealth of information and to whose authors I am deeply indebted, are listed as follows:

Augusta, Joseph, with illustrations by Zdeněk Burian, *Prehistoric Animals,* Paul Hamlyn, London, 1960.

Berman, David S., and McIntosh, John S., "Skull and Relationships of the Upper Jurassic Sauropod *Apatosaurus* (Reptilia, Saurischia)," *Bulletin of Carnegie Museum of Natural History,* Number 8, Pittsburgh, 1978.

Colbert, Edwin H., *The Age of Reptiles,* W. W. Norton & Company, New York, 1966.

———, *The Dinosaur Book,* McGraw-Hill Book Company, New York, 1945.

———, *Dinosaurs (Their Discovery and Their World),* E. P. Dutton & Co., New York, 1961.

———, *Men and Dinosaurs (The Search in Field and Laboratory),* E. P. Dutton & Co., New York, 1968.

De Camp, L. Sprague, and De Camp, Catherine Crook, *The Day of the Dinosaur,* Doubleday & Company, Garden City, New York, 1968.

Desmond, Adrian J., *The Hot-Blooded Dinosaurs (A Revolution in Paleontology),* The Dial Press/James Wade, New York, 1976.

Gilmore, C. W., "Osteology of the armored Dinosauria in the United States National Museum, with special reference to the genus Stegosaurus," *Bulletin of the United States National Museum,* 89, Washington, D.C., 1914.

Good, John M., White, Theodore E., and Stucker, Gilbert F., *The Dinosaur Quarry,* National Park Service, Washington, D.C., 1958.

Gregory, Professor J. W., F.R.S., D.Sc., *Geology of To-Day,* Seeley, Service & Co., London, 1915.

Hotton, Nicholas, III, *Dinosaurs,* Pyramid Publications, New York, 1963.

Long, Robert A., and Welles, Samuel P., *All New Dinosaurs and Their Friends,* Bellerophon Books, San Francisco, 1975.

Lull, Richard Swann, "A Revision of the Ceratopsia or Horned Dinosaurs," *Memoirs of the Peabody Museum of Natural History,* Vol. 3, No. 3: New Haven, Connecticut, 1933.

———, "Triassic Life of the Connecticut Valley," revised edition, *Bulletin of the Connecticut Geological Natural History Survey,* 81, 1963.

———, and Wright, Nelda E., "Hadrosaurian Dinosaurs of North America," *Geological Society of North America,* Special Papers, No. 40, Baltimore, 1942.

McLoughlin, John, C., *Archosauria, a New Look at the Old Dinosaur,* The Viking Press, New York, 1979.

Madsen, James H., Jr., "*Allosaurus fragilis,* A Revised Osteology," Utah Geological and Mineral Survey, Bulletin 109, August, 1976.

Marsh, Othniel Charles, "The Dinosaurs of North America," *Sixteenth Annual Report of the U.S. Geological Survey*, 1896, pp. 133–244.

Olshevsky, George, *The Dinosaurian Taxa*, privately published, Toronto, Canada, 1976.

———, "The Archosaurian Taxa (Excluding the Crocodylia)," *Mesozoic Meanderings*, No. 1 (1978), and 1979 and 1980 supplements.

Ostrom, John H., "Cranial Morphology of the Hadrosaurian Dinosaurs of North America," *Bulletin of the American Museum of Natural History*, Vol. 122, article 2 (1961).

Owen, Ellis, *Prehistoric Animals (The Extraordinary Story of Life Before Man)*, Octopus Books, London, 1975.

Piveteau, Jean (editor), *Traite de Paleontologie*, Vol. 5, *Amphibiens, Reptiles, Oiseaux*, Macson, Paris, 1955. (Albert F. de Lapparent and Rene Lavocat wrote the section on dinosaurs.)

Ratkevich, Ronald Paul, *Dinosaurs of the Southwest*, University of New Mexico Press, Albuquerque, New Mexico, 1976.

Romer, Alfred Sherwood, *Man and the Vertebrates*, Penguin Books, Baltimore, 1933.

———, *Vertebrate Paleontology*, third edition, The University of Chicago Press, Chicago, 1967.

Russell, Dale A., *A Vanished World, The Dinosaurs of Western Canada*, National Museums of Canada, Ottawa, 1977.

Scheele, William E., *Prehistoric Animals*, The World Publishing Company, Cleveland and New York, 1954.

Špinar, Zdeněk V., with illustrations by Zdeněk Burian, *Life Before Man*. Thames and Hudson, London, 1972.

Steel, Rodney, Handbuch der Palaoherpetologie (Encyclopedia of Paleoherpetology), Part 15, "Ornithischia" (1969), and Part 14, "Saurischia" (1970), Oskar Kuhn, ed., Gustav Fischer Verlag, Stuttgart and Portland.

———, and Harvey, Anthony, eds., *The Encyclopedia of Prehistoric Life*, McGraw-Hill Book Company, New York, 1979.

Swinton, W. E., *Dinosaurs*, third edition, Trustees of the British Museum (Natural History), London, 1967.

———, *The Dinosaurs*, Wiley-Interscience, London and New York, 1968.

———, *Fossil Amphibians and Reptiles*, Trustees of the British Museum (Natural History), London, 1965.

———, *Giants, Past and Present*, Robert Hale, London, 1966.

Tweedie, Michael, *The World of Dinosaurs*, William Morrow and Company, New York, 1977.

White, Theodore E., "Catalogue of the Genera of Dinosaurs," *Annals of the Carnegie Museum*, Vol. 44, article 9, Pittsburgh, December 31, 1973.

Wood, Peter; Vaczek, Louis; Hamblin, Dora Jane, and Leonard, Jonathan Norton, *Life Before Man*, Time-Life Books, New York, 1972.

Zangerl, Rainer, *Dinosaurs, Predator and Prey*, Chicago Natural History Museum Press, Chicago, March 1956.

Zittel, Karl A. von, *Textbook of Paleontology*, Macmillan & Co., London, 1932.

ILLUSTRATION INDEX

287